WOMEN AND QUA...
IN THE 17th CENTU...

Front cover: A Quaker Meeting from Geoffrey Makins' illustration on front cover of *Margaret Fell, Mother of Quakerism* by Isabel Ross. *Sessions Book Trust 1984.*

A Quaker woman in action
Illustrations by Geoffrey Makins for *Margaret Fell, Mother of Quakerism* by
Isabel Ross. Sessions Book Trust 1984.

Women and Quakerism
in the 17th Century

by
Christine Trevett

Sessions Book Trust
The Ebor Press, York,
England

ISBN 1 85072 087 8

Printed in 10 on 11 point Bembo Typeface
by William Sessions Limited
The Ebor Press
York, England

Contents

List of Illustrations

★ By kind permission of the Library Committee of London Yearly Meeting of the
   Religious Society of Friends.
† By the artist Robert Spence.
‡ By the artist Geoffrey Makins.

Introduction and Acknowledgements

I STARTED TO WRITE THIS BOOK because no-one else had. The more I read of Quaker history, the clearer it became to me that *women's* story was relatively little represented in it. The more of the work of modern feminist historians and theologians I read, the more apparent it was that *they* believed there had been something distinctive about seventeenth-century Quaker teaching and practice where women were concerned. Yet British Quakers did not seem to be responding to this enquiry about their history. This was different from the situation in the USA.

The feminist writers who had shown such interest nevertheless remained largely unaware of the struggles and the heartsearchings about women and ministry which had occurred within Quakerism itself. In fact very little of women's story was being told, either within or outside of Quakerism. The kinds of observations which writers had made were true: it *was* within non-hierarchical and charismatic groups like the Quakers that greater possibilities had been laid open to women (Ursula King, *Women and Spirituality*, 1989, p. 38; Karen Armstrong, *The Gospel According to Woman*, 1986, p. 239 seq.); it *was* in sectarian groups, rather than in the mainstream Church, that women's theological status had been most notably improved and of all such groups it had been the Quakers – 'the tradition most richly endowed with women saints' – who had aimed consistently at restoring the pre-lapsarian relationships between the sexes (so Susan Dowell and Linda Hurcombe, *Dispossessed Daughters of Eve*, rev. edn. London, 100; Rosemary Radford Ruether, *Womenchurch*, 1985, p. 18 and *Sexism and God-Talk*, 1983, p. 35 and p. 102). Other writers knew that Quaker women had been 'immensely bold and fearless' in claiming their own experience and in relying on divine authority (in a group which was suspicious of the human kind). Hence such Quaker women had made it 'particularly hard for the men to sanctify any attempt they might have made to discipline their women' (so Sara Maitland, *A Map of the New Country*, London 1983, p. 9-10). There was truth in all of these assessments so far as the seventeenth century was concerned, just as writers were correct to comment on the wealth of inspiring stories about women which was part of Quakerism, from the seventeenth century through the reforming, abolitionist and peace-promoting women of the Religious

vii

Society of Friends, into our own day. Yet British Quakerism was almost entirely silent about its 'herstory' and as a result, it seemed to me, most British Friends were functioning with scarcely any knowledge of their foremothers. So early in 1986 I began work for this book.

Writers who are not specialists on British history of the seventeenth century are well advised to keep away from it. There is an incredible wealth of primary source material (or so it seems to one who specialises in *second century* history) and a great fund of books and articles by scholars who disagree one with another. I found this when I first embarked on my journey of discovery into seventeenth-century Quakerism and realised that it could not be described in isolation from other aspects of the society and religion of that century, nor its women apart from the lot of their sisters outside the Quaker fold. My initial plan had been to provide an 'overview' study of women and Quakerism to the present day. I soon realised that that was an impossible task for me. I did not have the time to spare from my 'real' research work, teaching and family and in any case I had discovered just how much seventeenth-century source material on Quakerism there was readily to hand in the Library in Friends House in London, as well as in the British Library. It became a subject of great fascination for me. The result is this introductory examination of women and Quakerism *in the first half century of its existence* and mostly concerning Britain, the area of its origin.

The subject became my hobby. I inflicted it on student societies in universities which had been kind enough to invite me to speak, on post-graduate students doing Women's Studies courses in religion, on audiences at conferences. It has been, nevertheless, the work of an amateur in the field. I have read voraciously but – I expect experts to think – probably at times without the discrimination that *real* historians of the seventeenth century would have shown.

I took on this task with trepidation. It happened after a lot of vacillation and for three reasons:

(a) I had well-developed interests in church history and in feminist theology. As I said at the outset, my reading in both had made me aware of contemporary comments on Quakerism. Whether in discussion of enthusiasm, of 'prophetic' sectarianism, of women in Christian history or of the history of the struggle for female emancipation, Quakerism appears regularly in the footnotes of books. Yet apart from Mabel Brailsford's 1915 study of *Quaker Women* and valuable biographies of individuals (such as Isabel Ross's examination of Margaret Fell) there were in fact few books on women and the Society of Friends. There were none, it seemed to me, given exclusively to telling the story of women in the formative first half century of Quakerism and none which took account of the very considerable body of published material about the seventeenth century and about Quakerism in particular, which has emerged in recent years. There seemed to be a gap to be filled.

(b) I was teaching religion for Cardiff University's MSc course in Women's Studies and alongside the role-models of female leadership in the early Church, the medieval and later mystics and the feminists of the Evangelical tradition, there were also the prophets and preachers of radical Protestantism to be considered. The Quaker women of the seventeenth century were not to be ignored in that presentation, but I could find no easily manageable source book on them to offer my students. No-one was coming forward to write one.   _ Mack².

(c) I was being made aware of a growing academic interest in *women* and Quakerism. A number of stimulating articles had appeared; a plan had been formulated in the USA to publish a collection of seventeenth-century writings by Quaker women and Phyllis Mack was doing further work on prophets; a number of books (including several by Margaret Hope Bacon, one by the Stoneburners and the edition of Potts Brown and Mosher Stuard) on Quaker women in America appeared in the 1980s and Elaine Huber had examined women and the authority of inspiration, paying special attention to the second century Montanists, the American Antinomian movement and the Quakers. Women and Quakerism featured in several current British PhD research projects of which I knew and also in Britain students and colleagues of Dr Michael Mullett at the University of Lancaster had produced interesting studies relating to women and Quakerism, with special reference to the North of England. But still there was no 'overview' of women's lot in the first half century of Quakerism in the land of its birth.

Because the reclaimers of women's religious history had become aware of Quakerism and of some of its writings they were beginning to make their interest known to the Religious Society of Friends in Britain. So I was invited to prepare a new edition of Margaret Fell's 1666-7 work *Womens Speaking Justified*, which was also to include brief references to other writings on women and Quakerism in the seventeenth century. This small item was published in 1989 by Quaker Home Service. I then 'tested the ground' by writing an article which was published by the Journal *Religion* ('The women around James Nayler, Quaker: a matter of emphasis', vol. 20 (1990)) and that exercise taught me a lot. It gave me confidence that I had done quite a lot of research and had managed to learn *something* about a field which was not my own while at the same time its anonymous expert reader, to whom the article was referred, taught me very much more. I had decided by this time, then, that I was going to launch into waters I had not properly charted. I had also decided that this could not be a comprehensive work. It would not provide biographies of individual women and no woman's story would be told fully. Instead individuals figuring in this book represent aspects of, or trends in, seventeenth-century Quakerism.

This study is only a small beginning. There is very much research and publication to be done on women and Quakerism of the seventeenth century.

In preparing this I have referred deliberately in the notes to sources which I think will be most easily accessible to the interested (rather than to the expert on the seventeenth century) reader. Thus, for example, it is the Nickalls' edition of Fox's *Journal* which is quoted and *published* letters, as reproduced in well-known works of Quakerism, rather than in the manuscript collections, that have been cited wherever possible. I hope it will be readable for all – that is for those within and beyond the Religious Society of Friends, for students of Women's Studies, for lovers of the seventeenth century. In *Women and Quakerism in the Seventeenth Century* I have tried to take account not only of the factors which gave to Quaker women a remarkable status and freedom in that century but also of the 'warts and all' struggles within Quakerism itself when it was defining and dealing with that status and freedom.

In writing these chapters I have also made use of the American convention of referring to women using both their maiden and married names, or the name from more than one marriage: e.g. Margaret Fell Fox or Gulielma Springett Penn or Hannah Stranger Salter. This is of course an anachronistic usage. Women did not refer to themselves in this way in the seventeenth century. I hope nevertheless that it will make for clarity and will help to avoid confusion when a woman is referred to at intervals and in relation to different stages of her life.

Each of the chapter headings in this study is a quotation and each is referred to in the body of that chapter.

> **No more than a goose** (Chapter One) comes from the *Journal* of George Fox and refers to a statement he heard that women had no souls – 'no more than a goose'.
>
> **Women's Speaking Justified** (Chapter Two) is the title of a writing by Margaret Fell, published in 1666. This work defended strongly the right of women to public Christian ministry.
>
> Finally, **This my Friend** (Chapter Three) echoes part of the marriage declaration made by men and women Quakers alike, when they announced 'I [Mary Jones] take this my Friend [John Smith] to be my husband . . .'

I owe a great debt to many people. Some of those I shall mention have given me valuable advice and put me right on matters where I was going astray but only I am responsible for the shortcomings which remain in this study.

In particular I must mention libraries and their staff: Malcolm Thomas and the staff of the Library, Friends House; Christina Lawson, the Librarian of Woodbrooke College, Selly Oak; the staffs of the British Library and the Dr Williams Library, London and of the Humanities and Social Science Library, University of Wales College of Cardiff. I must thank for helpful conversations, referrals, observations, corrections and encouragement Prof. Catherine Belsey of the Department of English in Cardiff, Dr J. Gwynfor Jones of the Department of History of Wales, Dr Michael Mullett of the University of Lancaster, Edward H. Milligan, formerly Librarian of the Friends' House Library; the American historian and Friend Kenneth Carroll and the publishing Sessions family of York.

My thanks go to the ever-enthusiastic first cohort of MSc students of women's religious history in Cardiff – to Margot Cronin, Dr Noragh Jones, Liz Rowlands, Carolyn Sansom, the Rev'd Pat Stephens and Viv Turner; to Prof. Rosemary Radford Ruether, who assured me she was *not* making an identical study; to the encouraging editor and previewing reader of the Journal *Religion*; to my friends and colleagues who put up with my reading of papers at the conferences of the British Association for the Study of Religion; and to those on the *Religion and Gender* panel of the International Association for the History of Religions; to my friends in the European Society of Women for Theological Research; to John Banks; to the Literature Committee of Quaker Home Service, especially Clifford Barnard and Carol Gardiner; to the 'Seventeenth Century Working Party' of the current *Quaker Book of Discipline* revision committee, *viz.* Edward Milligan and Malcolm Thomas again, Janet Scott and Arthur White; to the Friends of Wakefield (Yorkshire), Thornbury (Bristol) and Chepstow (Gwent) Meetings.

Finally there must be special mention of my family. This includes Nathan, whose birth and constant efforts still did not prevent my finishing this task.

This study is for my Friend, the long-suffering Peter Trevett, who is amused that after sixteen years (not our whole married life) of boring him with the *second* century, when now I speak of 'the 60s' I mean the *sixteen* sixties.

Department of Religious Studies
POB 911
University of Wales, College of Cardiff
CARDIFF CF1 3AT   September 1st 1991

Abbreviations Used

BDBR	R. Zaller and R. L. Greaves (eds.), *Biographical Dictionary of British Radicals*
BQ	W. C. Braithwaite, *The Beginnings of Quakerism*
EHR	Periodical, *English Historical Review*
EQW	H. Barbour and A. O. Roberts (eds.), *Early Quaker Writings*
FF	M. Ferguson (ed.), *First Feminists*
FPT	N. Penney, *First Publishers of Truth*
FQ	Periodical, *Friends Quarterly*
FSM	L. Stone, *The Family, Sex and Marriage . . .*
JEH	Periodical, *Journal of Ecclesiastical History*
JFHS	Periodical, *Journal of the Friends Historical Society* and its Supplement series
Journal =	J. L. Nickalls' edition of the *Journal* of George Fox
MF	I. Ross, *Margaret Fell, Mother of Quakerism*
PP	Periodical, *Past and Present*
QER	B. Reay, *The Quakers and the English Revolution*
QH	Periodical, *Quaker History*
QM	Periodical, *Quaker Monthly*
QPE	H. Barbour, *The Quakers in Puritan England*
QW	M. Brailsford, *Quaker Women*
RDM	K. Thomas, *Religion and the Decline of Magic*
SDEQ	R. T. Vann, *The Social Development of English Quakerism*
SPQ	W. C. Braithwaite, *The Second Period of Quakerism*
Sufferings =	J. Besse, *A Collection of the Sufferings of the People Called Quakers*
TWTUD	C. Hill, *The World Turned Upside Down*
TWV	A. Fraser, *The Weaker Vessel*
WFC	E. Potts Brown and S. Mosher Stuard (eds.), *Witnesses for Change*

Quaker Glossary

RELIGIOUS SOCIETY OF FRIENDS (QUAKERS) is the official name of the society. 'Quaker' originally a term of derision, is now generally accepted. Thus the terms 'a Quaker' and 'a Friend' are interchangeable.

Preparative Meeting — The business meeting of a Friends' Meeting, or Particular Meeting; a Meeting forming part of a Monthly Meeting.

Monthly Meeting — The business meeting of a group of Meetings in an area, as set up in 1666 by George Fox.

Quarterly Meeting — The business meeting of a group of Monthly Meetings, originally organised on a county basis before 1666 by George Fox; now replaced by General Meetings on a similar regional basis.

Meeting for Sufferings — The Executive Committee of London Yearly Meeting now held monthly on a Saturday; originally set up to take action over the distress caused by persecution.

General Meeting — Established in 1656 and replaced in 1678 by Yearly Meeting.

Yearly Meeting — The annual national assembly of Friends lasting several days. This was established in 1678 and London Yearly Meeting has met regularly ever since.

Women's Meeting	Friends recognised women from the outset as both temporal and spiritual helpers and established Women's Meetings for this purpose. From the beginning Women Friends were influential leaders of the Quaker movement, notably Margaret Fell (widow of Judge Fell of Swarthmoor Hall and later wife of George Fox). Women's Meetings were held separately until 1896, concerns being brought in person from Women's to Men's Meetings and vice versa.
Business Meetings	All business meetings, held in the spirit of worship, deal corporately with both spiritual and practical aspects of Christian discipleship. There is never a vote, but instead a careful endeavour to find consensus.
Elders	Friends appointed to have special concern for the pastoral care of members.
Minister	In 1723 Yearly Meeting decided Friends must produce a certificate from their Monthly/Quarterly Meeting before being recorded as a minister, who was a Friend whose speaking in Meeting for Worship was recorded by his Monthly Meeting as acceptable: a practice discontinued in 1924. Travelling ministers were voluntary unpaid Friends who visited other Meetings after obtaining a travelling certificate.
First Day	Sunday, the first day of the week. Friends declined to use the names of pagan gods for the names of the days and months. Thus 'First Day', 'Second Day' to 'Seventh Day' and 'First Month', 'Second Month' to 'Twelfth Month'.

Discipline	Religious teaching, or the regulation of life by religious teaching, or a body of such regulations: thus 'The Books of Discipline'.
Meetings for Discipline	Meetings for the business of the Society (not now current).
Truth	Spiritual reality or the gospel in the experience of Friends: hence the phrase 'Friends of the Truth as it is in Jesus', or just 'Friends of the Truth'.
Weighty Friend	Those whose ministry in Meeting and whose advice and conduct were such as to make their words and council carry weight (now only used in its historical connotation).
Concern	A compulsive course of action taken under deep religious conviction, which in early days often entailed visits to Meetings in order to visit and minister in other areas of Britain or frequently abroad. From an early date it became the practice that an individual's concern needed to be brought before P.M. or M.M. If the concern was endorsed it would often go forward to Q.M., Meeting for Sufferings and eventually Y.M.

As I was going to a meeting, I saw some *Women* in a *field*, and I discerned them to be *Witches* and I was moved to go out of my way into the field to them, and declare unto them their *Conditions*: telling them plainly, *They were in the Spirit of Witchcraft*.
George Fox his *Journal*.

R Spence

CHAPTER I

'NO MORE THAN A GOOSE'
The seventeenth century

Setting the scene

IT IS THE 1640s IN ENGLAND and witchcraft is still a statutory offence. In 1647 Matthew Hopkins, witchfinder, is completing his definitive work on his unpleasant vocation – *The Discovery of Witches*. The offence remains ✔ statutory until 1736 and for now the old and the isolated, the deformed and the eccentric, the unpopular, the unmarried, the widowed and the autonomous, the mentally disturbed, those without patronage, the malicious, the healers and people with an eye to the occult continue to be at risk: almost all of those accused are women. Most of the cases tried end in acquittal but the fear of accusation is real indeed. The country is troubled and scapegoats are needed. This is a suspicious, ferment-ridden decade, when many liken Roman Catholicism and its practices to witchery; when the Anglo-Catholicism of Archbishop Laud (sentenced to the Tower in 1641)[1] and his like is feared and witch fever achieves new vigour as the King's authority wanes. Still things have never been as bad as in other parts of Europe. There the terror of heresy and the theological definitions applied to witchcraft took their toll over many decades and the Inquisition fanned the flames of witch-hatred.[2] In England it has been three decades and more since the last heretic, an Anabaptist, was burned. Already the first breezes of the winds of scepticism can be felt but still superstition is rife and the names of Paracelsus and Nostradamus, of Merlin and Mother Shipton resound in some circles.[3]

1647 in England is the fifth year of civil war. There has been revolutionary turmoil for longer. In just two years into the future the King, Charles I, God's anointed, will be beheaded and it will seem to many that yet again the unthinkable has happened in the land. To some of them it will be a sure sign that God's intervention is indeed imminent. Those who are awaiting the millenium cannot know that in fact the monarchy will be restored in 1660. Instead they, with prophetic social and religious idealists of many persuasions – with Familists and Levellers, Seekers, Fifth Monarchists, Grindletonians and others – look forward to a better day and a more just social order.[4] Shortly Ludowick Muggleton will be sure of his vocation and the Muggletonians will be born.[5] Shortly the Ranters will rise to infamy. There are not as yet any called Quakers. Politics and religion are not to be separated. On the European continent the *Thirty Years War*, Catholic against Protestant, is in its final year.

It is 1647 and apocalyptic hopes abound. From the highest to the lowest people are offering to identify 'the Beast' (of Revelation) and 'the Antichrist' (of the first letter of John) in their midst. These figure large in preaching and writing. The Beast is no longer associated only with things Popish and Romish, but with bishops and priests generally and with the panoply of hierarchies and powers both ecclesiastical and governmental.[6] 'Liberty of conscience' is a recurring cry. The requirement to pay tithes to the Church is hailed as a mark of the Beast, and in 1647 (as in many other years throughout the seventeenth century), there are some who think that this is the year in which Antichrist will fall.[7] In this atmosphere anything seems possible. People are seeking new answers to perennial questions. They are joining groups which offer a radical redefinition of the world and the self. Food prices are beginning to rise and the North seems threatened with famine.[8] The army, with Agitators and Levellers in association, is alive with ideas about democratisation.[9] Women of many religious persuasions are challenging their God-given roles in seemingly unprecedented ways. Like many men and women of the time Bathsua (Bathusa, Basua) Pell Makin, learned woman, radical educator and tutor to the daughter of the King, has been pamphleteering. She has been writing to challenge imprisonment for debt. The world is being turned upside down.

It is the 1640s in England and to many it seems that heresy has reached plague proportions. The doctrine of the Trinity is challenged by the unlearned. The authority of the scriptures is denied. Untutored laypeople are declaring infant baptism to be an abomination and the Church's creeds are set at nought. Anti-episcopacy and general anti-clericalism are commonplace. Even traditional ideas about heaven, hell, original sin, the resurrection of the body and the historical person of Jesus Christ seem to be ripe for reinterpretation or abandonment. More conservative Christian writers deplore the spread of such schismatics and heretics who are rotting the fabric of religion and society. Thomas Edwards, Presbyterian and scourge of sectarians, has been working on *Gangraena* (1646) in which (*p. 3*) there are itemised hundreds of errors, heresies, blasphemies and pernicious practices. Such things will multiply, he believes – monstrous bastard children will be produced, for they await only 'the midwife and nursing mother of Toleration'. There will come, he fears, the promotion

2

of that atheism which is already a mark of the age. The age is one of profound change.[10]

It is the prevailing view that where there is heresy there too will be women. They have been condemned down the Christian centuries for their love of sectarianism, their witchcraft and blasphemies, their appropriation of 'rights' to preach and teach. Women, so it is maintained, are frail of body and mind. Women, so runs the prevailing wisdom, are easily disposed to error and are prey for seducers, as was their foremother Eve; they are vulnerable because of their lustful natures and drawn to offers of power and knowledge which are not rightfully theirs.[11] Those with a knowledge of history remember that there were prophesying, preaching and troublesome women among the errorists of the past, from Jezebel of Thyatira (*Revelation* 2:20-23) through the tattling women of the Pastoral letters (1 and 2 *Timothy* and *Titus*), the Montanists, the Albigensians (Cathars) and the Anabaptists to the present day.[12] Those with a knowledge of history deplore, but are not amazed, that in the current turmoil they find the public activity of upstart women.[13]

It is 1647, George Fox, shoemaker and son of a Leicestershire weaver, is experiencing a change. After years of uncertainty and seeking he is finding enlightenment. He is becoming what others will call a Quaker. He will outlive those men and women whose enlightenment is similar and who will preach and practice the Quaker message fervently. He will tell the story of the group in *his* way and become the father figure of Quakerism. Its message will soon be preached the length and breadth of Britain and it will be taken perilously to the New World. There, history will show that in terms of Quaker numbers it will bear a fruit greater than in its homeland. Its message is in many respects like that of other groups which are active at this time. Not a few of the 'heresies' known to *Gangraena* (*pp. 18-36*) will be recognisably Quaker too. In other respects, however, Quakerism offers an additional twist in that upturning of the world, its values and order, which is happening. Thus Quakerism will strike dismay in the hearts of those who are conservative but it will delight others. Among the latter will be many women.

Setting the scene: mid-seventeenth-century women

In the seventeenth century, which was a time before anaesthesia and adequate knowledge of hygiene and antiseptics, a pregnant woman might surreptitiously prepare her own shroud. If literate, as a small but growing number of women were becoming, she may have tried to leave in writing a legacy for that child she feared she would not live to see. Some confessed in a Journal their terror of the pain and peril to come. In 1648 Elizabeth Duncome, wife of Sir William Brownlow, gave birth to her nineteenth child in twenty-two years. It was her last birthgiving and the child was the sixth to survive. Such a level of infant and child mortality was not uncommon, but it is less certain how many mothers died in childbirth. It may have been as many as 150 per thousand.[14] Even among the aristocracy up to 45% of women died before the age of fifty, a significant number due to complications of childbirth. Those women were better housed than their poorer sisters, but the general dirtiness and their dietary deficiencies, when added to the fads of upper class women, conspired against their good health. Undernourishment was common among the poor.[15] The starvation and misery which Alice Clark discovered in her study of *Quarter Sessions* records

> but represent the ordinary life of women in the wage-earning class . . . the hardships suffered by the women . . . proved fatal to their children . . . few children of the wage-earning classes were reared. Of those which reached maturity many were crippled in mind and body . . . this appalling loss and suffering was not due to the excessive work of married women but to their underfeeding and bad housing . . . the sacrifice of the wage-earners' children [as distinct from those in husbandry, for example] was caused by the mother's starvation.[16]

Seventeenth-century observers were saying that more men and women died before the age of thirty-five than lived beyond it. John Graunt, writing in the infancy of demography, claimed that in London 36% of children who survived birth died before they were six, and that 60% did not see a sixteenth birthday. Graunt may have been exaggerating, and things were probably better in some country areas, but for no-one was a long life to be assumed.[17]

Theirs was not a comfortable age. Paradoxically, lavish display often combined with and helped to mask an almost barbarous discomfort. Chronic illnesses were commonplace. There were smallpox and plague, with severe outbreaks of the latter in 1625 and 1665.[18] The mother who survived childbirth found her offspring disfigured, weakened, or struck down by disease. Religion was looked to for explanation and also for relief from the seeming social and moral chaos all about. But increasingly conventional religiosity was not enough. Churchmen, some of them negligent incumbents, were seen by many to have failed. Other leaders were no less blamed for not giving a lead. Social contagion and the breakdown of order were discussed and written of a great deal, as were those who failed to stem them. They

> scramble at the shearers feast
> and shove away the worthy bidden guest . . .
> The hungry sheep look up and are not fed,
> But swoln with wind and the rank mist they draw,
> Rot inwardly and foul contagion spread

declared John Milton in *Lycidas*.

It seemed that the English, and scarcely less the Scots and Welsh, had become an ungovernable people.[19] Some women were ungovernable too. Sections of the country's womanhood had risen to their feet. Some were on the march. There were upper-class heroines, active in the civil war and faithful to the Royalist cause. There were those who preached and prophesied, published and petitioned. There were still radically minded medical practitioners as well as nurses and midwives, though this would change.[20] There were women in religious orders who were struggling for the right to ministries outside the cloister, like those associated with Mary Ward (d. *1645*). They believed passionately that girls should be properly educated, and worked tirelessly for that end. Mary Ward had petitioned the Pope and found herself forced to flee the country. She was imprisoned and with her sisters was accused of trying to usurp the rightful activities of men. But for some such women under vows of poverty, chastity and obedience, freed from the burdens of marriage and childbearing and freed for piety, study and a degree of autonomy, the cloister could be a privileged existence. Nevertheless it was one frowned on by the Puritan detesters of 'Popery'.[21] For women in the world there was very much unelected poverty. Obedience was to fathers and husbands, their lot was minimal education or none and childbearing.[22] In the seventeenth century few of them had cause to question the veracity of the *Genesis* curse of Eve (*3:16*):

> I will greatly multiply thy sorrow and thy conception; In sorrow thou shalt bring forth children; And thy desire shall be to thy husband, and he shall rule over thee.

In 1641 strictures on the press were removed and a spate of religio-political publications followed. Women were among the writers. Publication allowed them access to the public sphere without so much compromising femininity and reputation by polemicising in person. They wrote pamphlets. But also for some time better-educated women had been writing poetry, plays and more, most of which never saw public performance beyond a few friends.

A small number of *prophesying* women had their revelations printed and thus knowledge of their words and deeds (and not just hostile accounts of them) has survived for our own age. These women prophets did not shrink from the public domain, however, and they had no need of the intermediary of print as protection. Whether published or not, their names were well known in the decades which preceded and included the civil war and in the Interregnum too: there were Mary Cary (later called Rande), who called herself a 'minister' in her work *The Glorious Excellencies of the Spirit* (1645). The Baptist Anna Trapnel, daughter of a Poplar shipwright, had had a mother whose dying words had been 'Lord double thy Spirit upon my child'. Anna had had visions from the age of nine, she claimed.

5

Both she and Mary Cary were millenarian Fifth Monarchists in outlook. There was Mary Gadbury, visionary, labelled a Ranter, who was involved with the disreputable William Franklin in one of a number of 'holy family' situations which existed at this time. Franklin recanted and disowned the bewildered Mary. Jane Hawkins was a pedlar woman prophet and we know too of Elizabeth Poole, Elizabeth Joceline, Elinor Channel and others. The young and immensely popular Sarah Wight, whose spiritual experiences started when she was sixteen, was part of an Independent Baptist congregation and the child of a gentry family. The significant prophesying Welshwoman Eleanor Douglas, whose insights had been variously respected by the Queen and branded false prophecy or treasonable, was well born and well married, first to the poet Sir John Davies. On the 28th of July 1625, the remarkable Lady Eleanor reported (see *The Lady Eleanor, her Appeal* 1641) that she had awoken to a voice from heaven: 'There is nineteen years and a half to the day of judgement, and you as the meek virgin'. She authored some thirty-seven publications between 1641-1652.[23]

It can be seen that such women emerged from more than one class of society, though historians and sociologists remark rightly that prophecy tends to be associated with the powerless and the marginalised. Whatever their class, women in the seventeenth century were almost always among the powerless. Moreover the prophets were to be found among Baptists, Congregationalists and others and they differed from one another both in theology and mode of prophesying. There were many women active on the religious front, as Dorothy Ludlow reminds us, who did not just *declare* the word of God but who 'harangued prelates and country priests, tore down altar rails, smashed stained glass windows and cut up surplices with their sewing shears'.

Radical Puritans acknowledged the spiritual equality of men and women. They also allowed (as the Apostle Paul had done) that a woman directly under the inspiration of the Spirit might prophesy. But since the exposition of scripture in the light of their revelations tended to be the form prophecy took, and since the right to interpret Scripture was not given to women, there was always scope to accuse the women prophets. Such prophecy smacked of teaching and of usurpation of the rights of men. The women's activity in the public sphere called into question their morals and their sanity too, as well as their religious orthodoxy, so that the lot of many such women was periods spent in the Bridewell House of Correction, in Bedlam or in the Tower. The fact was that these prophets, active before and contemporaneously with the beginnings of Quakerism, were, on the whole, troublesome women. They declared in song and rhyme, had fits of delirium and went into lengthy states of trance. They sometimes attracted large audiences and seemed to pose a threat to order. The results were predictable. Anna Trapnel recorded in her 1654 work *Report and Plea* (which was also an account of her travels in Cornwall)[24] that

> England's rulers and clergy do judge the Lord's handmaid to be mad, and under the administration of evil angels, and witch, and many other evil terms they raise up to make me odious and abhorr'd.

So it had always been throughout Christian history, since the reverence for the likes of Philip's daughters and Ammia of Philadelphia had faded and the second-century Montanist prophetess Maximilla observed

> I am driven away as a wolf from the sheep, I am not a wolf, I am word and spirit and power.[25]

In the 1640s publications by women were not hard to find. Indeed, and given that there had been decades of social and religious upheaval, they had been around for some time. However, the use of pseudonyms sometimes makes it hard to be sure that a writer was indeed a woman. Such authors responded to the events of their day and some of them challenged as feminists those who tried to deny them rights. Mary Tattlewell and Joan Hit-Him-Home deserve mention for their work of 1640.[26] In this, *The Womens Sharp Revenge*, they asked angrily

> . . . what poor woman is ever taught that she should have a higher design than to get her a husband?

Even earlier there had been published replies to particularly unpleasant misogynist outpourings. Thus in 1617 Esther Sowernam in *Esther Hath Hang'd Haman* had answered Joseph Swetnam's *Arraignment of Lewde, Idle, Froward and Unconstant Women* of two years previously. Rachell Speght did the same in 1617, writing *A Mouzell for Melastomus* and so did Constantia Mundi in *The Worming of a Mad Dogge*.[27] Swetnam's diatribe was immensely popular, reiterating as it did the accusations of the early Fathers of the Church, that women were of the devil, beset by filthiness and lust and were snares for men. Answering publications of the Sowernam, Speght and Mundi kinds (and of other kinds too) do indeed indicate that there was

> a seventeenth century feminism that questions assumptions about gender, challenges some of the norms and values of patriarchy and masculine culture, and sometimes offers alternative values or straightforward opposition.

It did the women little good, however, but merely fueled the suspicion and derision which 'forward' women had to endure.[28]

Faced with such women of radical social and religious views and their petitioning, preaching and prophesying sisters, their seventeenth-century opponents over the coming decades penned couplets; as for example in Samuel Butler's *Hudibras* (1662-3, 1678), an attack on Puritanism:

7

the oyster women lock'd their fish up
And trudg'd away to cry 'No Bishop'.

There was *Lucifer's Lackey* of 1647, which said:

When women preach and cobblers pray
The fiends in hell make holiday.

and the accusatory lines in a skit by those who feared women's autonomy:

We will not be wives
And tie up our lives
To villainous slavery.

(*Rump, or an Exact Collection of the Choycest Poems and Songs* ii, London 1662, p. 196).

Despite the lack of encouragement, some women hoped still to be literary figures. A few were quite prolific writers but their efforts were not appreciated. An exception was Aphra Behn, who wrote in the latter half of the century. She did become the first British woman to make a living by her pen and her works run to six volumes in the Montague Summers edition of 1915. But in general, as Anne Finch Countess of Winchelsea knew, women, 'debar'd from all improvements of the mind' were themselves expected to be 'dull',

Whilst the dull manage of a servile house
Is held by some our utmost part and use.

Her poetry had to be for friends only, for as she wrote:

Did I my lines intend for public view
How many censures would their faults pursue[29]

Anne Finch, dismissed later as 'a blue-stocking with an itch for scribbling', complained in *The Apology* that the Muse always had to be followed in private:

To some few friends and to thy sorrows sing
For groves of laurel thou wert never meant.

The works of not a few of these seventeenth-century women poets and biographers too have survived to be read today. Among them were the mystic poet Jane Lead, and Anne Bradstreet who had left England at eighteen and whose brother arranged the publication of her poetry without her knowledge. Biographers and autobiographers included Anne, Lady Halkett and Mary Rich the Countess of Warwick, Anne Lady Fanshawe and Lucy Hutchinson. Their class had allowed them the opportunities both for learning and leisure time, such as were denied to the vast majority of women. Margaret Cavendish, Duchess of Newcastle, was of a different and more determined turn of mind than most such women:

8

I confess my ambition is restless because it would have an extraordinary fame. And since all heroic actions, public employments,
powerfull governments and eloquent pleadings are denied our sex in
this age, or at least would be condemned for want of custom, is the
cause I write so much[30]

(Epistle in preface to her autobiographical *Natures Pictures Drawn by Fancies
Pencil to the Life*).

Samuel Pepys (hardly an impeccable source) mocked the Duchess for
her outlandish dress and her poetry – 'the most ridiculous thing that ever
was wrote'. And Dorothy Osborn's letters to William Temple in the 1650s
suggested that

The poor woman is a little distracted, she could never be so
ridiculous else as to venture at writing books and in verse too.

In short, as Dorothy observed, 'there are many soberer people in Bedlam'.
In contrast her contemporary Bathsua Makin (probably with an excess of
enthusiasm for female assertiveness) declared the Duchess a genius, who
lacking 'any timely instruction over-tops many grave grown men'. In our
own century Virginia Woolf has probably come nearest to the sad truth:
'Margaret too might have been a poet', she commented, but

as it was, what could bind, tame or civilize for human use that wild,
generous, untutored intelligence? . . . What a waste . . . the crazy
Duchess became a bogey to frighten clever girls with (*A Room of
One's Own*, 1929).

Margaret Cavendish was certainly eccentric and by the standards of her
day oddly dressed – though a kind commentator might surmise that her
sartorial oddities were themselves signs not of instability but of reaction
to gender-related norms. She was elitist and no ardent feminist[31] but she
pinpointed accurately the paucity and poor quality of education for girls.
She thought that convent enclosure was preferable to unhappy marriage
and an enforced marriage, she added, was an invitation to adultery:[32]

Women live like bats or owls, labour like beasts and die like
worms

the Duchess told her contemporaries.

In his book *Women in Stuart England and America* (12 seq.), Thompson
observed that such literary women shared a common strain of
abnormality, 'be it sexual, social or familial'. They were women who
were free of those constraints which normally would have prevented a
woman writing. Childlessness, late marriage or a compliant husband,
these were advantages few women enjoyed. Thus, he maintained, their
creativity

does not really argue any great freedom of intellectual endeavour
for women in seventeenth century English society.

9

He was surely right, yet such women were nonetheless remarkable and their own struggles make those of their less privileged and articulate sisters seem all the more harrowing.

The incipient feminism of the women petitioners of the 1640s and later, of those who fortified cities, rhymed prophecies and expounded doctrine, found little echo in the literature and drama of the time, as Shepherd noted in his study of *Amazons and Warrior Women* (65 seq.). The Puritan road to feminism was reviled. Yet there did exist 'a positive resistance to anti-feminism' which had some influence in the pre-revolutionary period. It was present in the 'warrior woman' figures which appeared in literature. These female figures would also appear later in the religious pamphlets as well as on the lips of petitioners and of those who discoursed on the nature and status of women. There were in such sources appeals to Boadicea and Deborah, to Esther and others. There *were*, then, militant, even militant scriptural female models to be looked to. Generally, however, woman was 'visible only as model of invisibility' in the drama of the time as Catherine Belsey observed in *The Subject of Tragedy* (p. 168). Woman had 'uncertain place', for 'in the family as in the state women had no single unified fixed position from which to speak.'[33]

In the seventeenth century there was plenty *for* women to advise them on their place and behaviour.[34] It came in publications like that of John Dod and Robert Cleaver's *A Godlie Form of Household Government* (original 1598 but thereafter in many editions). Apart from their equality in salvation with their husbands, Dod and Cleaver wrote, women might expect no other kind:

> (the husband and wife are equal, in that which is the chiefest . . . they have everlasting life given them, which otherwise are unequal.)–

Women were in almost all ways subordinate. The 'complete' woman, however, was no frail dunce but immensely capable and hard working. According to Gervase Makham's *The English Huswife: containing the inward and outward Vertues which ought to be in a compleat woman* (1615), such a woman was modest and temperate. She was to be a skilled household manager, overseer of servants, able in 'bakery, cookery, physic, banquetting stuff and distillation'. Other influential works included William Gouge's *Of Domesticall Duties, Eight Treatises,* (3rd edn. 1634) and Richard Brathwaite's 240 page *The English Gentlewoman* (1631 and its 1630 parallel for gentlemen). Marriage sermons further distilled men's wisdom about femininity. Thomas Gataker's *A Good Wife God's Gift', Two Marriage Sermons* of 1624 was a typical example.

Daniel Rogers in his *Matrimoniall Honour* of 1642 repeated familiar warnings of the day against marriages in which too much passion figured – 'woeful imps' would be the progeny (p. 32). Moreover, such writers observed, no husband should jeopardise by his loving behaviour his God-given status. As Dod and Cleaver put it,

> We would that the man when he loveth should remember his superiority

A wife, as they pointed out, was to be dutiful, faithful and loving:

> In her business, diligent and painful. To her neighbours modest. Humble, kind and quiet . . . A wife is called by God Himself and an helper and not an impediment or a necessary evil, as some unadvisedly do say . . . 'It is better to bury a wife than to marry one'.

Dod and Cleaver were indeed in some respects quite enlightened, if patronising:

> Women are as men are reasonable creatures, and have flexible wits, both to good and evil . . . she is not therefore to be neglected because of her infirmities, is so much the more to be born withal of her husband . . . the honour of all dependeth only on the woman.

But Bathsua Pell Makin knew the realities of social prejudice and she put it more sharply in her *Essay to Revive the Ancient Education of Gentlewomen,*

> Had God intended women only as a finer sort of cattle, he would not have made them reasonable.

Husbands and wives, Gouge told his readers, had distinct duties. Two words summed up their relationship — love and fear:

> Love as sugar to sweeten the duties of authority . . . Fear as salt to season all the duties of subjection which appertains to a wife.

The Apostle Paul's injunction had been quite clear – no wife should rule over her husband. A sober religious matron she might be, married to

> a man of lewd and beastly conditions, as a drunkard, a glutton, a profane swaggerer, an impious swearer and blasphemer,

but still her duty was clear:

> Though a husband in regard of evil qualities may carry the image of the devil, yet in regard of his place and office he beareth the image of God.

So marriage or submissive daughter status was woman's lot. In almost every way she was secondary. *T. E.* in *The Lawe's Resolutions of Women's Rights* (1632, 6) made the matter quite clear,

> Women have no voice in parliament, they make no laws, they consent to none . . . All of them are understood either married or to be married.

In short, as the language of the age put it, 'every feme covert is a sorte of infant.'

11

It was just such lack of identity and enforced self-effacement which the frantically-composing Duchess, Margaret Cavendish, feared. She longed for fame, knowing that if her husband took another wife after her death even the memory preserved in her title would be obliterated. At the same time, however, even Margaret paid lip service to the prejudices of her day, claiming in *Natures Pictures* (p. 297) to be a 'silent' woman,

> because I am addicted to contemplation, unless I am with my lord, yet then I rather attentively listen to what he says than impertinently speak.[35]

It is a sad picture.

In reality, as I've observed, many of the 'quietly submissive' women in the less exalted strata of society, if they were 'complete', were women of considerable skills and remarkable energy. As Antonia Fraser wrote:

> if modesty and deference were to be displayed in theory, in practice a woman needed a formidable combination of organising ability and sheer physical dexterity . . . strength and executive ability were actually required in the 'compleat woman'.[36]

Such a 'formidable combination' emerged triumphant in some of the seventeenth-century women who also ventured into more public spheres. The Quaker women were prominent among them. It is time to give place to these Quaker women. They entered against the background of the troubled years of civil war, in an era of religious and political dissent and one in which, as we have seen, some women's perceptions of themselves had been changing. In just a few years they found themselves centre stage. The seventeenth-century writers who had been deriding women's preaching and prophesying, who had idealised the silent woman, bound to hearth and home and who thought their more militant sisters were unfeminine or witch-like, had seen nothing yet.

Coming to Quakerism

Just like the first followers of Jesus Christ the first Quakers (or *Friends of Truth* or simply *Friends*, as they came to call themselves) joined the new movement from a variety of backgrounds. Many were from the yeoman class, some were in trade. Not all of them stayed the course of the decades of persecution which met them and some of them had not grasped fully those things which Friends (as I shall call them in this study) came to see as the bases of their message. Yet among those who did there were very many remarkable women.

The teaching of the early Friends was in many ways similar to that in other dissenting groups. Indeed there is much truth in Barry Reay's assessment of events in *The Quakers and the English Revolution* (p. 9), where he wrote that

12

the birth of the Quaker movement was less a gathering of eager proselytes at the feet of a charismatic prophet [George Fox] than a linking of advanced Protestant separatists into a loose kind of church fellowship with a coherent ideology and a developing code of ethics.

The Quakers were not even first in the seventeenth-century field in allowing forms of public preaching ministry to women. What marked Friends out from the other groups, however, was the consistency and coherence of their positive teaching about women's nature and about female ministry. Women Friends' new-found freedom bore fruit in action, as they responded to the 'leadings' of God and as a result they suffered with an intensity which was unmatched in this period, except in the experience of Quaker men.

In the period before 1647 George Fox, father figure of Quakerism, had been finding 'openings'. These were moments of enlightenment about matters which had troubled him greatly. It was at this time, so his *Journal* records (pp. 7 seq.), that he came to realise that believers needed no *human* teacher to instruct them and that God dwelt in human hearts, not in buildings made with hands. There should be no clergy or academics' monopoly on the interpretation and teaching of scripture, for even the book of *Revelation*, the source for so much speculation in his day, was not really 'sealed' (*Rev.* 5:1; 10.4; 22:10) from the likes of him, as priests and professors (i.e. those professing religious belief) maintained. Many such things were now being revealed to him.

Previously the spiritually confused Fox had travelled around, meeting with adherents in many religious groups. In this formative period he had also begun to clarify his views on women and on what their place should be in the new order he was coming to understand. On one occasion he had encountered (according to *Journal* p. 8 seq.)

> a sort of people that held women have no souls adding in a light manner, no more than a goose.

Fox responded scripturally, as was his usual manner. He was typical of his age in his abundant knowledge of the Bible:

> But I reproved them and told them that was not right, for Mary said 'My soul doth magnify the Lord, and my spirit hath rejoiced in God my Saviour'.

On that occasion he had in fact met some of the diehard prejudice of the period. It was not commonly *taught* that women had no souls.[37] More common was the dictum which Samuel Torshell echoed in *The Womans Glory* (1645, pp. 2, 10 seq.), namely that 'the soul knows no difference of sex'. This was the theologically impeccable opinion, but as Christopher Hill observed, 'it was socially imprudent to emphasise that in the 1640s'![38] Society was androcentric. Theology and anthropology were inextricably bound together and thinking about women was still to a great extent associated with mistaken views about biology. While it might be conceded (by some at least) that woman, like man, *was* in God's image and enjoyed *spiritual* equivalence, it was still pointed out that since she (Eve) was taken *from* man (Adam) and *for* him, God therefore had ordained the subordination of the female.[39] This double current in Christian thinking was long established, though there had even been times in Christian history when its allegedly greatest thinkers had denied that the woman was in the image of God.[40] Neither the gradual spread of education for women nor the growing Puritan emphasis on mutuality in marriage ('an helper and not an impediment' as Dod and Cleaver noted) stemmed the common tide of misogyny and acerbic comment about women. But George Fox's view of them, and that of his followers men and women, was one of the elements of newborn Quakerism which outraged onlookers.

Women were attracted to Quakerism in large numbers but this was certainly not because the first ministers were advocating a new brand of feminism. Certainly they defended women's equality of souls, but so did others. They were not even trying to undermine the doctrine that a husband, in likeness to Christ's relation to the Church, was 'head' of his wife (*Ephesians* 5: 23 seq.). This was a view Friends held also, as is shown in Fox's writing of 1656 on *The Woman Learning in Silence* (p. 2). In fact Quakerism, on the face of it, did not offer women social equality at all, but it offered them unheard of opportunities for action in the sphere of religion and a rationale for public activity which was liberating. Since Friends did not acknowledge rigid distinctions between the religious, the social and the political, Quaker women found themselves with rights, indeed obligations, to have views on essential issues of the day.

The opposition remarked on the presence of many women at early Quaker gatherings. The polemicist Richard Baxter asked who made up the Quaker following and it was 'young raw professors and women', he concluded, plus 'ignorant ungrounded people' (*One Sheet Against the Quakers,* 1657, p. 11). The table of membership in Buckinghamshire, Norwich and Norfolk in 1662, which Vann compiled in *The Social Development of English Quakerism* (p. 82) indicates respectively that in fact 44.9%, 50% and 43.3% of Quakers in those areas were women. The women would have been especially noticed, given the assumptions of the age, and in any case it would have been hard to ignore them. They courted disfavour in the most hallowed spheres, in churches, in the colleges of Oxford and Cambridge and in the courts of law.

Women Friends preached publicly, often to large gatherings. They travelled to minister, usually two at a time but sometimes in larger groups. They shared the charismatic experiences of their ministering brethren,

14

indulged in shocking 'prophetic' public gestures, harassed the clergy, refused tithe payment and the swearing of oaths and were punished accordingly. Of the 360 Quakers recorded as involved in the disruption of church ministry between 1654-59, 34% were women. Of those Quakers who made the hazardous crossing to America between 1656-63, 45% were women.[41] Like the preaching, prophesying, writing women who had preceded them and who were active at the same time, they were thought to be unfeminine and dangerous, lewd and probably heretical. Their own defence was based on fervent belief (a) in the in-breaking of a new Christian order (b) in the Inner Light, of which they preached[42] which knew no gender-based distinctions and (c) in the fulfilment in Gospel ✓See times of the prophecy of *Joel* (2:28-32), that God's Spirit was poured out on *all* flesh, so that sons and daughters alike should prophesy. Under the 'Gospel-order' which they believed to have been inaugurated the pre-Fall status of the sexes was restored. Men and women who had appropriated to themselves the sacrifice of Christ could be 'helps-meet' once more. 'Christ is sufficient', George Fox wrote in a letter in 1672, 'who restores men and women up into the image of God as they were before they fell.' This also implied that appeals to tradition and even to well-worn passages of scripture in support of women's subjection would cut no ice with Quakers. Where there was no scripture to be appealed to for the Quaker viewpoint on this or any other matter, there was the sufficiency of Christ and the Spirit. Without the Spirit, Friends argued, the scriptures could neither have been written nor understood. The first Quakers preached the good news of Jesus Christ from the standpoint of transformed individuals.

As we shall see in the next chapter, the men and women Quakers who preached and published in support of women's public ministries did not fight shy of using the Bible. If they had, they would have been doing less than other groups of the time who were also egalitarian in outlook and scripture-based in propaganda. Fox and others upheld women's right to prophesy using *Joel* (2: 28-32), which had been a favourite text since Montanist times.[43] They also made extensive use of the writings of Paul which had provided 'loopholes', allowing prophecy, at least, to the female sex. These are matters which will be discussed more fully in the next chapter. While Quakers argued that scripture did not necessarily have the final word, and while prophecy was not the only right at stake, they knew such things were not to be ignored, even if Paul had to be neatly circumnavigated sometimes. Fox did so, for example, in *The Woman Learning in Silence*, referring his uncritical readers to *2 Peter* 3: 16 which stated that Paul's letters

> contain some obscure passages, which the ignorant and unstable misinterpret to their own ruin.[!]

15

The war of words on women's rights and obligations was well-established in Fox's day (indeed twentieth-century readers of feminist theology will find many of the arguments dispiritingly familiar). Despite the vociferousness of the opposition[44] Quakers made their position clear. They were insistent that women as well as men had the right to function as priests, i.e. as representatives of Jesus Christ and vessels of his word. Thus Fox wrote in a *General Epistle* of 1667:

> What, are women priests? Yes women priests. And can men and women offer sacrifice without they wear the holy garments? No . . . the priests surplice? Nay . . . it is the righteousness of Christ . . . the royal garment of the royal priesthood which everyone must put on, men and women.

Such determination was of course bred of a visionary view of the Christian community and as a result it is not surprising that as Keith Thomas observed ('Women and the Civil War sects', 47) 'it was of course among the Quakers that the spiritual rights of women attained their apogee'.

In the early decades Quaker organisation was loose. As in all groups in which leadership was of a charismatic kind and every individual might be expected to know 'leadings', there was among Friends the opportunity for unhelpful individualism and bizarre (even by Quaker standards) behaviour. As we shall see in the following chapters, a formidable organisation developed and individualism was curbed, but at first Quakers were notorious for their outlandish behaviour and their socially divisive teachings. It was these things, rather than their revivalism, philanthropy or spiritually invigorating silent gatherings for which they were known. In the rest of this chapter, then, I shall concentrate on some of the colourful figures of these first decades. Jane Holmes, Susannah Pearson, Martha Simmonds and Hannah Stranger were names which in their day would have brought a frown and more to George Fox. They will figure in the following pages. Elizabeth Hooton's name would have evoked quite a different response. It is fitting that any account should begin with her, the first Quaker woman preacher, indeed possibly George Fox's very first convert.

Elizabeth Hooton of Skegby was the comfortably-off wife of a Nottinghamshire farmer and the mother to four surviving grown-up children when she met and was 'convinced' by Fox around 1647. She was nearing fifty years old and was twenty-four years Fox's senior when they met. At the time he was visiting one of many separatist groups and in hers encountered 'tender people, and a very tender woman'. So he recorded later in his *Journal*. Fox's arrival was sometimes unnerving to such gatherings. Often he was travelling in great privation and at times this 'man in leather britches' had to sleep in the open. He was fervent in his speech and occasionally extravagant in his behaviour and language.

'Repent thou swine and beast' he told an obsequious Ranter. 'Woe to the bloody city of Lichfield', he declared as he walked through it barefoot, seeing in his mind's eye its market place awash with blood. Oliver, one of Elizabeth Hooton's sons, later wrote of this man's coming. Certain people, he said, had been 'startled, and some came no more'.

Previously Elizabeth had been a Baptist and a preacher [Baptists] shared things in common with the Friends: both rejected the rite of infant baptism and disliked oath-taking. They objected (as did many people of the time) to the payment of tithes and they allowed women to preach (though such preaching had been more circumscribed among the Baptists). Even teaching about the Inner Light had existed in some Baptist circles. Baptists would come to excommunicate Quakers, however, as they did Ranters, while as time went on Quakers strongly attacked both. Yet there was common ground between them.[45] After her 'convincement' Elizabeth Hooton condemned the Baptists and their 'deceit'.

Her skills as a preacher were soon put to good use. She left her husband, who had objected to her vocation, and with other Friends she became a minister in the North. Quakers, 'the dregs of the common people', as Ephraim Pagitt called them[46] were 'thickest in the North parts'. Traditional Presbyterian Puritanism was shallow there. Familism, Grindletonianism and the Levellers, common labouring 'mechanic preachers', Seekers and 'shattered' Baptists developed some roots there and so Quakers might seek converts among the disaffected of many kinds.

The Quaker message was usually delivered in a direct, even intemperate way. In an age of ceremony Quakers shunned the signs of good breeding: their ministers' plainness challenged the niceties of dress, their speech patterns (particularly in their use of 'thou' as an address to all, a word normally used for inferiors) seemed offensive and threatened to dissolve barriers of rank and status. So too did the refusal of 'hat honour', of bowing or kneeling. The conventions of polite society were flouted openly and such flouting seemed all the more threatening of social chaos when it was associated with women. Parents, clergy, magistrates and others objected. Opposition to these Friends was inevitable. The likes of Elizabeth Hooton and her daughter (who in later years became a companion in travel) were particularly strongly censured. The authorities suspected Quakers of 'some Levelling design', as the Friend John Audland reported in *The Innocent Delivered out of the Snare* (1658, p. 8) [and they disliked ministers in pairs]– 'Morris dancers', coming two by two. The law, or local officials' interpretation of it, fell heavily on such Friends.[47]

By seventeenth-century standards Elizabeth Hooton was already a woman of advanced years, but so indomitable that she became a role model for later Quaker women.[48] Not long after Fox's first imprisonment in 1650 (for alleged blasphemy) she found herself with him, incarcerated in Derby. Her crime had been to reprove a priest who had then applied to a magistrate to punish her. Such a pattern of events became familiar in Friends' experience. This was the initial period of Quaker 'sufferings' and by 1659 twenty-one of them had died in prison or as the result of ill-use. Many more had been crippled or had had their health otherwise ruined. Dissenters of the time discovered quickly that 'freedom of conscience' was at odds with a clerical authority which was being strongly defended. In fact the Quakers' denunciations of the clergy as 'conjurors' or 'hireling priests' were neither particularly harsh nor unusual in this period. Friends proved to be more than usually vociferous and determined, however, and so they had to pay the price of determination. [49]

Itinerant ministers like Elizabeth Hooton, who organised and attended gatherings ('conventicles') in the houses of sympathisers, who met with others and preached on street corners and elsewhere and who challenged clergy in their own 'steeple-houses', were bound to fall foul of the 1650 *Blasphemy Act*, the two *Conventicle Acts, The Five Mile Act, The Quaker Act, The Lord's Day Act* and other prohibitions against the interruption of ministry, all these dating from the 1650s to 1670. Then there was the extension of the Elizabethan laws on vagrancy, which bore on travelling and masterless Friends. [50] These and more ensured that frequent spells in prison were inevitable for those who refused fines or oaths and who, moreover, would not give sureties. Elizabeth Hooton was one such Friend.

'Met several poor creatures carried by, by Constables for being at a Conventicle. They go like Lambs without resistance would to God they would either conform or be more wife, and not be catched.'   *Pepys Diary.*

18

In prison a Quaker might still preach to inmates and gaolers and might still write letters. A letter signed by Hooton in 1651 is among the earliest of Quaker documents to have survived.[51] A copy signed by Fox exists too, with rather better spelling, though his own could be very unreliable. It was addressed to Noah Bullock Mayor of Derby and this was probably the first of what would be very many addresses by Elizabeth to people in power. Bullock, who lived in comfort, should heed the oppression which was rife, for 'the day of the Lord is coming', she warned.[52] The following year, in prison in York Castle for a similar offence committed at Rotherham, Elizabeth was with the Quakers Jane Holmes and Mary Fisher. She spent sixteen months there and in that time berated Cromwell about the corruption among prison authorities and the intolerable conditions:

> Your judges judge for reward. And at this York many which committed murder escaped through friends and money, and poor people for lesser facts are put to death . . . two great tyrants viz. the gaoler and the clerk of the Assize . . . keeps many poor creatures still in prison for fees . . . they lie worse than dogs for want of straw.[53]

In the same year came another moving plea, this time from Lincoln Castle (*Elizabeth Hooton, Prisoner in Lincoln Castle, pleads to him in authority to reform the Abuses of the Gaol*). A vicious female gaoler had made things hard for her and she was locked away from even visits by the occasional priest ('drunken' she maintained) who offered in any case (she said), only 'invention or imaginations' to the prisoners (one suspects she was isolated because she could not be relied upon to keep silent!). Prison conditions were often inhuman, with prisoners heavily dependent on the good offices of gaolers and having to find funds for their own board and lodging ('ten groats the week' for a bed, she reported). The system was rife with abuse and Elizabeth Hooton pre-empted by a century and a half many of the observations of Elizabeth Fry.[54] Prisons were places of 'drinking and profainness and wantonness', she recorded. Male and female prisoners should be segregated. The use of alcohol should be controlled, as should 'disorder in carding and dicing'. Prisoners should surely be given useful employment. In 1819 the Friend Elizabeth Fry visited Lincoln prison, and those in Nottingham, York and Wakefield too. Reform was still needed. If anything Elizabeth Hooton's reception in the New World was even worse. She was not the first female Quaker minister there. Elizabeth Harris and (in her early twenties) Mary Fisher had been before her. The unfortunate Mary Dyer, after a previous reprieve when she was already at the gallows, had finally been hanged on Boston Common on June 1st 1660, the only woman to suffer execution through disregard of Puritan authority, though some men Friends suffered the same fate in Boston. She had refused to conform to their 'bloody laws'. 'Are you a prophet?'

19

demanded the governor at her final hearing. 'I spoke the words that the Lord spoke in me', she replied. A court official remarked that 'she did hang as a flag for others to take example by'. He had more insight than he knew.

Mary Dyer's punishment was regarded in (Restoration) Britain as an extreme one even for a Quaker. It was probably the outraged response to it which saved Hooton and some others from Mary Dyer's fate.

The now widowed Elizabeth had Joan Broksop[p] (or Brocksoppe) with her as companion in mission as they sailed to the Massachusetts Bay Colony. In fact it was impossible to land in Boston – there were hostile laws of 1657-8 and a promised fine of £100 for any sea captain who deposited Quakers in the region. Indeed the Americans were well appraised of the mother country's view of Quakers. Many a propagandist pamphlet hostile to Friends had reached them, for publicity was bad for Quakers in Britain at the time. In the early months of 1661 some five thousand Friends had been rounded up and imprisoned, following an unsuccessful Fifth Monarchist rising which had been nothing to do with them. Anti-Quaker feeling had been running high, hence Quakers like Joan and Elizabeth were not wanted in the American Colony and they had to land elsewhere. They determined that they would *walk* to their destination from Virginia and by this time Elizabeth was around sixty years old. As it happened they obtained part passage by boat.

Religious freedom was relative so far as the leaders of the Massachusetts Puritans were concerned. Their own people had been refugees from persecution but that did not temper their harshness. The two women Friends were met with great hostility whenever they visited the Colony. Elizabeth was whipped in the towns of Cambridge, Watertown and Dedham, stripped to the waist. She was imprisoned, left without food, more than once taken under armed escort and deposited in wilderness country:

> At night we lay in the woods without any victuals but a few biscuits that we brought with us and which we soaked in the water . . . many wild beasts both bears and wolves and many deep waters where I waded through . . . but the Lord delivered me.[55]

Once she and her companion had been reduced to following wolf tracks in the snow in order to find a way. Still she preached. Undaunted she debated in churches and argued for the welfare of Friends. Her sense of justice was acute. 'Clergy and the gentry hath the land betwixt them', she observed, and in the light of her own experience she declared that

> The professors of Boston and Cambridge, who call themselves Independents who fled the bishops formerly . . . behaved the worse than the bishops did to them by many degrees . . . which causeth their name to stink all over the world because of cruelty.

It was a point which Joan Broksop made too, when she wrote *An Invitation of Love . . . and a Lamentation for New England* (1662, p. 14) and not a few women ministers, Alice Ambrose and Mary Tomkins among them, told of great suffering in New England and elsewhere in America. In her *Lamentation for Bosston and Camberig* (Boston and Cambridge) Elizabeth Hooton wrote of their 'unrighteous decrees' and of those two towns as the breasts of New England. From there, she declared, 'all cruelty' was nursed, to produce blood suckers and persecutors.

On her return to her homeland she gave the King, Charles II, little peace. It was her hope to secure some land, better conditions and a 'safe' house for Friends in the Colony, so that they might propagate their Gospel there. She hoped too that a safe burial place would also be found. The reality at that time was that a fine of £1 per night was levied on anyone who sheltered a Quaker. To further her seemingly hopeless cause she went where the King did. Charles II was known for his appearances in certain London parks, where petitioners would approach him. Elizabeth Hooton was one of them:

> I met him in the Park [St James's] and gave him two letters, which he took at my hand but the people murmered because I did not kneel but I went along by the king and spoke as I went . . . and [I] watch for his going up into the coach in the court.

Eventually she did obtain the permission she wanted, for even the King had read the Bristol Friend George Bishop's indictment *New England Judged*. In Boston, however, the authorities were unimpressed when she returned to them with her daughter as companion, despite the fact that the King had instructed that persecutions should cease.

Elizabeth Hooton had thus far been imprisoned in Derby, York, Lincoln and Boston, New England, for public speaking, refusal to take an oath in court and for disturbing the peace. She had been humiliated, pelted, whipped, sometimes half naked and at a cart-tail. She had seen her son fined for oath refusal, and property to the value of £20 confiscated. Her farm had been sold at considerable loss. She had felt the effects of the first *Conventicle Act*[56] and was again in England when the second such Act was initiated in 1670.[57] She continued to harass the monarch. 'I wait for justice of thee, o king', she cried, this time when she was following him from a game of tennis.

> How oft have I come to thee in my old age, both for thy reformation and safety, and for the good of thy soul, and for justice and equity.

We know nothing of Charles's response to this old woman who had once sat at the gates of his palace in sackcloth and ashes (as she had once reminded Noah Bullock of Lazarus at the rich man's gate, *Luke* 16:19). We may only imagine his reaction to Elizabeth's advice that he should

> not give up thy kingdom to papists nor thy strength to the women.

21

There is a personal record from another ministering woman Friend, Elizabeth Stirredge, who had delivered her own testimony to the King in the eleventh month of 1670. This had been done 'in the dread of the Most High' and trembling, so she had recorded in *Strength in Weakness Manifest* (London 1711). On that occasion, at least according to Elizabeth Stirredge, a paleness had come over his face, and 'with a mournful voice' he had responded 'I thank you my good woman'.[58] But we know only of how *Quakers* responded to the ministrations of Elizabeth Hooton.

She was greatly respected. From the very beginnings of the movement she had lent her house for Meetings (Fox's *Journal*, p. 43, records that a 'possessed' and 'roaring' woman was 'set free' at one such gathering there in 1649). She had laboured hard as an itinerant minister and had not compromised Friends' *Testimonies*. Indeed we find her in 1664 in New England (with Jane Nicholson and Ann Richardson, women of 'Ranter's spirit' and 'a subtle serpent' their opponents declared), publicising George Fox's position against the teachings of the schismatic Friend John Perrot. She had had extensive experience of persecution and it was probably this which led London Friends in 1671 to appoint her their overseer of the Fleet prison. They were too late, however. She was aboard a ship with George Fox, ten other men Friends and Elizabeth Miers, already *en route* to the West Indies. She died in Jamaica in 1672 and was buried about a week after they had landed there, as William Edmondson reported in a letter to Margaret Fell Fox. The West Indies Diary in Fox's *Journal* preserves the following:

> We travelled many hundreds of miles up and down in Jamaica among Friends and the people of the world . . . many were convinced and loving and very tender . . . and not a mouth was opened against us . . . Elizabeth Hootton is deceased in Jamaica. She was well up on the sixth day of the week and deceased on the next day about the eleventh hour in peace like a lamb.

One of her last acts before leaving the country was to petition the King yet again. This time it was for Margaret Fell Fox's release from prison. 'Thou hast suffered more than many have expected' she told the Quaker matriarch, who had been George Fox's wife since 1669. Margaret's freedom came in April 1671. Elizabeth Hooton had been no less noteworthy in suffering. She had once reported of herself that people found her witness before King and commoners alike remarkable. Some had said it was of the devil, she observed,

> and some present made answer, and said they wish they had that spirit.

There was a Baptist woman sick in that Town. John Rush of Bedfordshire went along with me, to visit her; and when we came in, there were many People in the House, that were tender about her: and they told me, She was not a Woman for this World. So I was moved of the Lord God to speak to her, and the Lord raised her up again to the astonishment of the Town and Country. Her Husbands Name was Baldock.

G. Fox his Journal, 1655   R.S.

'Contrary to her own inclination': naked and 'eyric' women

The other women Friends who will be considered in this chapter make Elizabeth Hooton look a pillar of respectability and caution. Their actions have to be understood in the light of some of the characteristics of early, unorganised Quakerism with its teaching on freedom in the Spirit and response to the leadings of God. 'Signs and wonders' accompanied Quakerism's rise. Fox recorded 'miracles'.[59] Quakers were notorious not just for the quakings in their gatherings, which formed the basis for the 'Quaker' epithet and their tears and partial paralysis. Such things also served, as Phyllis Mack has observed, as statements against ritual, self-glorification and control. But they were infamous too for their startling public acts. John Toldervy plunged his hand into boiling water, thrust needles into his flesh and 'lay as if dead for three quarters of an hour in public'.[60] There were less tortuous symbolic gestures, such as when Thomas Aldam encountered Cromwell in 1655, tore his hat and threw it to the ground, as a sign that Cromwell's power 'should be rent from him'. Then there was going 'naked for a sign'.

Solomon Eccles, formerly a teacher of music, had once made his way into a pulpit and had sat there sewing before the congregation. In response to a savage raid on Friends' Bull and Mouth London meeting place he went naked through Bartholomew Fair with a vessel of burning coals on his head, reminding observers of fire, brimstone and Sodom. In his *Diary* for July 29th 1667 Samuel Pepys recorded just this mode of action in the Westminster Hall:

> a man, a Quaker came naked through the hall, only very civilly tied about the privities to avoid scandal, with a chafing-dish of fire and brimstone burning upon his head . . . crying 'Repent! Repent!'

In 1654 a pamphlet noted that eight such cases had occurred in Kendal, Hutton and Kirby Stephen the previous year (*A Further Discovery . . .*, Gateside) and the Friend William Pearson, who died in prison in the course of punishment, had been moved to strip himself naked

> a figure of all the nakedness of the world . . . for the naked truth.

George Fox and other Quakers did not condemn such actions.[61]

A few women Friends performed the same 'sign' too. This prophetic gesture was not made lightly or in a spirit of exhibitionism, indeed some Quaker women found this particular 'ministry' very burdensome. Nevertheless they said they felt called to it. This was a time of great persecution and bloodshed and feelings ran high. Also there was biblical precedent for the action in *Micah* 1:8. So with Elizabeth Leavens (later Holme) as companion, a teenage girl of Kendal gentry family, one Elizabeth Fletcher ('a very modest and grave young woman'), went 'naked' through Oxford, so as to point out the hypocrisy of the religious profession there. The action had been 'contrary to her own will or inclination' wrote Thomas Camm.[62] Less flamboyantly Elizabeth Harris, perhaps the first Quaker minister on the American mainland, preferred entry into churches dressed in sackcloth and ashes. She 'hath much peace in this service' reported John Stubbs to George Fox in a letter of 1660. Elizabeth herself was well aware that even among Friends 'there was some seemed rather to be against it' and so she sought guidance from Fox on the matter.

Public 'nakedness' was not a new phenomenon. Earlier some Anabaptists had done as much;[63] but when it was added to other Quaker 'signs' – i.e. to their prophesyings, 'discernment of spirits', interruptions of church services and rowdy outdoor gatherings where

> men women and little children are strangely wrought about in their bodies, and brought to fall, foam at the mouth, roar and swell in their bellies

as the *Lancashire Petition against Quakers* to the Council of State reported in 1653 – then people in wider society were bewildered and indeed fearful. The Friends were seen to be an additional force for disorder in the land.

It has to be said that in the mid-seventeenth century the remarkable was becoming almost commonplace. There were reports of (non Quaker) women who sat naked and surrounded by the curious, waiting to give birth to the Antichrist. There were those (and the previously mentioned Ranter Mary Gadbury was one) who hailed their sexual partners as Jesus Christ or who claimed to be with child by the Holy Spirit (as did Mary Adams and Jane Robins[64]). Not surprisingly, then, there were women on the fringes of the nascent Quaker movement too, and some firmly within it, whose behaviour worried Friends. Organisation was loose in the early decades of Quakerism, eschatological fervour was infectious[65] and Quakerism was fertile ground for the unstable persons and for the exhibitionist, as well as for the insightful ones. There was ever-present hostility to Friends and they did not wish to arm the opposition. Jane Holmes and Susannah Pearson, who will be considered next, were just the kinds of sources of embarrassment they could do without.

Jane Holmes was a woman with personal charisma. Those who encountered her as a preacher and counsellor felt drawn to return to her, despite themselves. In 1652 she had been at the centre of an incident in the town of Malton, where George Fox had established sympathetic contacts with such as the linen draper Roger Hebden. 'The spirit of prophecy' was at work in a group of Quaker ministers there and when Jane Holmes preached, 'the Power' broke out in the town. Jane Holmes received a ducking. This was a common punishment for 'scolds' and this, along with the humiliating and painful metal scold's 'bridle' which was used to punish assertive women, was punishment suffered by a number of women Friends. In 1655 the Friends Dorothy Waugh and Anne Robinson were led through the streets of Carlisle in 'bridled' fashion. Jane had been ducked because of local outrage. The Friends' message at Malton had brought into the open shopkeepers and woollen drapers who had set alight quantities of silk ribbons and other fine materials, as a witness against pride and injustice.[66] Jane Holmes, it was alleged at the Yorkshire Assizes, had been 'an instrument of the disturbance of the whole town' and an 'instrument for the desertion of wives'. The truth was also that there had been a successful Quaker mission there. She had shown no respect to the minister of the church, it was claimed, and in addition had poached its congregation. She had been at Meetings at strange hours and her message had disrupted families. Thomas Dowley's son had said that he had no more loyalty to his father than to any other man. Major Blaydon could not 'keep his wife at home'. None of this is surprising, of course. Sectarianism has always divided families. Friends did hold Meetings in odd places and at peculiar hours, as they felt moved so that it was probably true, as her accusers claimed, that local women were still out at midnight. Aspects of Quakerism's message must indeed have seemed liberating to Major Blaydon's wife. All things considered, it was inevitable that at this time Jane Holmes would be suspected of witchcraft.

It was a common enough accusation against Quakers that they were witches or that they dabbled with the paranormal. In America in

25

particular, Elizabeth Hooton, Mary Fisher and others like them might certainly expect to be 'searched'. In Britain the authorities seldom took such accusations seriously, though the flamboyant prophet Anna Trapnel *was* searched for signs of her witch status, as the *Report and Plea*[67] recorded. Sometimes bizarre accusations about Friends did reach the magistrates. It was claimed that in 1657, for example, in Cambridgeshire a widow named Morlin had turned an apostate Friend into a bay mare and indeed had then ridden her to a midnight feast. The accusation came two years later and the case was dismissed, though John Bunyan seems to have encouraged belief in the story.[68] Sometimes disillusioned former Quakers claimed that they had been 'bewitched' and George Fox was regularly suspected.[69] Fox and other Friends certainly believed in witchcraft; they believed in the power of malediction, in ghostly appearances and that a person's presence might preserve a ship from harm or damn it.[70] Given prevailing ideas it was inevitable that the spectre of witchcraft hovered around *women* Friends in particular. With her reputation Jane Holmes was a marked woman.

Witnesses and her accusers held that Jane Holmes had carried a mysterious bottle, one whiff from which was enough to send someone into a state of trance. She had allegedly diagnosed one Anthony Beedall as having 'an evil spirit', and he had gone to her for counselling and to have his sins uncovered. Having drunk from the bottle, it was said, he fell into a trance and then vomited, which Holmes declared to be the workings of the Spirit in him. She advised a fast, which would make him 'as good as Christ'[71] and the allegation was that she had told Beedall he might walk across the Derwent, rather than take a boat. For all his co-operation with the authorities the said Beedall acknowledged a desire to go to Jane again.

Jane Holmes was incarcerated in York Castle at the same time as Elizabeth Hooton and Mary Fisher[72] were there. It is probable that the mutual support network which Friends tried hard to maintain was not very effective at this time, for Thomas Aldam, also in prison there until December 1654, recorded that there was 'freedom to come amongst Friends very little'. Jane was involved in a dispute about aid distributed to prisoners and it may be that she was also showing signs of mental disturbance. On the other hand, it may be that she was an early example of some Quaker women's refusal to allow male Quakers to 'reprove' them and to escape some of the implications of the Friends' philosophy of the Spirit and of womankind. Jane, it was said, manifested

> a wild and eyrie [i.e. airy] spirit which was exalted above the cross, which kicked against reproof.[73]

William Dewsbury and Richard Farnworth, Friends and friends of the ministry of women, visited and remonstrated with her in York, but she had 'run out' in her mind.[74] This was the phrase Friends used to describe straying from the path of Quakerism, scarcely defined though it was at

A QVAKER

Weake as you say we are, yett wee command,
all flesh to fall, that doth against us stand.
The light within us, of such force is found,
should satan come, twill lay him on the ground.

The Light they talke of keepes a heavy rout.
ile search all corners, but ile find it out.
By yea and nay, she is a dareing Curle,
ile it ... tell or els Iam a Churle.

With face of brass, this woman that you see
most Impudently doth afirm, that shee.
The mind of God, in all poynts, more doth know,
then from the Sacred Scriptures, ere could flow.
Presumptious wretch; it were more fitt that shee,
at home showld keepe, and mind hir howsewifery.
And if noe meanes to live on, woorke for bread
then idlye gossop with hir magot head

Their light within doth so prevayle.
it makes them hot about the tayle.
Exsept afreind that poynt doth cleare.
they could them selves in pecces teare.

The Quakeress and the Devil (Engraving c.1700 by Egbert van Heemskirk, 1645-1704)

27

this stage. She would not be the last Friend to be so described. Though we know of her imprisonment Jane Holmes disappears thereafter from the records. Perhaps she died. Perhaps, on the other hand, she was one of the subjects of that process of 'cleansing' Quaker history which occurred in the final decades of the century. Quakers, great chroniclers of their own history, were aware that in the beginning anarchy had been the danger in their midst. They preferred not to be too much reminded of it. Some decades further on, however, *some* of the colourful characters of the early years had been persuaded onto less dangerous paths, and so they continued in the Quaker fold. One of them was Susannah Pearson.

In these remarkable times of prophetic happenings there were some who believed that the dead, even the long dead, might be raised. After all, it was observed, the Hebrew prophets and the first Christian Apostles had achieved resurrections in their own God-governed days. So for example John Robins, a Ranter,[75] claimed to have 'raised' even a redeemed Cain, Judas, Jeremiah and other prophets. Ludowick Muggleton, who gave his name to the Muggletonians, was taken in by Robins for a time, though later he denounced him for 'the witchcraft spirit of Quakerism'.[76] Quakers, too, believed that theirs was an age of grace, guided by the Spirit which through those 'in Christ' could bring healing and *resurrection*, so it is not entirely surprising that a Quaker should attempt such a feat. Susannah Pearson of Worcester was just such a Quaker.

The events concerned the corpse of William Pool who had embraced Quakerism but later, in 1657, he had committed suicide by drowning. His mother was distraught. The unfortunate man's corpse was exhumed though Susannah Pearson signally failed in her attempt to revive it. The Quaker Thomas Willan described the whole affair coolly in a letter to George Fox. The marginal note – 'mad whimsy' – may come from Fox himself[77] but opponents of Quakerism were less sanguine. The title of an anonymous publication of 1657 well illustrates the tone of the publicity:

> A sad caveat to all Quakers . . . containing a true narration of one William Pool an apprentice, and a known Quaker near Worcester, who on Friday, in last Febr. the 20, boasting that he had that day Christ by the hand, and must according to appointment go to him again, did . . . drown himself in the river . . . As also the most barbarous usage of some Quakers who digged him out of his grave. And the most unparalleled presumption of one Mrs Susan Pierson, who undertook to raise him again to life . . .[78]

Susannah's 'presumption' had involved fervent prayer and she had 'laid her face upon his face, and her hands upon his hands', reported the news-sheet *Mercurius Politicus* (no. 351). There was no place in an ordered society for latter day recreations of Elisha's actions with the Shunnamite's son or Peter with the late lamented Dorcas (2 Kings 4:18 seq. Acts 9:36 seq.).

Such acts were, to say the least, an embarrassment to those Friends who cherished already a hope for peace, acceptance and order. Yet Susannah did *not* disappear from the Quaker records. I would assume, nevertheless that her later associations with Friends were more sober. Her name appears more than once in Besse's account of their *Sufferings*.[79]

Such strange events were not confined to the seventeenth century, of course. In 1707 the French Camisard prophets in exile created a tumult so that the militia had to keep order in the London streets. The crowds were awaiting the promised resurrection of one Dr Emes, an event foretold before his death. Then in 1786 the American Quaker, Jemima Wilkinson of Yates County, New York State, was said by her detractors to have portrayed herself as resurrected, as an incarnated Christ and capable of miracles which included walking on water.[80]

> For us, no doubt, these are case-histories of hysterical women and lack significance,

Geoffrey Nuttall wrote, referring to the non-Quakers Sarah Wight and Anna Trapnel, as well as the Friends Susannah Pearson and the women around James Nayler. The fact is that some seventeenth-century Quakers did move in those circles in which prophecy and 'raisings', fasting, trances and 'hysterical' women figured[81] but sometimes other Friends felt it necessary to disassociate themselves from certain kinds of action, thereby creating precedents for their developing discipline.

One such action took place in 1656 and it helped to change the face of youthful Quakerism. The movement was shaken by it. Country-wide, from parliament to the ballad-mongers and pamphleteers, Friends were derided. The episode is of particular interest to me. This is not just because the man involved, James Nayler, was an apologist whose writings and spirituality have enjoyed something of a renaissance in Quakerism of the present century. It is of interest because the actions of the disgraced Nayler have frequently been presented as due to manipulative and hysterical women. Students (such as myself) of the ancient heresies of the patriarchal Church are very familiar with presentations of this kind. I shall begin this tale, then, by quoting some modern writers on James Nayler and the women. Most of the writers concerned are in fact Quakers.

Martha Simmonds and the women around James Nayler

Historians have pronounced as follows:

(a) The admiration of his women followers was to prove his undoing (Brailsford *QW,* 253).

(b) . . . the strains of controversy and ministry appear to have blurred his judgement, particularly in relation to some of the fanatical women the movement attracted (I. Breward, *BDBR* 2, 257).

(c) James Nayler allowed the enthusiasm of two women followers to overturn his judgement (M. Hope Bacon, *Mothers of Feminism,* 19).

(d) . . . always his loyalty to Fox and his teachings was destroyed by the extravagance and adulation of Martha . . . the influence of Martha Simmonds, a hysterical woman, almost drove Nayler as early as 1655 to quarrel with Howgill and Burrough (Ross, *MF,* 105, 101).

(e) A group of women in London began to disrupt meetings . . . treated James Nayler with exaggerated respect . . . he allowed himself to be used by unbalanced people (Punshon, *A Portrait in Grey,* 75).

There is consistency in these presentations. As Knox wrote in *Enthusiasm* (pp. 160, 165 seq.)

> Nayler was a tool in the hands of admirers who all held, and continued to hold, that their actions were inspired by the inner light . . . the story . . . is usually told as that of a muddle-headed Quaker who underwent a brief apotheosis at the hands of a few crazed women.

The seventeenth-century records, Quaker and otherwise, indicate that women played a significant part in what occurred. Some of the women later repented of their roles in the affair and to the modern reader both the language of the event and the event itself seem remarkable. Yet writers' (not least Quaker ones') accounts seem to me to treat the seventeenth-century language with a literalism which is not usually found among those who look coolly at the religious language of those times. It is striking, too, that (with notable exceptions among specialists on the seventeenth century who have made a detailed study of Nayler) scarcely a writer refers to those *men* who figured in what happened – no less extravagant or 'hysterical' in their actions. Moreover there is an almost universal failure to enquire *why* some Quaker women were acting as they did, beyond it being asserted that they were responding to belief in their own inspiration and the Light. Let us turn, then, to James Nayler and the events of October 24th 1656.

James Nayler had been a cavalry quartermaster and a preacher before he became a formidable apologist for Quakerism. He had one of the finest minds among early Friends[82] and he wrote prolifically and powerfully for them.[83] After Nayler's disgrace people speculated on what his earlier associations had been. Had he perhaps been among the Leveller rebels at Burford? Nayler's was just 'the old spirit of the Ranters', declared the Quaker Samuel Fisher in 1679 (*The Testimony of Truth Exalted,* p. 621).[84] Sir Henry More, the Cambridge Platonist, observed in his correspondence with Lady Conway that surely Nayler (a man 'at least equal with Fox') was 'tinctured with Familism'.[85] Nuttall and Bittle, authors of two valuable studies of Nayler, differ as to just how significant had been Nayler's contact with those who, in turn, *did* associate with the Familists and the

James Nayler 1618-1660
The Quaker Indicted
by Parliament

des Quackers
IACOB NAYLORS Einzug in BRISTOL

likes of Anna Trapnel and Sarah Wight. What is not in doubt was that Nayler was a leading and popular Quaker and he was probably one who was familiar with some of the more exotic shores of seventeenth-century religion.

The farmer from West Ardsley near Wakefield had met George Fox in 1651. God, he declared later, called him to leave his land, to say goodbye to his wife and children and to become a preacher in the Quaker cause. He did continue to provide some support for his family and at a later date we catch occasional glimpses of Ann Nayler, cheering the imprisoned James, gaining the ear of Cromwell for his welfare and supporting her husband in his broken state.

By 1656 he was a man of considerable stature and reputation among Friends. He was at that time ministering in London and in the summer of that year his co-workers Francis Howgill and Edward Burrough rejoined him, after a period of work in Ireland. George Fox at that time was suffering a hard imprisonment in Launceston Castle, unable to visit established or new groups of Quakers and in the light of certain recent developments in London, probably very frustrated. For in London factions had been emerging. Some had been saying they were for Nayler, others for Howgill or for Burrough.[86] It was reminiscent of Paul's experience with the church in Corinth. The Friends' gatherings in the capital had been suffering disruption for some time. The troublesome people concerned were at least on the fringes of Quakerism and some were firmly within it. Some supporters of Nayler were being held to blame. Even at this early stage of Quaker history it was not new to find disagreements in the ranks[87] but we may discern a fear in the air that the 'James' camp was precipitating a crisis in the movement.

Martha Simmonds is usually cited as the ringleader. Hannah Stranger (Stringer), Judy Crouch, a woman called Mildred (a close relative of Judy), Mary Powell, Dorcas Erbury, Ann Gargill (Cargill) and others figure among the accused over several years. Nayler, it must be said, was not just an associate of 'fringe' or extravagant Quaker women. Sarah Blackbury and Rebecca Travers, pillar 'mothers in Israel' were numbered among his close friends. So it is hard to see why events took quite the course they did. Nayler had probably been overworking and he was under strain. He was certainly a victim of his own success in some respects and a prey to certain emphases in early Quaker teaching. George Fox was not guiltless.

Martha Simmonds (b. 1624), sometime nurse to Oliver Cromwell's sister, was the wife of Thomas Simmonds and the sister of Giles Calvert, both men being London printers for Friends. She had been 'convinced' in 1654 and it was only a short time before she was both imprisoned and an author. She had published *A Lamentation for the Lost Sheep of the House of*

Israel and *O England thy Time is Come.* These tell of a long spiritual search and of restlessness before her own convincement among Friends, when God had shown her 'a measure of himself in me' (*Lamentation* p. 6). It was necessary, she wrote, to seek the true teacher, the 'one of a thousand who brings the glad tidings' (*idem.* p. 3). As early as 1655, however, there had been signs of strain between Martha and male ministers in London. Howgill and Burrough had reproved her for her behaviour and she had gone to James Nayler for redress. Nayler neither condemned his co-workers nor sought to discipline Martha, so that he was temporarily estranged from Howgill and Burrough and Martha declared 'How are the mighty fallen . . . I came to Jerusalem and behold a cry!' (2 *Samuel* 1:19, 25; *Isaiah* 5:7). The estrangement did not last long[88] and even as events took a turn for the worse in the next year, correspondence shows that relations between Nayler, Fox and other Quakers were not irrevocably bad.[89] Nevertheless, two decades later, when he was composing his *Journal*, George Fox claimed that it was in the summer of 1655, soon after Howgill and Burrough left for Ireland, that he had had a premonition of Nayler's downfall.

Martha and other women had been disruptive and as some Friends became concerned about James Nayler's state of mind and his association with his ardent admirers, so too the rumours began that this same Martha had bewitched him. Those who visited Nayler commented on his lapses into fits of weeping. There are unspecific references to his having strayed from the Quaker way. Writers observed that, hopelessly and unhappily under Martha Simmonds' influence (as his visitors thought he was), Nayler had never been the same since the time he spent three days in the Simmonds' household, after the 'how are the mighty fallen' incident.

Martha Simmonds had alienated leading Quakers. Richard Hubberthorne described her to Margaret Fell as 'an exceedingly filthy spirit'. Fox condemned both Martha and Hannah Stranger alike as lying, slandering women. It seems to me that there was probably a leadership crisis in the air. Yet although there survives a very great deal of evidence about the Nayler affair, in fact much of the language of the Quaker records is opaque. Hence it is not easy to determine what exactly was happening or what the women's wishes and grievances were. Nayler's own ability and popularity were obvious, however. Certainly Corinthian-type 'parties' existed among London Quakers. Fox was cut off from public ministry and oversight through being in prison and in any case the position of leader of Friends was an unregularised one. Baxter in *Reliquiae* (i, 77) described *Nayler* as the Friends' 'chief leader' and More, later, was to describe him as 'at least equal with Fox' (see n. 85). A clash of personalities emerges in a letter from Margaret Fell to Nayler, which was sent in response to one that he had written. In his own letter he had declared his loyalty to George Fox.

Howgill had seen the document, however, and maintained that it was 'full of cunning and subtlety' and Margaret Fell replied sharply:

> . . . thou hast confess'd him to be thy father and thy life bound up with him and when he sent for thee and thou would not come to him where was thy life then . . . thou saith George is burying thy name that he may raise his own.

Nayler was in prison in Exeter when this letter was sent. He was a weakened man who had been fasting and was confused by the mixture of adulation and ill-feeling he was experiencing from different quarters.

James Nayler had been arrested *en route* to visit George Fox in Launceston Castle. In Launceston, to Fox's bewilderment and anger, Martha Simmonds and Hannah Stranger had managed to visit him. They had not shown him the respect he expected and just as was happening in disrupted London Meetings Fox had had to put up with loud singing. Martha was much in evidence during Nayler's Exeter imprisonment too, or so visiting Friends claimed. Richard Hubberthorne reported to Margaret Fell that

> . . . after a little time his heart was opened towards me . . . but there came Martha Simmons . . . and when at any time we were together she would have called him away . . . and he was so much subject to her . . . in her filthyness still.

Nayler never seemed to criticise his devotees (men as well as women) and Margaret wrote to him about 'siding with unclean spirits' and of 'the spirit that rebels'. But it was already too late. In Fox's opinion Nayler had 'run out' in June of 1656 and an important letter probably did not reach him before he made the fateful public entry into Bristol on October 24th.

Established men Friends had had a difficult year as workers in London. For reasons that are not made plain, there was disaffection in the ranks, or on the fringes of, women Friends, and the men had suffered as a result. Richard Hubberthorne, 'a man of small stature, of a weak constitution of body' as the *Piety Promoted* obituary series described him (i, 43) had encountered problems and he had written to tell Margaret Fell of one remarkable Meeting where he had faced up to Mildred:

> . . . yesterday which was the 5 day of the week, we had a meeting at the Bull and Mouth and Mildred was there . . . and I having spoken something in the living power of the Lord to the people, she was tormented, and she resolved so to speak as that I should not speak any more . . . And when she had spoken until her natural breath was spent, she again still did strive to speak . . . I was kept and moved to stay. The meeting began at the 3 hour, and we stayed almost until midnight . . . she did so strive in her wickedness until all her natural parts was spent, and her senses distracted and she was even really

34

Bull & Mouth Inn – turned – Quaker Meeting House in London.

> mad . . . she said that at the next meeting she would come in more
> power . . . but she did not come at all . . . she is so hoarse that she
> cannot speak at present.

Mildred was sternly rebuked by Fox, as were Hannah, Martha and others,
but to no avail.

Here was a dilemma. Quakers had supported the public ministry of
women and they had preached the free working of the Spirit. Without
doubt they proved to have a better record of proclaiming and defending
the spiritual equality of women and their right to public Christian ministry
than any group of the period. Now, however, as in all religious groups
which have to face the implications of charismatic freedom, questions of
good order and of 'testing the spirits' were to the fore. On the one side
there were challenges to those who were coming to represent (male)
authoritative leadership. On the other there were accusations of
unruliness, madness and more. The dominant faction criticised the
doctrine and extravagant language of the other, while disregarding
parallel tendencies in its own ranks. None of this was new in Christian
history. [90] It was clear to seventeenth-century observers (and must have
been evident to Fox), that Nayler and later John Perrot were not just
charismatic figures for many, but were also attractive to women. As John

35

Harwood recorded in 1666/7 (*The Life of Innocency Vindicated* . . . British Museum Library, unprinted)

> JN and JP in their day was amiable and beautiful in the eye of the chaste virgins in Israel as David was when he conquered Goliath . . .

The aftermath (made stronger by the Perrot schism of a few years later) fitted a familiar pattern too – there came greater institutionalisation in Quakerism, organisation and discipline, the marginalisation of women's charismatic authority and the near disappearance of the likes of Susannah Pearson, Jane Holmes and Martha Simmonds.

This is what happened on October 24th 1656: James Nayler rode into Bristol with his hands clasped before him, with Martha Simmonds and Hannah Stranger at either side, two male riders behind, sometimes John Stranger and sometimes Timothy Wedlock in front and on the last stage of the journey a dismounted woman at the rear, leading her horse. Garments were spread before him. Nayler had been out of Exeter prison less than a week and he was forty years old. The party was rainswept and it had been sometimes ankle-deep in mud trudging through Martha's native Somerset. Their singing had deteriorated to humming. The language which admirers had addressed to Nayler was certainly uncompromising:[91] 'Everlasting Son of Righteousness' Hannah Stranger had written in a letter to him, but it was John, her combmaker husband, who added the postscript 'thy name shall be no more James Nayler but Jesus'. Just the year before Hannah had published a short piece beginning (and entitled) *Consider I beseech you how clearly the Scripture is fulfilled*. Now she hailed Nayler as 'fairest of ten thousand, thou only begotton Son of God'. 'Holy, holy holy' sang those who had gathered round him in Exeter prison, 'dear and precious son of Zion, whose mother is a virgin'. 'King of Israel and Son of the Most High', praised Thomas Simmonds.[92] 'James Nayler shall sit at the right hand of the Father' was Dorcas Erbury's reply to the magistrate who examined her. Dorcas, it was claimed, being 'two days gone', had been 'raised' by Nayler in the gaol (cf. *Acts* 9:40). The event had been witnessed by her mother, or so Dorcas told her interrogator. 'Holy, holy, holy, Lord God of Sabaoth . . . Lord God of Israel' sang Nayler's entourage on the way to Bristol.

The response from the ballad-mongers, rumour-makers, the pamphlet writers and from parliament was swift. The ten day parliamentary case which followed involved the participation of 103 members. It seemed to some that a religious toleration which could give rise to James Nayler was toleration taken too far. Yet the perfectionism to which Nayler had fallen prey, his certainty (put into practice) that the believer might be in totality 'in Christ', inhabited by Him, were ideas familiar to other Friends. Even the language used was in fact not far removed from that favoured by some Friends when writing to others.[93] 'Thou would not be subject to him

[George Fox] to whom all nations shall bow' Margaret Fell had written to Nayler in the letter already quoted,[94] and Margaret herself addressed her future husband with the words 'O thou bread of life . . . fountain of eternal life'. Fox wrote of her in terms of the woman clothed with the sun of *Revelation* 12.[95] Nayler's replies to his questioners were circumspect and do not suggest insanity on his part. When asked if he were indeed the Son of God he answered:

> I am the son of God but I have many brethren . . . where God is manifest in the flesh there is the everlasting Son, and I do witness God in the flesh.

He did not deny that the kind of language cited had been used by his companions, but there was one title which he denied with a vehemence which is unusual in the trial reports. Martha Simmonds, he stated, had never been called 'mother' by him or any others. He was told that George Fox had said it was so. 'George Fox is a liar and a firebrand of hell' he replied. He had received no support from Bristol Friends.[96]

In December of 1656 there was a move to inflict the death penalty on Nayler (but not his followers) and the biblical penalty of death by stoning was talked of. The motion was defeated.[97] *Clemency* was the order of the day! Nayler was to be pilloried and in midwinter brutally whipped through the cities of London and Bristol. His tongue was to be bored with hot irons and the *B* of blasphemy was to be branded on his forehead. Finally prison with hard labour would follow. The sentence was carried out

> The blood and wounds of his back did very little appear at first sight by reason of abundance of dirt that covered them

noted his friend and now his nurse, the Quaker Rebecca Travers.

Reay in *The Quakers and the English Revolution* noted that by 1655 Quakerism had become 'a national problem rather than a regional nuisance' (p. 11) and in *The World Turned Upside Down* (pp. 219 seq.) Christopher Hill explained succinctly:

> Nayler was leader of an organised movement which . . . had swept with frightening rapidity over the southern counties . . . whose aims were obscure, but which certainly took over many of the aims of the Levellers . . . recruiting former Levellers and Ranters . . . Bristol was the second city of the kingdom.

South.

Historians also write of the struggles which feature behind this case. There were moderates, like Cromwell himself, and those who wanted very much to stem the effects of religious toleration. Cromwell, a man not tolerant of blasphemy, seems nevertheless to have been dismayed at the course of action:

we . . . do desire that the house will let us know the grounds and reasons whereupon you have proceeded.

It was Cromwell who let Ann Nayler visit her husband and take him provisions. At Ann's request he allowed James Nayler candlelight and fire in 'The Hole' in the Bridewell.[98] It was Cromwell's secretary, William Malyn, who went to enquire about the sick Nayler in August of 1658, and offered a physician (which was refused). It was probably due to ill-health that Nayler was released briefly in the winter of 1657-8 but otherwise he was incarcerated until September 1659.

The determined adulation of his supporters (of what, exactly, who can say?) and opposition to other leading Friends did not cease with James Nayler's arrest and punishment. Four were taken with him to London, though Samuel Cater, Timothy Wedlock and Robert Crab (who died soon after), all of whom had been associated with the Bristol entry, were discharged.[99] There was singing all the way to London according to the Friend Thomas Taylor's report to Margaret Fell. Not for the first time they knelt before him and sang in the prison. When he was pilloried as part of his sentence, Martha Simmonds, Hannah Stranger and Dorcas Erbury – in likeness to the women at the foot of the cross (*John* 19:25), it was said – gathered round. Robert Rich had already besieged parliament and its members with his letters and petitions, standing at points of access where he could not be missed, and according to John Deacon's *Exact Historie of the Life of James Nayler* (1657, 35 seq.).[100] Rich had marched around the pillory. He had sung to and kissed the injured Quaker, even licking his branded forehead. Rich it was who set up the sign 'This is the King of the Jews', in case the likeness to Christ's suffering should be missed.

Sympathetic and singing followers accompanied him on the Bristol stage of his punishment, with Rich crying 'holy, holy, holy' again. London Quaker gatherings and some elsewhere were still being disturbed the following year by Mildred, Judy and others. 'Ranters and loose persons', Fox commented dismissively. It is not improbable that disruptive people *were* taking advantage of the Friends' discomfiture and unjustly were being branded 'Naylerites'. Associates of Martha Simmonds unnerved Quakers in the Salisbury area. Ann Cargill was named as a Naylerite in reports to Margaret Fell from ministers in the Low Countries. The noisy singing of Robert Rich (subsequently an associate of the schismatic John Perrot) troubled Quaker gatherings in the West Indies long after Nayler had repented of his actions[101] and it is Rich's own writing which sheds some light on the strains between Nayler and Fox, as between Fox and John Perrot later.[102]

When Nayler emerged from his imprisonment Rebecca Travers, formerly a Baptist and married to a London tobacconist Friend, was again

38

there to meet him. Rebecca came to be a pillar of London Quakerism and much more prominent than her husband, linked as she was with the disciplinary Six Weeks Meeting and having the Morning Meeting use her house for its deliberations. She was sister to Mary Booth, who was also an associate of James Nayler (Mary had written the preface to his published *Milk for Babes*) and Mary emerged later as confidante and supporter of the schismatic John Perrot. Rebecca at the time of the Perrot affair remained firmly within the mainstream and she was no lover of Perrot and his vision but now on the release of James Nayler she did not abandon the man who had been responsible for her own 'convincement'. She, like her sister, had written prefaces for Nayler's tracts, and at the time of his punishment she had washed and dressed his wounds. Rebecca had requested parliament to dispense with any more punishment and other Friends had done the same. But this 'mother in Israel' who became the author of seven pamphlets, had not been part of that entourage which had done the fateful deed. Her presence is a salutary reminder, nevertheless, that James Nayler had sympathisers in more than one Quaker camp. Similarly John Perrot, troublesome in the next decade, was known to many as a man of great spirituality and honesty.

Crowds gathered to be with Nayler in the house of Jane Woodcock.[103] Jane was part of that Giles Calvert-Thomas Simmonds circle which seems to have been closely associated with radical ideas within Quakerism[104] and it is notable, too, that some of the same women (and men including Robert Rich and John Harwood) came to be associated with the schism initiated by John Perrot, whose actions represented 'an extension of the already existing controversy represented by Nayler'.[105]

Quakerism would never be the same again. Perhaps it could not be. Thereafter, as Cherry remarked:

> Quakers ceased to indulge in miracles or even discuss them, the individualistic appeal was de-emphasised, organisation and discipline received more emphasis[106]

There is truth in this, but the shift did not occur overnight. The accusations against Friends, of all the kinds referred to, did not cease in the anti-Quaker publications. Nevertheless it is the view of Kenneth Carroll, American Quaker historian (who has made studies of Martha Simmonds, John Perrot and Elizabeth Harris among others) that

> there is evidence that after the Nayler episode . . . Fox became somewhat distrustful of women in the movement, especially in positions of leadership.[107]

In my view Knox's assessment in *Enthusiasm* was not far wrong. It was *schism* rather than heresy (or at least as much as heresy) which Quakers were most fearful of at the time. Loyalty to George Fox seemed to be in jeopardy:

It was not that he was attempting to make himself equal to the Saviour of the world but that he was attempting to make himself equal with George Fox.[108]

It is striking, too, that despite the clear evidence in contemporary records that *men*, as well as women, were closely associated with the actions of Nayler, writers (not least Quaker ones) have continued to stress the influence of irrational or unscrupulous women, to the exclusion of much else. It is clear that the causes of female Quaker disaffection, after only a decade of the movement's existence, have been insufficiently studied.[109] The possibility should not be ignored that some women were conscious of a gap between preaching and practice where Quaker testimony to the spiritual equality of women was concerned. Perhaps, indeed, they were seeking an equality which went beyond the spiritual. For whatever reasons, Martha Simmonds and others were challenging the 'natural' superiority of some male leaders in the mid 1650s, as other women did during the tensions between John Perrot and Fox's circle in the 1660s. Despite the Friends' great interest in recording their own history, there is much that their records do *not* say. I think it will be difficult to discover with certainty what Martha Simmonds, Hannah Stranger, Judy, Mildred and others had in mind. They did not write the records.

In the late 1660s Hannah Stranger married Henry Salter. She had repented of her former associations and was once again in sisterhood with Bristol Friends. Indeed in the spring of 1657 John Perrot ('convinced' by Edward Burrough during his time in Ireland and no admirer of Nayler) with two others was writing to Friends in Waterford, Ireland, reporting that supporters of Nayler

> would come creeping on their bellies to be owned yea: Martha their miserable mother this day hath been with us, and all her witchery and filthy enchantment is set at naught.

Margaret Fell Fox's release from prison in 1671 came about after a number of Friends had appealed to the authorities. Elizabeth Hooton had been one of them and so too was Hannah Stranger Salter. She went on to settle in the New World.

Martha Simmonds' first expressions of regret came just a year after the events and she too was reconciled with the Friends. She died on her way to Maryland in 1665, the same year in which one Mary Powel (perhaps the associate of Judy Crouch and the hoarse-voiced Mildred) was transported. If this transportation occurred because of determined public attendance at Quaker gatherings, then she too had not abandoned the Friends – though who knows whether she was, by their reckoning, now 'respectable'. Judy and Mildred were perhaps never reconciled, for 'ranterish' disturbances and separations did not cease.[110] In 1657 women were still disrupting London Meetings, crying out to the men 'you have lost the power'. The accusation is probably significant.

In this chapter I have concentrated almost entirely on events in the first two decades of Quakerism. I have paid special attention to women who seem to have been in one way or another innovative and extraordinary. There were, as I shall show, many other extraordinary women Friends too, remarkable not for their travels, their public confrontations, their prophetic gestures or their publications but as quieter, though no less intransigent, souls, showing great tenacity in adversity. They struggled in enforced separation at home with their children while partners were absent or imprisoned; they faced the opposition of unconvinced members of their families. They will figure in the next two chapters with many other sorts of women Friends, for Quakerism was fortunate in that at the outset it had foremothers who were role-models of many kinds.

It is beyond its scope to do justice to all or any of the women referred to in this study. Indeed although there exists a great deal of evidence to be sifted, the stories of some of the women have never been recorded and their lives never researched – Ann Nayler is one such example as is Elizabeth Perrot, beloved wife of John. There is very much work to be done. Nevertheless feminist historians and students of literature, at least, and occasionally some others too, are now conscious that the study of Quaker women brings with it a wealth of stirring tales and also questions about the stages of women's onward march towards freedom of action. In her book *The Underside of History* the American historian and Friend Elise Boulding wrote that:

> In its beginnings Quakerism did not create individuality in women, it attracted women who were already autonomous individuals.

I think this was true of some, but the statement does not go far enough. From its inception Quakerism offered to women occasions of greater autonomy. Its teachings offered a rationale for what some women had known instinctively but had never acted upon and for some, Quakerism, itself born in a time of social and religious upheaval, allowed them to break through the bounds of 'femininity' so that by adopting the biblical (primarily male) prophetic role, they might transcend the very, womanly, self. I have sympathy with Phyllis Mack's reading of the situation. It was not that Quaker women were 'convinced' because they wanted freedom from their families or to act like men, 'like young women dressing up as soldiers in order to find adventure and see the world'. In the seventeenth century, in fact, most of them continued to work out their Quakerism close to hearth and home, as we shall see. They acted as they did because the time had come – a time of change, and they felt, and were encouraged to believe, that they could do no other. Women in the Protestant traditions

41

have not infrequently 'taken on new roles in an unsettled situation'.[111] Quaker women did no less. In the seventeenth century the effects of persecution upon such women and the traumas they overcame in pursuing ministries despite themselves *bred* autonomy, even in the hesitant. The birth was not painless.

CHAPTER II

'WOMEN'S SPEAKING JUSTIFIED'
Defending and travelling in public ministry

LET US MOVE BEYOND THE EARLIEST decades of Quakerism and look harder at the women Friends who had joined the ranks of exceptional seventeenth-century women. Like them, the Quakers preached, prophesied, travelled, published and petitioned. When they made their own forays into these fields they did not offer *original* arguments in defence. Instead what distinguished them was their dogged *determination* in evolving and defending their Testimonies, in furthering women's public religious activity and in being willing to suffer the consequences. Yet so far as the experience of women Friends was concerned, things did not stay the same in all respects.

Quakerism altered in the 1660s and later it became more ordered, less enthusiastic (in its religious sense) and more overtly patriarchal. For much of the seventeenth century, women Friends lived lives shadowed by insecurity. They were in fear of the knock at the door, of the impoverishment born of absent, often imprisoned, husbands and all Friends were conscious of the suspicion and hostility their choice of belief had brought. Quakerism also grew to deplore destructive individualism and in the early decades some women had figured among the most striking individualists. Dissent in their own ranks had brought Quakers into the public eye and into greater disrepute. In any case their teachings were all too readily misunderstood and misrepresented so that their influential figures felt the need to curb 'unprofitable' ministry which might offer ammunition to its opponents. Hence a complex organisation evolved and as the century progressed functionaries, who were elders and overseers, became much in evidence.

Ministers had to be 'accredited'. Channels for women's ministry were opened up (especially through the creation of the Women's Meetings) which in fact led them into more recognisably 'feminine' tasks. These new forms of activity for women *complemented*, rather than replaced entirely the other kinds; for there were still women Friends who travelled as ministers, who published warnings to cities and preached. Moreover, through their own business Meetings women found other means of recording opposition to acts of injustice, to the payment of tithes and so on. They did this in solidarity with their sisters. Nevertheless it was not the Quakerism of the early, heady decades.

By the end of the seventeenth century a quieter Quakeress had emerged than some of their foremothers. By that time Friends knew the benefits of the *Act of Toleration* (though this did not solve all their problems) and they were more concerned with security than with impending judgement. By that time, also, they had made public commitments to pacificism and were much perceived to be less of a threat. Their deviations in terms of speech, dress, lack of paid ministers, marriage practices and so on remained, of course, but after 1700 there would be fewer published jibes accusing Quakers of fanaticism, witchcraft, sexual indiscretions and perversions.[1] 'Even the Quakers', Knox wrote in *Enthusiasm*, 'had felt the chill air of the Age of Reason.'[2]

These changes had impinged on the lives of women Friends. There had been criticism of unco-operative women Friends since the 1650s, notably when they stirred up opposition to male preachers. But with increasing emphasis on good order, 'the definition of "inappropriate" was extended to much less frenzied exhortations', and the general rule-of-thumb developed among Quakers, as in other religious groups: 'if she was infringing on "male authority" . . . she could not be acting under divine direction'.[3] Indeed had they been asked what Martha Simmonds should have done when she was 'moved by the power . . . to go to James Nayler?'[4] within a short time of the event most Friends, men and women alike, would have said that she should not have gone. Still it is important to note that *despite changes of emphasis*, which did bear on the ministries of male and female Friends, Quakers did not cease to defend *women's* right to public Christian ministry. With such changes, too, there came the need for other forms of defence: in support of women's organisational and disciplinary roles in the church. Most of 'the world's people' and not a few amongst the Friends themselves, did not approve of developments. Quakers made the defence of their practices in print, in their preaching and in the courts of law. It was part of their vision of the new order; but since much of it concerns the structure of the Women's Meetings, it will be left until the next chapter.

Arguments about Silence: mother Eve, the prophet and the Apostle

It was first Paul of Tarsus and then that 'Paul' who wrote the letters to Timothy and Titus who provided much of the case against the liberty of women. The Apostle (so the Reformer John Knox had noted approvingly in 1558), had deprived women of

44

all power and authority, to speak, to reason, to interpret, or to teach, but principally to rule or to judge in the assemblies of men.[5]

Paul was not really the arch-villain but in an age when scripture was a formidable weapon in any war of words, Paul's teachings had to be taken into account. Then there were the Christian Fathers' interpretations of the Eve myth to be countered. Eve had been the devil's gateway, the bringer of death, seducer and prime example of women's susceptibility to error, they said. Given the precedent of Eve their foremother, women should not seek to instruct or preach.

It was not just Quakers who opposed such views. Others had been doing so for decades. In the sixteenth century the pseudonymous Jane Anger had proclaimed the superiority of women, who had been first witnesses of the resurrection. Adam had been created 'of dross and filthy clay', she observed, but woman was of Adam's *flesh*, and not on that account secondary or inferior. Rather, it was

> that she might be purer than he [and] show how far we women are more excellent than men . . . from woman sprang man's salvation. A woman was the first that believed . . .[6]

Anger's was a spirited apology for women. Men, she declared, were unfaithful, greedy, lustful and rampantly egocentric. But women, she argued,

> are contrary to men because they are contrary to that which is good.

Rachel Speght, who was referred to in the previous chapter, declared in her work *Mouzel for Melastomus* that as the last work of creation woman was surely its final glory.[7] Certainly Jesus had never intended the denigration of women and indeed they *had* been first witnesses of the resurrection. Yet even such truths became ammunition in the hands of men, as the polemicist Mary Astell showed:

> . . . some men will have it, that the reason of our Lord's appearing first to the women, was their being least able to keep a secret; a witty and masculine remark and wonderfully reverent![8]

As for the men in the seventeenth century, Baptists, Independents, Congregationalists and others were having to assess the significance of Paul's words for their congregations. In 1610 John Robinson had defended among the Separatists the right of both sexes to 'bind and loose'. Women, it was agreed, might make public confession, sing psalms, witness an accusation, but 'authority over the man' was not to be theirs. Only in extraordinary circumstances, 'namely where no man will', might a woman offer reproof in a church. There was *one* important exception, however, that of the prophet. Justified by the precedent of Anna (*Luke* 2:36) and the tacit approval of Paul, a female prophet who was, by definition, extraordinarily and miraculously inspired, 'might speak without restraint'.[9]

In the 1640s outrageous women seemed to be multiplying and, just like other churchmen were doing, the Massachusetts Congregationalists had to consider 'The Woman Question'. It seemed to some that the key passages of *1 Corinthians* 14:34 and *1 Timothy* 2:11-12 implied that women had no voting rights, in churches or elsewhere. This was because a vote 'imports some kind of government, authority and power'.[10] But British Presbyterians attending the Westminster Conference of Divines were less than impressed with some of the disclaimers from the New World. Robert Baillie knew that in New England there were women as leaders and 'chief pastors' in churches, though Independents, he acknowledged, did not willingly give 'any public ecclesiastical power' to women. That was an aberration you would have found in *London* churches:

> . . . in this our London Independents exceed all their brethren, who of late begin to give unto women power of debating in the face of the congregation and of determining ecclesiastical causes by their suffrages.[11]

It was inevitable that Paul's teaching would touch women's secular lives too. With monotonous regularity his strictures appeared in the Domestic Conduct Books and when women wrote, their disclaimers and apologies very often included a genuflection in Paul's direction. Women were denied a right to knowledge and education because of New Testament language.[12] What Paul had said about silence in the churches, women's submission to, and learning from, their husbands, could be used to ensure that they acceded to servile and domestic roles, with limited access to study. Thus Brathwait in his advice to *The English Gentlewoman* held that in the company of elders or of men a young woman should be silent. When she was permitted to speak, she should make

> choice of such arguments as may best improve your knowledge in household affairs.

Even in private there was to be no discussion of contemporary theology, for

> Women, as they are to be no speakers in the Church, so neither are they to be disputers of the controversies of the Church.[13]

Indeed Mary Astell noted that Anglicanism required women only

> to know their catechism and a few good sentences, to read a chapter and say their prayers, though perhaps with as little understanding as a parrot.

There were women who dared (if circumspectly) to disagree. Notably the learned Bathsua Pell Makin knew how to make use of the worst prejudices of her contemporaries. If women were indeed Eve-like and susceptible to error, she argued, easily deceived and in turn liable to be a bad influence on their families, then would not *education* help to counter such frailty?

> This will be a hedge against heresies . . . Women ought to be learned, that they may stop their ears against seducers.[14]

None of these arguments had come from the pens of Quakers and in reality, as my opening chapter showed, there *were* women who were far from circumspect and who were unresponsive to the prevailing interpretations of the Apostle's words. They were preaching and prophesying. In the 1640s some of the female preachers were operating at fixed venues preaching weekly, or sermonising in houses. There were groups which refused to listen to male preachers and others frequented by preaching women where 'they break bread also, and everyone in their order'. Thomas Edwards reported many such aberrations in *Gangraena* in 1646. The anonymous author of *A Spirit Moving in the Women Preachers,* again in 1646, was critical of the 'affronted, brazen-faced, strange, new feminine brood' of his day, some of which preached to mixed gatherings. John Brinsley in *A Looking-Glasse for Good Women* (1645) commented that such women, denied participation in the government of the Church proper, had grown discontented, disaffected and 'open to Satan's delusions'. So great was the concern about these matters that in 1646 in London a complaint was made to the House of Commons regarding 'private meetings of women preachers'.

When the Friends came on the scene their writers also had to take account of teachings about Eve, about women's silence and the 'weaker vessel' image of the female sex which the Bible had provided. *Prophecy* of the biblical kind was of particular interest to them as were the loopholes in Paul's ecclesiology through which prophesying women might slip into the public sphere. Something must be said, then, of their treatment of scripture and the Quaker view of the prophesying female.

In 1648 George Fox was debating in a Leicester 'steeple-house' used by Presbyterian, Baptist, Independent and 'Common Prayer' preachers. A woman in the gathering asked a question of the priest, who forbade her to speak ('though he had before given liberty for any to speak', Fox recorded). So 'in a rapture' Fox stepped forward and discoursed on the true nature of the Church and the role of women in it. He acknowledged that according to the scriptures there *were* some kinds of women who should not be allowed to speak. Nevertheless, he told them, there were others who might rightly prophesy and speak. While those present turned against him for his words, it is not surprising that 'the woman that asked the question aforesaid was convinced'.[15]

The Quaker ideal was prophetic and so Friends used prophecy to defend prophecy. Hence the egalitarian sentiments of *Joel* 2: 28–32 appeared quite often in their writings about ministry. The passage was well known to those with prophetic inclinations and it had figured in the teachings of dissenting groups since the time of the second-century Montanists.[16] On one occasion George Fox had written that

> . . . the prophet Joel was not against the daughters prophesying, nor the apostles were not against it, but said 'despise not prophesying' [from 1 Thessalonians 5:20]. . . touch not mine anointed and do my prophets no harm,

adding that Paul had had female 'yoke-fellows' in his work and that he had recognised 'the wise Priscilla' as an instructor. Just like George Fox, other Friends sifted the scriptures for examples of women's ministry which might be used to counter the claims of churchmen, and like others who were not Friends, the Quakers returned often to *Joel* 2:28 seq. Churchmen, in turn, had been noting and deploring this sectarian usage. In *Gangraena* Thomas Edwards (somewhat obsessed with the activities of a Mrs Attway) had written of the Cheapside Lace-seller, a woman of Bell Alley in Colemanstreet, who was also preaching the fulfilment of Joel's prophecy:

> . . . and after this speech she made a prayer for half an hour.[17]

Agrippa in his work *The Glorie of Women* had remarked on the popularity of the prophecy with the 'vulgar':

> . . . men do forbid them publicly to preach for it appears unto each vulgar eye that Joel saith, women shall prophesy; So it was done in the Apostles' time.[18]

Contemporaneous with the beginnings of Quakerism the Fifth Monarchist Mary Cary had referred to Joel in her *New and More Exact Mappe of Description of the New Jerusalem's Glorie* of 1651 (pp. 236 seq.) as did the Lady Eleanor Davies Douglas. We find it, too, in the anonymous works of 1641 and 1646, *The Discovery of Six Women Preachers in Middlesex . . .* and *A Spirit Moving in the Women-Preachers* and in Vicars' *The Schismatic Sifted* (1646). Opponents of these prophets argued, of course, that the promise and its fulfilment appertained to the Apostles' time and was long past. This was a much-used passage but most people remained unimpressed.

> Beware of a young wench, a prophetess and a Latin woman

ran a familiar proverb.[19]

Undaunted and despite the widespread cynicism and bewilderment among those they were addressing ('Jesus I know, and Paul I know, but who are ye?' the writer of *A Spirit Moving . . .* had asked at the end of that work), the Quakers, too, looked to the prophetic promises of a new or restored order.

Friends were not concerned primarily with the finer points of scriptural interpretation. It was to the in-breaking of the new that they appealed, to the sufficient grace of Jesus Christ and to the need for personal response to the activity of the Spirit. Personal 'convincement' of the indwelling Christ ensured renewal, they said. It altered perceptions and brought courage beyond expectation. Quakers were called to know 'truth in the inward parts', in fulfilment of the prophet Jeremiah's New Covenant promise (*Jeremiah* 31:31 seq.). No longer would a priest or ordained minister determine the ways in which the Lord might be known. The women Friends, no less than the men, knew the 'I' of personal convincement but that was especially liberating for the women, who were now freed to respond to leadings other than those of father, husband or other male guardian. Such Quaker teachings ensured that Paul's prohibitions availed nothing when a woman was 'convinced' of the rightness of the leadings: 'this was no voice of a woman', declared the Quaker prophet Dewens Morrey to the challenging minister of Hawkchurch in Dorset – it was the voice of God. She was 'whipped until the blood did come'[20] Nevertheless these women Friends did debate about the scriptures also, and they were capable of great ingenuity and wit in so doing. In fact they were sometimes naughtily selective in the use of quotations to serve the logic of their cause (though the opposition, it should be said, has always been no less selective). Thus for example Priscilla Cotton and Mary Cole in *To the Priests and People of England* (1655) shifted, step by step, the usual course of the argument against women which was based on *1 Corinthians* 14:31.

> For the Scriptures do say that all the church may prophesy one by one . . . and that women were in the church, as well as men, do thou judge . . .

So far so good – women therefore must have been among those prophesying.

> And the Scripture saith, that a woman must not prophesy with her head uncovered, lest she dishonour her head . . .

or so *1 Corinthians* 11:5 had said. Well then, said Cotton and Cole almost teasingly,

> thou wouldst know the meaning of that head . . . [*1 Corinthians* 11:3], the head of the man is Christ. Man in his best state is altogether vanity, weakness, a lie. If therefore any speak in the church, whether man or woman, and nothing appear in it but the wisdom of man and Christ, who is the true head, be not uncovered – do not fully appear – Christ the head is then dishonoured.

A neat twist, but one which disregards, of course, Paul's *actual* argument in the texts.

Dewens Morrey, Priscilla Cotton and other women like them were no longer (in their own eyes at least) female, weaker vessels trespassing

49

on male preserves. Guided by the Light, they (like male Friends too) had transcended carnal humanity and were innocent of socially offensive, 'unfeminine' behaviour, even while ranting at clergy or going 'naked'. A woman might indeed be acting 'contrary to her own (human) inclination'. The notion of 'womanhood' was thus tranformed in some Friends' writings, to mean now that part of the self, in male and female alike, which was weakness or God-lessness. *This* was the 'woman' which Paul and Paul's disciples had wanted to debar from speaking in the Church, as Priscilla Cotton and Mary Cole argued further in *To the Priests and People of England* . . . (pp. 7-8):

> Thou tellest the people, women must not speak in a church whereas it is not spoken only of a female, for we are all one both male and female in Christ Jesus [*Galatians* 3:28]: but its weakness that is the woman by the Scripture forbidden . . .

Male Quaker writers made similar observations. Edward Burrough, for example, writing in *An Alarm to All Flesh* (London 1660, p.p. 7-8) bade his readers 'wholly root out the whorish wo-man within yourselves . . .'

Phyllis Mack in her study of 'Gender and Spirituality' has drawn attention to this Quaker alteration of 'the womanly' as popularly understood:

> holding to it as a negative abstract while rejecting its descriptive value for individual, sanctified women, must have seemed . . . the only possible argument, both theologically and strategically – that could justify the public authority of female prophets.

But such a distinction – between the individual still ensnared in 'womanhood' and she (not under the Law but the Gospel) who had died to her 'womanhood' so as to function 'in Christ', could also be used to apply sanctions internal to Quakerism. Not only might it be used to distinguish the false from the true prophet but also, if need be, to quench a spirit of madness, disobedience or dissent in women.

At the end of the century the Friend Ann Docwra acknowledged in print that

> it was true, there was some shatter-headed people amongst us

(*An Apostate Conscience Exposed*, London 1699, p. 18). There had been something of a 'leave well alone' policy amongst the early Quakers where such people were concerned, she said, a consensus that they should

> use them kindly, so long as they were morally honest . . . they were not to be disturbed, for that would make them worse.

She was not lying, it had indeed been so. Nevertheless action *was* taken against individuals and Friends' teachings about 'woman' together with the organisational and disciplinary structures which evolved within

Quakerism ensured that the activities and ministries of *women*, even more than those of the men, came to be overseen with diligence. This was so despite the teachings of men and women Friends alike concerning the Inner Light, the communality of 'womanliness' and the rights of all to prophesy and preach. But so far as we may judge from remaining records such judgemental oversight and curbing of ministry was the exception rather than the rule. Most women Friends of the first half century of Quakerism seem to have adopted and adapted to the evolving discipline without hearty argument and certainly from the outset, the women Friends were arguing that the Spirit of prophecy was indeed at work in them. They were not acting on their own authority they said, and they were only vessels of God's own activity. It was an argument which would stand them in good stead *inside* the Society, as well as outside it, for the rest of the century. The Fifth Monarchist prophet Anna Trapnel had written:

> Thy servant is made a voice, a sound, it is a voice within a voice, another's voice, even thy voice through her

(*The Cry of a Stone* 41 seq.). The women Friends understood such claims.

Quaker writers and preachers were not producing great academic or pastoral theology and little which was very good theology. They had not received the benefits (to them dubious 'benefits') of a theological education. They concentrated on a small number of themes. But they were 'restorationist' in outlook and they were certain that in the 'Gospel-order' for which they were a community in the vanguard the divinely-ordained male-female relationship (among other things) would be restored. The hierarchies and power structures characteristic of 'the world' (and which were the products of the Fall), would come to an end. The female would be truly a help-meet with the male.

As a result of such teaching Quakers refused to acknowledge the niceties of social and 'feminine' behaviour and of forms of address. This was intensely disturbing to the authorities but women Friends seemed immovable. Esther (Hester) Biddle, for example, had been hauled out of a Meeting by one called Lovel, who was a vintner, caught in the act of speaking while 'upon a form' (a bench). It was recorded in the 1662 *Brief Relation of the Persecutions and Cruelties that have been acted upon the People called Quakers* (one of many such works cataloguing Quaker accounts of injustice against them) that the jurymen (seemingly men isolated from the goings-on of the preceding two decades!) were shocked at Esther's case. 'They never heard of a woman to speak before.' But Esther merely reminded them of precedents in the New Testament ('the judge said that was a great while ago'!) and she reminded one of her accusers of some of his own pre-Restoration activities:

> Dost thou remember when thou prayest in the camp by Abingdon, and was that an unlawful meeting? Was that not a good day with thee, I am afraid thou will never see such another.

The preaching Quakeress. An engraving entitled 'Coacres et Coacresse dans leurs assemblees' after Egbert van Heemskirk (1645-1704).

Shunning the usual formalities of title she prefaced this address to the Bench and worthies present with the word 'Richard . . .'.

These Quakers, convinced of a change which was already inaugurated, also anticipated the millenium and the imminent conversion of the Jews which would surely precede it.[21] As women were called to their rightful places so too, as they saw it, were the Jews to be recalled from their Babylon of exile.

Yet this was no brand of radical feminism which was being offered, revolutionary though it was in its way. Nor had Anna Trapnel and the rest of the women prophets been feminists. It was *spiritual* equality which was being held out to Esther Biddle, Elizabeth Hooton, Dewens Morrey and others and it was to be worked out within the sphere of the church, as Quakers understood it. The church itself foreshadowed the eschatological order. In contrast, in the secular sphere (for example in the Quaker family), the trappings of patriarchy were still taken for granted. So it was amongst other radical groups like the Fifth Monarchists too. The 'headship' of the male in things temporal was accepted, and Paul's account of the divine-human order of superiority (God-Christ; Christ-Church; male-female) was accepted too. Incomplete as the Quaker offer of female emancipation was, it *was* liberating. Women Friends were certain of their complete personhood. They were assured that they were wholly in God's image[22] and that they had souls.[23] Quaker writings offered them a variety of imagery of the female, not all of it positive and much of it biblically – derived; the prophetess, the whore, the Church as female and bride, the virgin and the mother. They were told that they, like men, had the right, indeed the obligation, to respond to the guidance of the Inner Light and the promptings of the Spirit, even when response brought conflict with the social conventions, with prevailing prejudices and the law.

These women became less like the New Testament prophet Anna, declaring her vision to a few on her 'home-ground' of the Temple, or like the Spirit-filled Mary, giving out her song to her cousin in a domestic setting, than they were like the turbulent, politically threatening male prophets of the Hebrew tradition, or a Samson or a Joshua. It was inevitable, therefore, that Quaker teaching, consistently followed through in practice, brought unheard-of opportunities for activity beyond the home and it would have been an unperceptive observer who said of the publishing, prophesying, preaching women Friends only what Hugh Peters (surely with faint praise and little insight into his author) had written of the Fifth Monarchist prophet Mary Cary, in an introduction to her work *The Little Horn's Doom and Downfall* (p. 2). Mary had, he said,

> taught her sex that there are more ways than one to avoid idleness
> . . . they that will not use the distaff may improve the pen.

Their curiosity value brought crowds to hear the women Friends in action. Even after two decades of Quakerism, in the 1670s, Alice Hayes was attracted because

> I . . . heard a report about the neighbourhood of a woman preacher, greatly esteemed among the Quakers, and who was to be at one of their meetings . . . some of the neighbours, in curiosity, had a mind to hear and see, and asked me to go with them.

The presence of such *women* in active ministry doubtless helped to swell the numbers of women who came into Quakerism's ranks, but it was Quaker teaching generally which kept them there. Alice Hayes, once she had decided (after some years) to throw in her lot with the Friends, was warned by priest John Berrow that Quakers denied the Scriptures and the resurrection and owned no Christ 'except a Christ that was in them'. She told him she had not heard such things from them but with a response which is 'classic' in relation to fear of new religious movements he warned her:

It may not be yet, till they have got you, You do not discern the hook, or the pill that is gilded. It is a dangerous doctrine they hold, and damnable heresy they are in.

It was the very same 'dangerous' and subversive doctrines of Quakerism which its adherents found liberating, though externally they brought hardship and imprisonment for them.

The most comprehensively argued piece of Quaker writing about women's ministry came from Margaret Fell in 1666. This was *Womens Speaking Justified* . . . which she re-issued a year later with a Postscript.[24] Something must be said of it and of its illustrious author.

In the early 1650s Margaret Askew Fell had been touched by the teaching of George Fox and that of other leading men Friends. He had declared that all things were new and in Ulverston, preaching on that circumcision which was of the heart rather than outward (*Romans* 2:28-29) he had spoken of the Spirit as the hallmark of the regenerate believer:

> The scriptures were the prophets' words and Christ's and the apostles' words . . . and what had any to do with the scriptures but as they came to the Spirit that gave them forth . . .

he asked his listeners, adding

> You will say, Christ saith this, and the apostles say this, but what canst thou say? . . . what thou speakest is it inwardly from God?

Margaret Fell was moved and she became conscious of her own, and others' lack of spirituality. The first preachers had touched the heart of a woman who would come to be seen as the 'mother of Quakerism', who would be a good friend to the nascent Quaker movement, an empowerer of other women and eventually, after eleven years of widowhood, the wife of George Fox.

We are on familiar ground with *Womens Speaking Justified*. It echoes points made by other, non-Quaker writers, by Fox and the Friend Richard Farn(s)worth too (the latter writing much earlier, in *A Woman Forbidden to Speak* of 1654).[25] Its appeal to passages and personages in scripture is of a commonplace type. But it is special in the thoroughness of that appeal to biblical precedent, in its sometimes cautious, but often spirited, case for women, in its criticism of Church and clergy, and in its optimism. Margaret Fell was determined to present a thorough and well-argued case. In my view, however, *Womens Speaking Justified* lacks the charm and wit that we find in some other writings by women Friends.

Margaret Fell was no shrinking violet, though she has been fragrantly preserved in a lot of Quaker hagiography as the 'nursing mother' of Quakerism (a title Fox used of her[26]). She played the role in early Quakerism which has often been played by women in early religious

54

movements, when widows and the endowed 'give of their substance' in support, open their homes and so on. In her case she transcended that role. She was part of that 2% of the population which was landowning[27] and she was accustomed to comfort, yet she suffered imprisonments, hard journies and confrontations in the Quaker cause. Her published statements on Friends' Peace Testimony and on their marriage discipline were made when these things were just emerging. She had been married at 17, had mothered nine children (of which eight survived) and at the time of her 'convincement' was the wife of a judge. Once Margaret Askew Fell informed a Justice of the Peace that he was 'a caterpillar'.

In her Quaker days she became less than dutifully submissive to her husband Thomas Fell, but non-conformist sects before the Quakers had allowed to a woman a right of conscience in matters religious.[28] Here was something like the 'complete' woman of the Domestic Conduct Book type. She was pious (though not conventionally so), with oversight of the physical and spiritual welfare of her children, servants, the local poor and so on; she was involved in the family's business ventures, which included dairying and iron-smelting interests; she was generous. Here was an author too, an organiser and hostess for Friends on a considerable scale. Swarthmoor Hall, her home, was the postal 'sorting house' for a great deal of correspondence between the Friends at home, in America and on the European continent. She was more than a 'nursing mother'. Margaret Fell proved to be 'a powerful, dominant, argumentative and somewhat distant authority figure'. She had an 'everlasting tongue', observed a Justice at Lancaster Assizes in 1664. Margaret never 'went naked', usurped pulpits in 'steeple-houses' or tried to raise the dead. She did not follow the model of the prophetess, whose temporary state of inspiration alone validated her public activity and gave authority to an otherwise 'weaker vessel'. Margaret transcended that kind of model too. Hers became 'a model

*Swarthmoor
Hall*

55

The 'Great Hall' where Quaker meetings were held from 1652 to 1690. The panelling and carvings are part of the restoration of 1914.

for authoritative female public ministry',[29] as we shall see. While she continued to coo over her grandchildren and show concern about the health of her cattle, she ensured also that no ministering Friend lacked coat, stockings or shoes, determinedly ignored legislation against conventicles and saw to it that Quaker dissenters and errorists were reproved. Margaret Fell was of considerable significance in Quakerism's first half century (all of which she saw). But Quakers' interest in her significant role has tended to overshadow the work of the many other women Friends, leading, I think, to a distorted view of early Quaker 'herstory'.

In *Womens Speaking Justified* Margaret Fell argued that Adam and Eve alike had transgressed.[30] The corollary of enmity between the offspring of the serpent and of the woman (i.e. Eve and her antitype Mary from whom came the Christ and so the Church) was that

if the seed of the woman speak not, the seed of the serpent speaks

Hence those who opposed the speech of Christians, of either sex, were supporting the serpent's way and the triumph of evil. Those whom Christ had inspired were surely justified in speaking, just as the holy women of the past had spoken.

This work abounds with references to women of both Testaments and in the 'leisure' of her Lancaster imprisonment, when it was written, Margaret had mulled over the key issues in the 'women's speaking' debate. She examined Paul's injunctions about silence, the status of woman at creation, the Church portrayed as 'she' and Christ's bride, freedom 'in Christ' and the examples of ministering women in the age of the Gospel. Those opposed to women's speaking, she observed, had 'stopt' it in a number of ways.[31]

Some of Margaret Fell's sentiments in *Womens Speaking Justified* are strikingly familiar to present-day readers of feminist theology and the theology of liberation. She and her contemporaries shared assumptions about the world and God's intervention which are no longer our assumptions, but in the seventeenth century, too, they were reclaiming the religious history of women and declaring the activity of God for, and in, the weak and the oppressed.

The clergy, she told her readers, made money in quoting those words of women which were preserved in scripture, while in their own day they denied women a right to speak. Such opposition was at odds with the example of Jesus Christ himself, who had

> owned the love and grace that appeared in the women and did not despise it . . .

It seemed obvious, then, that

> those that speak against the power of the Lord speaking in a woman, simply by reason of her sex, or because she is a woman, not regarding the . . . Spirit . . . such speak against Christ.

Margaret Fell's optimism was remarkable. She believed change was in the very air. The 1666 version of *Womens Speaking* ended with the confident assertion that although 'a mountain' had been made of *1 Corinthians* 14:34 seq. and *1 Timothy* 2:11 seq.,

> the Lord is removing all this.

Quakers after her sifted the scriptures more finely for further examples to justify women's public religious roles and to argue for their

> talent of wisdom and spiritual understanding . . . and an office in the truth.[32]

They did not stop at the scriptures.

Richard Richardson, in a lengthy postscript to Friend Thomas Camm's work *The Fulfilling of the Promise* (1689, 18 seq.), also appealed to the witness of John Calvin, to Augustine of Hippo, the deaconesses referred to by Pliny the Younger early in the second century, to the *Stromateis* of Clement of Alexandria and the ecclesiastical historians Nicephorus and Socrates.

While such Friends, male and female, were being apologists in print for women's public ministry, the women themselves were actively engaged in the work. 'Ministry' is not to be understood in a narrow sense. For Quakers it encompassed not just preaching, prophecy and other overtly 'religious' activity, but also any witnessing to the faith, be it in the home, the marketplace or workplace, in the steeple-house, the law-courts and the prison. An example had to be set in all those places. There were converts to be won through all of them and hardship and hostility were realities in all of them too. Let us look, then, at some examples of Quaker women's ministry.

Varieties of gifts but the one Spirit

['Arise and be doing'] was the advice offered to all Quakers, regardless of sex and regardless of their station in life. There was to be no genteel idleness for women, but rather

> Every one to the ministry yourselves . . . England is a family of prophets, which must spread over the nations.

So read the Epistle from the General Meeting at Skipton on April 25th 1660, Minister women did.

> Thus saith the Lord,

declared Margret Killam (Killin) and Barbara Patison in true prophetic fashion in their 1656 *Warning from the Lord to the Teachers and People of Plymouth*:

> I have sent my sons and daughters from far . . . I have raised up prophets amongst you . . . but some of my messengers you have imprisoned and others you have evil entreated . . .

Almost from the outset they also looked to the needs of the poor. Quakerism knew the importance of not divorcing the religious message from social concern. To do so would have been to ignore the witness of the Old Testament prophets, of John the Baptist and Jesus himself. So they cared for the needy, especially their own, and it was not without cause that they were accused of 'some Levelling design'. Friends attacked strongly the flagrant disparity of wealth which showed itself in arrays of silks and laces while the streets teemed with beggars.[33] They responded to the changed fortunes of their co-religionists, some of whom had not been poverty-stricken at the time of 'convincement', but whose stand against seventeenth-century legislation and prejudice had brought distraint on goods, the sale of property and so on.[34] In addition, their understanding of the indwelling of Jesus Christ lent a special poignancy to Matthew's parable of the sheep and the goats, in which he had identified with the needy:

When I was hungry you gave me food; when thirsty you gave me drink . . . when I was ill you came to my help, when in prison you visited me.

While men Quakers ('ancient Friends') met and discussed 'Truth' in an upper room of the Bull and Mouth premises which had been used by Friends in London since 1655, the women Friends were not idle. They did not wait

> until the cry of the poor came to their houses, but where they did suppose or discover a want of help their charity led them to enquire . . . and to minister to their necessities.[35]

Friend Richard Hubberthorne claimed that there was not a beggar in the Quaker ranks. The claim is almost certainly exaggerated,[36] but the Quaker women's work, at first on an *ad hoc* basis, certainly helped to ensure that the incidence of penury among them was minimised.

The poor and powerless were also to be found in the places overseas to which Quakers travelled. As an instance of their response to need I shall take the Minutes from the 'trade-Meetings' of Quaker midwives in the West Indies.

Although Friends' condemnation of slavery did not come until the eighteenth century, in the seventeenth they were stressing the need to improve the lot of the slaves. Fox declared it was 'a slander and a lie' that Quakers encouraged the negroes to rebel[37] but he and others did want the slaves to be treated kindly, to be given freedom after thirty years, and to be educated in religion and encouraged to join in worship.[38]

The Quaker midwives who were working in the West Indies encountered owners and enslaved directly, and they served both. The following extracts from the Minutes of their Meetings between 1677–79 show how they sought to apply their Quakerism in their daily work.

> The woman being well and the child, we with those women then present do sit down and wait upon the Lord . . . a faithful testimony may be borne against . . . their ways, who as soon as the woman is delivered, do run into eating and drinking and foolish talk (11. xii. 1677).

They witnessed against extravagance and in favour of simplicity and therefore determined

> if . . . they should bring us laced linen to put upon the child, that then we call for plain,

For the slaves and the poor of other kinds, of course, laced linen was hardly an option. No money was to be requested from the poor, they decided,

> but rather help their necessity

(from Minutes of 7.ii. 1679 and 11.xii. 1677).

Though they did not refuse payment from slave owners for the delivery of a slave the midwives knew

> not to take anything of the poor negroes, but rather help the poor creatures, as the Lord shall enable[39]

Midwives figure in other documentation from Quaker women too. Through the segregated business Meetings which developed within Quakerism means were evolved by which a woman might be answerable to the group for her work and actions. This was especially important in the case of midwifery and so a Meeting might examine the competence of a midwife when a complaint occurred. This was something which was sorely needed in wider society.[40] Thus it happened that in February of 1675 the Women's Meeting at Swarthmoor was examining the midwife Mabel Brittaine. It instructed her to take on a competent midwife as assistant and the Minute drawn up by Sarah Fell (daughter of Margaret Fell) recorded and warned that

> Certain women have been long in travail, and have been delivered of dead children under her hands . . . in love and tenderness to women and children . . . if any do suffer making use of her, for the future, they must take it upon themselves . . .

It was part of the ministry of the women in that Meeting to pronounce on such matters.

Nine years later the forty-two year old Sarah herself had a child. Like all but one of Margaret's daughters she had married late. She was attended by Frances Kent, a famous midwife and a Quaker, who could command up to £25 for her services,[41] even though there must have been public reservations about her religion. Sarah wrote to her mother that Friend Frances had been 'a very tender and skilful woman for that employment'.[42]

The ministries of some women Friends were most difficult in their own families. Not a few of them had first discovered the depth of their loyalty to Quakerism when they showed solidarity with convinced and suffering partners. Sometimes quite suddenly they were thrust into situations they could never have envisaged. There are many fulsome Testimonies from husbands to the sufferings of their now dead wives. Just a few examples of their trials will be given here.

Mary Batt, on becoming the widow of Philip Tyler, found that two of her cows, valued at £9, were confiscated from her for daring to attend the funeral. Her next husband was imprisoned for non-payment of tithes and so she supplied 'his place in those affairs that more immediately concerned him'. Mary asked for her man to be released for two weeks, to see her over the birth of a child, but her request was refused. His statements about his dead wife told of her sufferings . . . far greater than mine . . . unreasonable men cleanse our fields of cattle, rummage our house of goods and make such havoc as that my dear wife had not wherewithal to dress or set food before me and her children.[43]

Friend Margrett Edmundson, too, 'took the charge of our outward concerns and family' recorded William her husband after her death:

I do not remember if ever she was terrified . . . when the cruel and bloody rapparees beset our house and they poured in shot . . . and they took me and my two sons from her barelegged and bare and left her stripped to her shift.[44]

The wife who supported a blind and helpless husband found herself confined in 'a nasty stinking cockloft'.[45] Country women struggled to run farms and care for growing children, not able to visit husbands in prison many miles away:

Though I would be glad to see thee here I am truly content to bear it . . . considering thy concerns in this season . . . being harvest time and the journey so long . . .

wrote John Banks from his prison in Carlisle.[46]

In Wiltshire in 1661 the daughters of William Moxon ('an honest, industrious husbandman, but poor and being a widower') had to bring in the harvest of corn themselves. This was because the priest who had had their father imprisoned for non payment of tithes threatened all who might have helped them. Next he subpoena'd the daughters into the *Exchequer* for their pains, but on hearing of their condition, 'the Barons' dismissed them, so Besse recorded (*Sufferings* ii, 41).

Women Friends were imprisoned too – for breaches of the peace (as we saw in the first chapter), for non payment of tithes and for having illegal 'conventicles' in their houses. They showed great solidarity in their adversity, whether their prisons were on native soil or abroad. For three years from 1659, for example, Katherine Evans and Sarah Cheevers were in the prison of the Inquisition in Malta, where John Perrot (who well knew the horrors of the Inquisition's attentions), sent monetary support.[47] Other women (Elizabeth Hooton and Mary Dyer among them) knew the insides of American prisons while others suffered in continental Europe. Women Friends often faced their own court trials and imprisonments without the presence and support of husbands:

. . . old prophetess, I know you of old . . . [your] husband careth little for you, I will warrant you, else he would have come with you and not have suffered you to be sent to prison by yourself; you are a troublesome woman

declared one Justice to Elizabeth Stirredge (Sturge). And for some (from all classes) there was distraint of goods and incarcerations again and again.

In his account of *Sufferings* (vol. ii, 24 seq.) Besse recorded that in Westmorland the widow Bridgett Gregg of Milthorpe had goods to the value of 6s levied in April 1678, a cauldron worth £1 taken in November and 5s for tithes in corn in the following year. Then in 1682 she was deprived of flax and candles worth 9s 4d for attendance at Meetings. At this same time the 'poor widow', Jane Swainson, was deprived of a bag of potatoes worth 10d, with which she was to feed her family. In 1684 widow Gregg was again listed among sufferers. She met demands for 6s for absenting herself from national worship.

The more privileged Loveday Hambly was imprisoned in her home county of Cornwall for several weeks in 1657, for not paying tithe of geese and pigs. Loveday had suffered distraint to the sum of 45s the year before and on one occasion she had been kept in Launceston prison after being taken out of a Meeting in her home and refusing to swear an oath. In 1663 cattle and horses to the value of more than £100 were seized from her, for a tithe demand of just 18s 4d. That time the bailiff had pretended that she was riotous and her doors had been broken down. With 'much incivility' the men had then kept her in an alehouse overnight before taking her to the Sheriff's prison in Bodmin. Thomas Lower, a relative of Loveday and the husband of Mary Fell, intervened when in 1670 goods to the sum of £127 10s 6d were seized, for some of them belonged to him. But though he obtained an order of restitution, they were never returned. Besse's account of the *Sufferings* of Friends (in this case in vol. i, 115 seq.) contains many hundreds of similar examples of distraint, physical abuse and imprisonment.

Marriages were made in prison, like that of Mary Fisher and her mariner partner. Her story is told later in this chapter. Babies were nursed there. Makeshift schools were established for the young and every day of incarceration offered its own opportunities for spreading the insights of Quakerism.

Not infrequently it was Quaker *women* who left the family home to travel in the cause of Truth. Either they left their children in the care of relatives (who were Friends) or else under the oversight of understanding husbands or older siblings. When the twenty-five year old Bridget Fell wrote to her mother Margaret, on February 3rd 1660, the family had not heard from its mother for many months, and there were three children still under thirteen to be cared for:

> It is a very hard time for money with us, corn of no sort is anything saleable . . .seizements and wages to workers must needs be paid, and them which brought corn last year hath several of them unpaid as yet. They keep men in custody that should till the ground, the time of seeding being now, it cannot be expected that we should be able to maintain them in prison.[48]

The women Friends had to bear in mind all contingencies. Before their deaths, for example, some of them made wills which took account of the likelihood of legal action against members of their families. Among those who did so was Mary Groves, a widow of the parish of St Martin in the Fields, Middlesex. She testified on the 20th of January 1682 that her grandson James Snead was to receive £100 after her death,

> and 40 more towards the defending any actions or suits of law that shall or may be at any time hereafter be commenced.

The ministries of the Quaker women were many and varied. There were many women like Jennet Bond of Chipping, who testified to her refusal to pay tithes, out of solidarity with her husband:

> and never shall [I] weaken his testimony.[49]

Then there were the likes of the

> two honest, grave, discreet and motherly women . . . Anne Merrick and Anne Travers

who provided hot food for those Friends imprisoned in the Bridewell who had no-one else to make provision. 'There wanted not among us a competent number of such guests', observed Thomas Ellwood drily.[50] There were also redoubtable travelling and adventuring women, of which Barbara Blaugdone will serve as an example.

Barbara described herself in her Journal as 'never hasty or forward'. It had been the unsought vocation of this former governess to travel in spreading Truth and it had brought her close to death on several occasions, as she recorded:

> . . . as Mary Prince and I was coming arm in arm from a meeting . . . there was a rude man came and abused us, and struck off Mary Prince her hat and run some sharp knife or instrument through all my clothes into the side of my belly, which if it had gone but a little farther, it might have killed me.

On another day she encountered a butcher armed with a cleaver, who swore to cleave her head in two, but

> a woman . . . caught back his arms, and stayed him . . .

At other times she was declared to be a witch, a 'great wolf-dog' was set on her, and more than once waves beat in on her on hazardous sea crossings. On one occasion on board ship, when a storm blew up, some people conspired to fling her overboard.[51] Grass-roots opposition to Quakers was additional to the general hazards of seventeenth-century travel which women faced.

There is one account of overseas ministry which deserves a special place. It concerns a former Selby servant girl, who was publicly flogged in Cambridge for her prophesying and who had been a pioneering missionary in America – there with a middle-aged mother of five called Ann Austin she was searched for signs of witchcraft. Her name was Mary Fisher.

In the late spring or early summer of 1657 six Friends set out. There were three Irish men, one of them John Perrot, Beatrice Beckley and two women who had already been banished from Boston the previous year – Mary Prince and Mary Fisher. Their intention ultimately was to reach Jerusalem. They crossed Europe and Mary determined that she would meet with the Turkish Sultan, the teenage Muhammad IV, who was encamped at Adrianople. The others, it seems, had abandoned such a plan. To accomplish this, she had a long overland journey to make through territory she did not know. It is uncertain that anyone shared the last of her adventure, though perhaps Beatrice Beckley did so. Mary Fisher was ignorant of Islam but she was firm in her intention to convert. Here was a thirty-five year old ill-educated, single woman, approaching the court of one of the mightiest and in a time of great tension between the Christian Venetians and the Ottoman Turks.

When she reached her goal, Mary Fisher was met with greater courtesy and sympathy than she had known in her native land. The Quaker William Sewel in his account of her actions recorded that she was treated tenderly. She was granted time to rest, to change her clothing and then she was given access to the royal presence. The Turks were kind and probably amused as well as impressed that such a one

> should take so much pains to come to them as far as from England, with a message from the Lord God.[52]

On being asked about the prophet Muhammad Mary confessed that she did not know him. Instead she discoursed on 'the true prophet', the Son of God (perhaps unaware that such Sonship was a concept anathema to Muslims). As for their own prophet, she told them, they should judge him according to the words of *Deuteronomy* 18: 20-22. If his words proved to be true, then they were indeed of God. That answer pleased them.

Her Muslim hosts offered her safe passage back to Constantinople but Mary preferred to make her own way. In that city (so its ambassador reported to the Protector in 1658), the Quakers were now involved in disturbing

> divine exercises and several notorious contempts of me and my authority.[53]

The powerful men who encountered Mary Fisher must surely have found her bewildering. In 1653 she and Elizabeth Williams had denounced Sidney Sussex College and its students as a cage of unclean birds and 'a synagogue of Satan' (*Revelation* 3:9). The Mayor had called them whores and when asked about her marital status Mary had informed him that she owned Christ alone as her husband. Christ it was who had sent her there, she said. As for her experiences among 'the heathen', Mary said she had discerned the Light in the Turk too.

They do dread the name of God

she reported to Thomas Aldam in a letter. With Aldam and Elizabeth Hooton she had been imprisoned in York:

> ... they are nearer the Truth than many nations, there is a love begot in me towards them which is endless.

This woman, who was for decades after pointed out as the one who had stood before the Grand Turk, went on to combine her ministry with marriage and children. In 1662 she married the Dorset mariner William Bayly, for whom she'd shown great concern in Newgate prison. Like most known men Friends in London that year Bayly had been rounded up and incarcerated. Through their meetings she had widened his understanding of ministry and he 'thought her worthy'.[54] She bore him three children.

Quakers of both sexes travelled in some numbers overseas – to Bermuda and Barbados; with addresses to the Kings of Spain and France; to Rome to try to convert the Pope (where the prison of the Inquisition received them); to Venice, Scandinavia, Germany, Newfoundland, Massachusetts, Maryland and to the Indians of Virginia. Mary Fisher and Ann Austin were pioneers in Boston, Elizabeth Harris in Maryland. The witty and redoubtable Esther Biddle travelled to Newfoundland[55] and two of the men Friends who were carrying Fox's letter to K'ang Hsi, Emperor of China, managed to reach Alexandria.[56] All of this showed great faith and adventurousness but many more women Friends bravely worked out their Quakerism at home.

Keeping the home fires burning

In the homeland of Quakerism women were petitioning. 15,000 signatures against tithes were presented to the remains of the Rump Parliament in June of 1658 and in the following month 7,000 'handmaids and daughters of the Lord' petitioned too: 'the women in the truth feels the weight as well as the men'. Later, individual women recorded their opposition to tithes in the records of their Women's Meeting, quite apart from any stand which the men were taking.[57]

The experiences of many of these women had been sobering. It was probably this which Anne Finch, Viscountess Conway (b. 1631) had in mind when she sought out Quaker maids because of their peacefulness. Anne suffered from severe headaches and she wanted peaceful people around her. The Quakers, she wrote,

> have been and are a suffering people . . . I find them so still and very serious.[58]

She was fortunate not to have encountered Quaker maids of the other sort, which would leave at short notice to preach on street corners or travel overseas! The Viscountess eventually became a Quaker herself and her view of Friends indicates that the sober and reserved Quakeress was to be found. Indeed some of them were being nurtured deliberately in families of the convinced. Even in the earliest days there had been families in which this was the case.

When Thomas Ellwood visited the Penington household in the 1650s he met again the daughter of the house, whom he knew, a girl 'of courteous mien'. Now, however she was so grave of look and sober of manner that Ellwood was speechless.[59] Isaac and Mary Penington, and with them Mary's daughter Guilielma Springett (later William Penn's wife), had embraced Quakerism only after marriage in 1654. This family's seriousness was as much a product of its general religious outlook as of Quakerism in particular. Their dinner, Ellwood remarked, though it was 'handsome', also 'lacked mirth'. In such families it was easier for women to follow through the implications of the Friends' *Testimonies*, as these touched dress, speech and worship. In homes where there was hostility to all things Quaker, a woman's decision to be an isolated convert brought her into an especially difficult kind of ministry.

Previously conformist women who had dared to embrace Quakerism now found themselves required to ignore the social niceties of the age. The peculiarities of Quaker speech challenged the hierarchical ordering of the family and of society. Refusal to pay tithes brought reprisals. For women who were as yet unconvinced, but who were married to a Friend, it was hard to come to terms with altered circumstances. Thus for example the wife of the minister Miles Halhead rather wished he had been a drunkard than a Quaker – then at least she would have known that the ale-house was the place to find him.[60] The untutored Yorkshire butcher Luke Cock had found the plain speech *Testimony* difficult enough but the call for honesty was harder still:

I'se be ruined of this butchering trade, if I mun not lie for gain.

Moreover on discovering that refusal of tithe-payment was required too, it was his unconvinced wife who responded

We's all be ruined: What art thou going stark mad to follow these silly Quakers?[61]

Almost anything seemed preferable to Quakerism. Alice Hayes, a woman Friend from Rickmansworth, found that her husband's father cursed her and exploded

do not thee and thou me . . . had you been a Baptist and gone to hear them every day of the week, it had not been as bad as this.[62]

there was at this Meeting one Elizabeth Trelawney daughter to one that was called a Baronet. She being somewhat thick of hearing came close up to me, and clapt her Ear very nigh me, while I spake; and she was Convinced. After, the Priests was done (here came some jangling Baptists, but the Lords Power came upon them. And Elizabeth Trelawney cried; George is over all)!

George Fox his Journal. Plimouth 1655.

Convincement of Elizabeth Trelawney by George Fox.

67

Her mother-in-law flew into 'a bitter passion', declaring, so Alice recorded, 'I would undo her child'. Thomas Ellwood's father threatened to knock his teeth down his throat for 'thou-ing' him and Lady Waller, who had never before been addressed as 'woman', attacked the Friend Ellis Hookes physically.

Women of good family who embraced Quakerism caused particular distress to their relatives. Thomas Lower, who was later to marry a daughter of Margaret Fell, had first been husband to Elizabeth Trelawney of Plymouth, daughter of the baronet Sir John Trelawney (d. 1664). Elizabeth's hearing was impaired but this had not prevented her responding to George Fox's preaching so that she had cried out 'George is over all . . .' (*Journal*, 234). As a result, however,

> The priests and other great persons and professors, her kindred, were in a great rage concerning her.

So Fox recorded; but Elizabeth had simply passed on their letters to Fox himself, and at first he had taken up the case for Quakerism on her behalf. In time, however,

> she grew so in the power and spirit and wisdom of God that she could answer the wisest priest and professor (*Journal*, 261).

Besse reported (*Sufferings* i, 116) of the Cornishwoman Anne Lepcot, the daughter of a priest, that she so incensed her family by her convincement that when they found her mending a torn waistcoat on the Sabbath her brother (who was a local Constable), obtained a warrant for her to appear before the Justices for Sabbath-breaking. Either 5s was to be levied or she was to be confined in the stocks. Her brother took the latter option and with her father he encouraged the rabble to abuse and jeer at her in the rain.

An unconvinced husband could prove a great trial to his wife and it is evident that violence sometimes marred relationships. One of Fox's early converts, Joan Sley

> met sufferings and afflictions from her own husband for a time,[63]

but once widowed, Joan went on to be an innkeeper. For more than four decades she bore her Quaker witness to 'soldiers and rude persons' at the Crown Inn in Alton, Hampshire. Alice Hayes again, suffered great marital difficulties as a result of her convincement. She had been impressed first by a woman Quaker preacher as well as by 'the solidity of the people and the weighty frame of Spirit they were under'. She had met Quaker men worthies such as Camm, Audland, Dewsbury and Halhead but before long Alice discovered the depth of hostility which Quakerism provoked. It was not just her husband's parents but her husband too who found it hard to come to terms with her changed status:

> My dear husband, who was so tender and loving to me all our days till now, grew unkind and his love turned into hatred and contempt

. . . sometimes when I went to dress myself to go to meeting, my husband would take away my clothes . . . 'If you do not leave off going to the Quakers, I will sell all that I have and pay every one their own and go and leave you' he'd declared to her (see n. 62).

Alice, like many a Quaker woman, found that 'all in this world that were near and dear to me, were turned against me'.

It is clear, then, that a woman did not have to be a Barbara Blaugdone, an inveterate preacher and traveller, to meet animosity and even violence. Her trouble might just as easily come to her at home.

Something must be said of Quaker businesswomen. A businesswoman such as the innkeeper Joan Sley was in a good position to further the cause, that is provided that her good business sense and honest dealings were sufficient to override local prejudices against her religion. Since it was important to ensure a livelihood for a woman when the men in a family might have to be absent for long periods, then in some families women were set up in trade. There were female converts, of course, who had been in trade before they had discovered Quakerism, just as there were other women for whom widowhood offered an impetus for change. The Friend Joan Dant was one such widow, formerly married to a Spitalfields weaver who had left her ill-provided for. Joan became an extremely successful itinerant haberdasher, involved in the import and export trade, and she appears now in Antonia Fraser's study of *The Weaker Vessel* as 'one of the few women *entrepreneurs* of the seventeenth century about whom some personal details are known'. Yet Joan never altered her frugal lifestyle nor did she abandon her simple house. So when she died in 1715 at the age of 84, she left more than £9,000 in her will. This came as a surprise to the Quakers, though her own comment was

> I got it by the rich and I mean to leave it to the poor . . . [to] do something for the poor, the fatherless and the widows in the church of Christ.[64]

Quaker men sometimes helped in their wives' business ventures, while giving much of their own time to public ministry and the administration of Quaker affairs. Both Samuel Bownas and Thomas Chalkely helped in this way. Elizabeth Stirredge and her husband worked in their shop. A few women were involved in the printing trade and so they helped to produce those 2,500 Quaker books and pamphlets which it is reckoned had emerged by the turn of the eighteenth century.[65] Among their number were the widow Inman, Elizabeth Calvert (a Baptist who carried on the work of the better known Giles, when he was arrested in 1661), Mary Westwood and Tace Sowle, who took over her father's business in 1691.[66]

Dorothy Ludlow has made a pertinent observation about such women:

the active commitment to their faith of these 'ordinary' women of the middling and trades classes is a more remarkable and significant phenomenon than the more outlandish antics of the women preachers and visionaries . . . one needs to account somehow for these women who apparently paid little or no attention to the legal, economic and religious restrictions which made them subordinate to men; who carried on their daily lives independent of these limitations and who apparently felt there was nothing 'unfeminine' or shameful about doing so.

('Shaking Patriarchy's Foundations', 115.) It must be said, however, that such women were privileged in their financial independence. To pursue an active public ministry, in particular, or even to support others in such work, money was needed and the luxury of time too. This is an important observation, I think, and it should not be overlooked. Local Meetings defrayed expenses for those who were otherwise too poor to follow their vocations, but some would not, or could not, seek such help. Just like their sisters 'in the world', Quaker women bore children at frequent intervals and so they too were cumbered with the tasks of housekeeping and childrearing. Travelling ministry and even local public ministry would have been beyond many women Friends because of their family circumstances. It was the unmarried woman (some women Friends remained unmarried until quite an advanced age by seventeenth-century standards) and the mature widow whose children were grown who had most freedom to travel. All such women needed money to follow their vocations.

Quakerism was keen to avoid the 'hireling' nature of Christian ministry, such as Friends condemned in the other churches. From the outset they had determined that the Spirit should not be quenched. Yet Thomas Ellwood's verse of 1685 shows their awareness of the dilemma:

May none beyond the seas go but can spare
Sufficient of their own the charge to bear?
Must Christ be so confin'd he may not send
Any but such as have estates to spend?

The answer to its question would have been No, and with all good intention. Nevertheless, even among Quakers the realities of most women's lives, and the economic powerlessness of most of them, were factors which helped to ensure that most 'public Friends', at home and abroad, were in fact male.

Women were generally much less educated and given the assumptions of the age they tended to be less socially confident at this time. Even among Quakers, then, women soon took it for granted that, in general, men were more 'serviceable' in the public sphere. Not a few of the Quaker 'mothers in Israel', we must remember – Margaret Fell, Anne Downer

(Whitehead), Loveday Hambly among them – were women who were relatively privileged, propertied, respected and they could expect even a degree of supportive patronage. In contrast many women Friends had burdensome family commitments combined with lack of resources. Barbara Blaugdone thought it worth remarking proudly in her memoirs that in all her travels she had relied on her own purse and was 'never chargeable to any'.

'A good example to her sex'

At the end of the seventeenth century a calmer and more conformist Quaker woman was to the fore. Remarkably she was sometimes the same woman who, a few decades earlier, had been roundly condemned by the world for outlandish behaviour and refusal of feminine stereotypes. Thus it was with Ann Audland Camm, one of the first *Publishers of Truth*, the 'prating wife' of John Audland, then wife of Thomas Camm (the son of her late husband's friend). Here had been a woman who was once threatened with death by burning and who had been imprisoned for her troublesomeness in frog-infested sewer rooms. Yet she was remembered by Sewel and in the *Piety promoted* series as

> . . . a good example to her sex; for without extraordinary impulse and concern it was rare for her to preach in large meetings where she knew there were brethren better qualified . . . and she was grieved when any, especially of her sex, should be too hasty, forward or unseasonable.

Some women, it seems, had slid gratefully into less publicly threatening roles.

Anne Downer Whitehead is often portrayed as the woman who had been 'secretary' to the imprisoned George Fox at the time of the Nayler scandal. At this time she managed not only the journey from London to Cornwall but also (a) the organisation of substantial prison and family relief (b) the making of converts and (c) taking shorthand notes for Fox. Anne, later a mainstay of London Meetings, was described as a scourge of the 'stubborn, idle and disobedient'. It is evident that this woman had many activities of her own to concern her, considerable organisational skills and she knew how to operate diplomatically in delicate political situations. Yet she saw herself in the role of dutiful, self-effacing and supportive wife to the younger George Whitehead! He had followed the pattern quite common among ministering Quaker men, of turning an eye towards a sympathetic widow and Anne had responded. Of all those things in her life which she might have reported with satisfaction she chose to report with pride of her marriage to him, saying

> . . . this I shall leave behind me, as that which is satisfaction to me . . . that I never did detain him one quarter of an hour out of the Lord's service.

She too disapproved of her own sex usurping the ministries which were, she thought, rightfully men's.[67] Not only Quakerism, but women Friends, had been transformed since the early days, though in Anne's case it must be said that she had never been a rouser of the rabble or a very widely travelled Friend.

There is a telling Minute in the records of the London *Second Day Morning Meeting* for 1701. This Meeting had been created originally to serve itinerant ministers, and one of its functions was to ensure the quality and availability of ministry. When women 'public Friends' expressed a wish to set up their own Seventh Day Meeting, the response from the men of *Second Day Morning* was revealing. The women's initiative was vetoed. Those who wished to 'attend public meetings under concern of service', they were told, should 'leave their names at the chamber'. Don't call us, we'll call you. In addition,

> Women should not interfere with their brethren in their public mixed meetings [or] take up too much time . . . in our public meetings when several public and serviceable men Friends are by them prevented in their serving.

The unregenerate Martha Simmonds should have been there at that hour! Indeed it is difficult for the twentieth-century reader to imagine that no eyebrow was raised at this response, especially among those surviving women who had been pioneer travellers and public preachers before the age of Toleration and some even before the Restoration. It is equally hard to imagine no raised eyebrows or voices some years earlier when Anne Downer Whitehead had brought back from the Men's Yearly Meeting the observers report from herself and twenty-three other women.[68] It was now considered (by the men, of course) that ministry in cities such as London, Norwich and Bristol was too weighty a task for women Friends. Moreover, the women should not court popularity and in their preaching should not seek 'to be seen or heard of men'. It seems probable that some rethinking did take place on these matters (at whose instigation we do not know), for in the *Cautions and Counsels to Ministers* issued in the Yearly Meeting of ministers in 1702 we read that 'brethren' should not discourage women's service. This counsel is found in association with another one, however, which at the same time told women not to 'hinder' the brethren.[69] It is evident that relations between 'public' men and women Friends were still not without friction!

The truth is that throughout the latter half of the seventeenth century there was a constant undercurrent of uncertainty among Quakers about the degree of freedom and participation to be accorded to women. There were Quaker men who neither understood nor valued properly the great variety of services which the women were performing. The undercurrent of uncertainty was present while the women themselves were out

72

preaching, prophesying, travelling overseas, publishing, petitioning, aiding the poor and imprisoned and maintaining piety in the Quaker home. Occasionally the fears surfaced strongly and in overt opposition to some female activities which other Friends welcomed. We shall see more of this 'surfacing' of opposition in the next chapter. It was because of just such fears and reservations *within* Quakerism, as well as because of the outrage and hostility to female ministry which was the norm beyond it, that over and over again women's speaking had to be justified in print.

It says much for the earliest converts that neither social conservatism nor public condemnation had deflected them from the way they thought was right. Nevertheless they too had been conscious of 'dangers' associated with their teaching about women. Their writings bear the marks of attempts to ensure that the 'right' kind of women ministered, and in the 'right' way. The language of the Bible served them well for this Thus the woman whose speaking was justified was not the woman 'in the disobedience of Eve' or still 'in the Law'. On the contrary, the acceptable woman was she who was 'led by the Spirit of God' and who was 'in the Gospel'.[70] When a moment of testing came, such distinctions proved useful, not least in ensuring that women did not lightly encroach on male territory and no more Mildred or Martha Simmonds figures emerged!

The end of Chapter One referred to disaffection among some of the women Friends, for reasons which are not clear. The present section, also, seems to end on a negative note. It should not be thought, however, that the opportunities for Quaker women were very short-lived. This was not so. The kinds of Minutes which have been cited above would never have been written and the 'official' male line so clearly stated, had it not been the case that women *were* fulfilling just those public functions which were under discussion. It is true (as we shall see in the next chapter) that from the late 1660s the emerging *Women's Meetings* did channel a lot of female activity into more stereotypically feminine areas. The discipline within those Meetings also helped to promote conformity and sobriety among the Friends. But the 'horses for courses' nature of Quaker ministry still ensured that appropriately gifted women retained opportunities to operate in 'unfeminine' ways. The constraints of family and economic power-lessness must have deterred not a few of them and the Quaker practice by the 1670s of vetting writings pre-publication took its toll of the works of women as well as men. Yet even having acknowledged these things, the fact remains that women Friends were active, and publicly so, in a great variety of ways.

One of my final observations in this chapter has to be about the extraordinary ordinariness of many of these women. They wanted their mundane daily lives to be impregnated with the experience of the Spirit and its fruits of love and peace and harmony. They went out into the streets, faced physical abuse and cried their message over baying opposition, then they went home to check the household accounts and feed and comfort their children. They foresaw the millenium, wrote letters to the King and served beef and beer at supper. Quakers, as Phyllis Mack observed in her study of 'Gender and Spirituality' (pp. 54 seq.)

> had to integrate moments of being 'in the power' with other aspects of their social and personal existence . . . one had to live on more than one level . . . to sustain the integration of ecstatic prayer with keeping a budget . . .

Even within the very real limitations of *spiritual* equality, these notable women forged roles for themselves which ensured that Quakers of future generations continued to take seriously women's insights and abilities. After the Restoration 'madness' was a frequent description among 'the world's people' for what had gone before and there was a growing cynicism about the possibility or desirability of change. Plagued by persecution, women Friends continued undaunted their public religious activities. In contrast, other groups and their women faded into oblivion.

CHAPTER III

'THIS IS MY FRIEND'
Marriage, children, education and the Women's Meetings

THE QUAKER PATTERN OF MARRIAGE and family life needs to be set against the background of wider seventeenth-century practice, so I shall begin with some introduction to that.

In his study of *The Family, Sex and Marriage in England 1500-1800* Lawence Stone wrote as follows:

> The many legal, political and educational changes that took place in the late seventeenth and eighteenth centuries were largely consequences of changes in ideas about the nature of marital relations. The increasing stress laid by the early seventeenth century preachers on the need for companionship in marriage in the long run tended to undercut their own arrangements in favour of strict wifely subjection and obedience.[1]

But historians differ as to the exact effects on family life both of the Puritan revolution and of the unrest of the civil war period. Despite those changes which *did* come about in this period, there was in those households of which we know most (i.e. not of the poorest classes) a hierarchy of relationships. Very often the household was still the basic unit of production. Spouses, children, servants and sometimes apprentices worked within it, and normally with a patriarchal figure at the head. It was the norm for father to lead the family prayers.[2] It was not the case, of course, that the meanest labourer in such a setting enjoyed status superior to the lady of the manor, by virtue only of being male. Careful lines of demarcation separated the strata of society. But such a man was lord in his own household.

The moralist William Gouge pronounced firmly that

> Though husband and wife may mutually serve one another through love; yet the Apostle suffereth not a woman to rule over the man.[3]

75

It was in the family that the wider commonwealth was to be seen in microcosm, so

> . . . necessary it is that good order be set first in families: for as they were before other polities, so are they somewhat the more necessary: and good members of a family are like to make good members of Church and commonwealth.

The seventeenth-century family differed from its modern counterpart, first in its size and then in what has been called 'the enormous mass of sociability within it'. Among the wealthier classes the presence of children also set it apart from similar families of the Middle Ages. Now the rich less frequently entrusted their children to strangers – though relatives still often found themselves in fostering roles.

> The child became an indispensable element of everyday life . . . a much more important character.[4]

Protestantism had preached mutuality in marriage and the 'helps-meet' ideal.[5] It had taught that marriage was holy and in our period John Milton summed up the usual Christian view by describing the three 'chief ends' of marriage as 'godly society, next civil, and thirdly that of the marriage bed'.[6] Archbishop Cranmer's Prayer Book of 1549 had referred to 'mutual society, help and comfort'. Real-life experiences of marriage not infrequently proved quite different and the problem of *divorce*, or lack of, remained. Throughout the century there was disquiet and some debate about what grounds for divorce might perhaps be allowed.[7]

It was widely agreed that parental consent was necessary for a marriage and that both parties to it should agree to it. In reality, of course, there was frequently coercion and just as married women were bound morally to obey their husbands, so too daughters owed obedience to fathers.[8] In many an arranged union there were financial interests at stake and so daughters might be unduly pressurised. Spectacular refusals to comply are recorded but there was also a great deal of enforced unhappiness.[9]

Marriage for love was not encouraged.

> He that takes a wife without money is a slave to his affections, doing the barest of drudgeries without wages,

wrote Francis Osborne in his *Advice to His Son*. Dorothy, another member of the Osborne clan, was typical of her class in disapproving of love-matches:

> To marry for love were no reproachful thing if we did not see that of the thousand couples that do it, hardly one can be brought for an example that it may be done and not repented of afterwards.[10]

Their 'betters' advised the poorer classes against passion too. Attachments were made with greater freedom among them, which was

76

something which some seventeenth-century writers deplored. Hannah Woolley, for example, wrote in *The Gentlewomans Companion . . . whereunto is added a Guide for Cookmaids etc . . .* that as a general rule 'this boiling affection is seldom worth anything'.[11]

In practice then, seventeenth-century women had plenty to complain of. The lot of many of them was far from happy, and this was so despite the preachers' insistence on mutuality in marriage, despite the legal and other improvements for women of which Stone wrote, and despite even the end of state patriarchy in 1688, as James II saw his support disappear and the enthronement of William and Mary came into view. The master of a houschold felt free to beat wife and servant alike. Even the patriarch of Protestantism, Martin Luther, had declared

When Katy gets saucy, she gets nothing but a box on the ear.[12]

Certainly there *were* more enlightened writers who disapproved of, or at least did not advocate, wife-beating, and with the Restoration in 1660 there did come a curtailment of a man's absolute right to chastise his wife. In this, as in other respects, Puritanism improved the lot of women. But the brutish views exemplified by Swetnam 'the woman-hater' (whose much reprinted work we met in the first chapter) were repeated and joked about.[13] At the start of the eighteenth century the poet Mary Lee, Lady Chudleigh, could still write of the god-husband, who 'governed by a nod'. Her poem *To the Ladies* began with the words

Wife and servant are the same
But only differ in the Name.[14]

The marital difficulties of all classes were portrayed briskly by Margaret Cavendish, Duchess of Newcastle, in Act Three of her play *The Convent of Pleasure*. Its characters were, on the one hand, well-born ladies who complained that their husbands lost estates through gambling at dice or cards or whoring ('in my house, under my roof'), so that all might be lost, even 'my portion'. One such lady told of the husband who 'hath forced me with threats to yield up my jointure'. On the other hand, 'mean women' characters were portrayed, who told of husbands who lay all day in ale-houses, who spent their wives' earnings and beat them 'black and blue', leaving their children unfed. Yet one of the Duchess's characters is made to say

. . . though some few be unhappy in marriage, yet there are many more that are so happy as they would not change their condition.[15]

Wealthy and well-born women were generally burdened with genteel and carefully cultivated idleness. It was suffocating for some of them and it remained a feature of their lives for centuries to come.[16] Margaret Cavendish and her peers knew that more interesting spheres of activity were open to them only if they flouted all the conventions of their class.

They would be regarded as unfeminine, mad, immodest, even unchaste. The sexual 'double-standard' was well established in the seventeenth century and women of all classes experienced its effects. Esther Sowernam had attacked it in her reply to Swetnam's work:

> If a man abuse a maid and get her with child, no matter is made of it, but by a trick of youth; but it is made so heinous an offence in the maid, that she is disparaged and utterly undone by it.[17]

The records which Quakers kept in their Meetings for business affairs show that they were well aware of the unpleasant realities of seventeenth-century society. All human life is there: birth and child mortality, marriage, death and widowhood, insanity, adultery, illegitimacy, violence and female poverty, marital incompatibility, imprisonment, drunkenness, fecklessness, business success and failure, philanthropy and fraud.[18] Through their own Women's Meetings female Quakers responded with immediate or continued support, with investigation and with censure. Modern observers wonder why *separate* Meetings for women were considered necessary at all. Quaker women had been meeting together for mutual support and to facilitate philanthropic work before formal Women's Meetings were inaugurated. The story I shall tell in this chapter is of the struggle to establish and to operate the mixed blessing of such Women's Meetings. It tells us a great deal about the sex-role stereotyping which existed among Friends, and which was more rampant still in wider society. It reminds us, too, that even in Quakerism there existed more than one view of a woman's place.

Establishing Women's Meetings

Thanks to occasional lulls in persecution Quakerism had developed an organisation by 1668. Between 1672 and 1676 George Fox and his supporters further consolidated this organisation. A brief explanation will be necessary of how it worked (and works today), for it was complex.

At the local level Quakers met and worshipped in their local groups and locally also transacted business in the Particular Meeting or what came to be known as the Preparative Meeting. It was there that preparations were made for the next level. The level concerned was the Monthly Meeting, where groups from a region or in an urban centre were represented. The Monthly Meeting was of considerable importance. It was there that births, deaths and marriages were discussed and registered; through the Monthly Meeting that apprentices and servants were settled, miscreants were admonished and poor relief and prison oversight were organised. In turn the Monthly Meeting reported to the Quarterly Meeting, which might relate to an area of more than one county. It was at Quarterly Meeting level that representatives for the Yearly Meeting were decided upon. From 1678-1905 Yearly Meeting was held in London and considerable influence was centred in it. More specifically, it was centred in the *Men's* Yearly Meeting business sessions, since for most of Quaker history women generally did not attend the business sessions concerned. They had little role in most of the other London-based 'power-house' Meetings either, whose work will be referred to from time to time.

The Quaker business Meeting was not entirely a novelty in 1668. There had been some moves towards organisation before that date, in the North in particular. Between 1558 and 1661, for example, there had been General Meetings held in Balby and Skipton, with another in Bedfordshire. Quakers had travelled to these from far and near, so they had been functioning rather like the later Yearly Meetings did. But it was in the late 1660s that organisation was formalised and established widely.[19] Meeting for Sufferings had initially met quarterly, but by 1679 its work necessitated a weekly gathering. As its name implies, it catalogued, drew attention to and sought ways to alleviate the many 'sufferings' of Friends. Its significance as a determining assembly grew apace but the women played no part in its judgements. However, by that same year (1679) a network of Women's Meetings to transact business had emerged, which operated parallel to the local, the Monthly and the Quarterly assemblies of the men. Fox and others had been advocating such a set-up since the late 1660s but the change was not welcomed wholeheartedly. There was dissent and disaffection in Quaker ranks about a number of organisational issues and the setting up of Women's Meetings offered a particular cause for complaint.

There were Friends who thought that Fox and other promoters of change were being imperious and heavy-handed. John Perrot in the 1660s,[20] John Wilkinson and John Story in the 1670s[21] did not want to see freedom 'in the Spirit' quenched through group judgement. They did not want institutionalised authority to replace the charismatic kind, group authority to usurp the individual's freedom, with organised Meetings bound to time and place. Twentieth-century historians of Quakerism tend to feel that the best of the emerging Society was on the Fox-Fell side (for where the Women's Meetings were concerned, for example, Margaret Fell was a stirring advocate) but even allowing for the polemical nature of the publications and the strong language of the age, it is clear from writings of the time that not a few Quakers were hostile to Fox and his innovations.

There were also defenders of the Foxian vision. Robert Barclay, with a backward look at past excesses, wrote *The Anarchy of the Ranters* and in this argued that it was a well-tested fact that *established* people should lead. Decision-making should be corporate:

> God hath ordinarily, in communicating his will, employed such whom he made use of in gathering his church . . . meeting together

> . . . and giving a positive judgement . . . will not import tyrrany
> . . . or an inconsistency with the universal privilege that all
> Christians have to be led by the Spirit.[22]

William Penn was equally positive. Without discipline, he maintained, the church would be overrun 'with lukewarm hypocrites and loose walkers'. What was in mind was no more than

> discipline in government, not in worship, formality in order, not in religion.

And as for the objections of the Wilkinson-Storyites to the setting up of Women's Meetings, these objections, Penn pronounced, were just 'heresy'.[23] It should be said that not all such objectors were male. George Fox remarked on women Friends 'that denieth women's meetings' though still they wanted to influence the Quarterly Meetings.

The reformers hoped there would be less extravagance and open-air disorder if Meetings were more disciplined. Elders and Friends appointed to practise oversight, as well as accredited ministers ('public Friends' as they came to be known) would do their work. These last were people who were recognised as having a special gift of vocal ministry. The advocates of change said that charismatic spontaneity need not suffer. The opponents were unmoved. In reality, of course, the presence of accredited 'public Friends', sitting raised above the rest of the Meeting from the 1690s onwards, *did* foster more silence in the unaccredited lower ranks.[24] It was true, on the other hand, that open-air Meetings did not cease entirely. There were still even the prophetic gestures, with Robert Barclay, no less, going in sackcloth and ashes through Aberdeen in 1672 and Thomas Rudd declaring woe to the city of Bristol two years later.[25] But patrician figures like Barclay and Penn had come to the fore. Quakerism was becoming increasingly bourgeois and conservative now that the first flourish of apocalyptic fervour was past. Persecution was *not* past, and it was believed that greater discipline would help to maintain that network of support which was needed and would show the Friends to be deserving of toleration. In some families in the 1670s the third generation of Quakers was in its infancy. Many of the early activists were dead.[26] Fox apart then, different Quaker men were at the helm and some of them were not entirely happy with the way the ship had been going.

The issue of separate Meetings for women figured in the Wilkinson-Story schism, though it was not about that alone.[27] The schismatics considered such Women's Meetings to be unscriptural and an unnecessary appendage in Quakerism. In fact, *power* was the real issue and the perceived danger of 'the monstrous regiment of women' (as Knox had put it in the previous century). There were Quakers who feared such 'female rule', and among those Friends who had stood at odds with the conventions of the 1650s and 1660s there were some who were social conservatives in this particular matter. Yet to the modern student of Quakerism what is most remarkable about the Women's Meetings (after the fact of their existence) is the *lack* of power associated with them. Indeed Braithwaite was right to refer to them as

> designed to give women some share in Church government but not an equal share with men,[28]

even if in his view such a statement was associated with 'hasty students of Quaker history' (*SPQ* 273). The Women's Meetings for business affairs were subject to those of the men. Men and women worshipped together (by the end of the century on different sides of the Meeting House, like Anglicans[29]). They sent representatives, as necessary, to the business sessions of the other, visiting 'under concern' or to discover the progress of business. But it was the men who controlled the purse strings. Certainly women Friends often administered considerable sums of money and their Meetings had other assets too, but the women submitted their Meeting accounts annually for male scrutiny while the men made no such submission.[30] Quaker men in their Meetings also had some control over women's freedom to minister, as we have seen, and they could forestall attempts at independent organisation. Even after the women won their own Yearly Meeting assemblies in 1784[31] it was in the Men's Yearly Meeting that the power lay.[32]

Yet despite what proved to be the reality of such relative lack of power for women the opponents of Women's Meetings were fearful. While Fox quoted scriptural precedents and maintained, in epistles of 1666 and 1673, that women were heirs in the Christian order – that they were priests, and should take up their inheritance and duties, he also indicated (a) that women should take instruction from their husbands at home, as Paul had taught and (b) that a convinced wife should instruct her unbelieving husband. Still other Quakers refused to be bound by female authority, especially where arrangements for the marriages of men were concerned.[33] The Friend James Lancaster berated the men in an epistle:

> You that stumble at Women's Meetings and think yourselves sufficient as being men: what was and is it that makes thee sufficient? Is it not the grace of God, and hath that not appeared to all men and to all women? Must not this be exercised in women, as well as men . . . born of it, the Spirit of God? . . . Thus being members of the Church, Christ Jesus being the head, male and female all one in him; therefore, dismember not the Body . . . look on them to be meet helps.

George Fox's own appeals to the relationship of Abraham and Sarah, with each obeying the other (*Genesis* 21:9-11) spoke only to the converted. In addition, John Wilkinson pointed out that Fox's use of scripture was suspect at times, 'unsound and impertinently quoted', not least when he

81

praised Micah's mother in the work *This is an Encouragement to all the Womens Meetings in the World.* As a more careful reading of Judges 17:1-4 would have shown Fox, Micah's mother was in fact idolatrous! The leader was on firmer ground when he returned to the familiar Quaker declaration that it was not even scripture which should determine such a matter. 'The foundation of the Womens Meetings is Christ', he wrote in 1674 in *To All the Womens Meetings.*

There was some half-hearted acknowledgment by the opponents that perhaps *in large cities* there was need of *some* administrative structure for the women's poor-relief, but the advocates of Women's Meetings had more than this in mind. The 'sober women' of town and country were to be told of the need to participate fully in Quaker work, 'that none may stand idle out of the vineyard'. The diffident women, and those who by dint of circumstances had not been using their gifts, were to be energised. This was the message, despite the existence of Quakers who continued to refuse 'arbitrary commands'.[34] Organisation went ahead.

The Yearly Meeting epistle of 1673 widened the existing rift by condemning the dissenters. *The Spirit of the Hat*, published that same year by Samuel Mucklow, had been openly hostile to Fox and his circle and Wilkinson and Story had a popular following which was not easily appeased. These two men had been among the first Quaker ministers and for decades they had laboured in their native Westmorland, in Bristol, Wiltshire and elsewhere. It was in just such places that opposition was most marked. Small groups held out against reform in Reading, Bristol and York. In Reading, Meeting House doors were shut by one faction against others, including against one of the Women's Meetings. Quakers of differing persuasions met separately in the same town and the schism continued into the eighteenth century in some places. Belief in the *spiritual* equality of the sexes did not prevent there being Quakers who thought women would be better employed fulfilling their domestic obligations than making decisions about church discipline. Elizabeth Tayler Stirredge (b. 1634), she who was once called 'an old prophetess' and 'a troublesome woman' by a hostile Justice, described this time of division as her greatest 'exercise', worse even than the persecutions she had known. She was one of those who faced up to Story in Meetings, daring to interrupt his lengthy and heavy sermonising:

> Woe to that spirit that dimmeth the glory of the Lord, and woe to that pot whose scum remains in it, for in it is the broth of abomination.[35]

His sermonising, she said, had prevented others from speaking.

Elizabeth Stirredge ventured deliberately into Wilkinson-Story territory and John Story told her that the evidence of God in her conscience was not enough. He had 'much reflected upon several women', she recorded, for bearing witness against his separatism. Two Quaker women, so she related in her autobiography, had left a Meeting in tears after Story had quoted St Paul's injunction against preaching. He had told them to go home and wash their dishes.[36] Yet Stirredge's writing also indicates that not a few were on John Story's side on some of the matters at issue. This was not Fox's view, however. Indeed he declared in print that Quaker men should not say

> . . . we can do our work ourselves and you are more fitter to be at home to wash the dishes.

In fact George Fox was adamant in the matter. When Nathaniel Coleman of Slaughterford showed his strong opposition to proposals for a Women's Meeting there, Fox observed that while he had a right to rule his own wife, Coleman had no such rights over the wives of other men, over widows or young women.[37]

During this period of disunity *women* Friends were working to promote and defend their own Meetings. Margaret Fell Fox and her daughters did so through their letters and personal contacts. William Rogers' 1680 work *The Christian Quaker*, which contains a lot of correspondence between the protagonists, tells (in Part IV) of a paper which 'George Fox's wife' caused to be read at a Quarterly Meeting in the eleventh month of 1672, and which was given in her name at Kendal. It had contained 'grievous accusations against our faithful Friend John Story', William Rogers reported. With other leading Friends Margaret had confronted and debated with opponents face to face, for Fox was absent, first in America (between 1671-73) and then in Worcester gaol. There was no love lost between her and the Wilkinson-Storyites and her role in the establishment of the Women's Meetings was more of a pivotal one than has been appreciated. In this, as in other matters, Margaret's own influence and leadership have probably been underestimated.[38] But other women were influential too.

They wrote and spoke out in favour of reform. Ann Powell Bryant, a Cirencester woman, took the opportunity to vilify John Story at a Meeting at fair-time in Bristol, in March of 1679. Some of the writers, by contrast, seem to twentieth century eyes to have been rather defensive in presentation. The defensiveness is a product, I think, both of the conventions of the age in women's writings and of their consciousness of the strength of hostility among some of the Friends.

Mary Elson and Anne Goddard Whitehead, in *An Epistle for True Love, Unity and Order* attacked hardened prejudice but wrote also of

> . . . the men Friends, who discharge their places, to whom the godly women always give the pre-eminence . . . not seeking rule over one another . . .

Their statement that

> Our God is the God of order, in all the churches of his saints, and
> not the God of confusion

has a chilling effect when it is married with what follows. The 'order'
under discussion concerned, not least,

> such things as are proper to us, as visiting and relieving the sick and
> the poor . . . and destitute . . . the children at nurse be rightly
> educated . . . the elder women to instruct the younger to all
> wholesome things, loving their own husbands, to be discreet,
> chaste, sober, keeping at home . . .

Here was no prophetic vision of *radical* change for women. Yet it is clear
that they, and women like them, valued the Meetings greatly. Moreover
they told of winning support from male Friends:

> Brethren from the Mens Meeting were soon expressing their unity
> with us . . . and this I can say, the more opposition we have had
> against our Womens Meeting, the more we have increased in the
> power of the Lord.[39]

Certainly there *were* male Friends who ventured into print in support of
Women's Meetings and some of them, too, adopted a reassuring tone for
the consumption of the opposition. While William Loddington in the tract
The Good Order of Truth Justified (London 1685, 5 *et passim*) expressed
Paul's view that the man was 'head' of the woman, he distinguished
between (a) rightful male headship 'in the temporals' and (b) equality 'in
Christ' where 'spirituals' were concerned. He concluded that:

> [women] may without the least suspicion of usurping authority over
> the men reason and confer together, in such things as are most
> proper and suitable for them, still submitting to the wisdom of God
> in the Mens Meetings.

But what exactly was 'proper' for women?

Propriety was a matter of interest in these debates. Those who were
more positive than to regard as improper *all* organisational and
disciplinary activity for women maintained that in Meetings for business
separation of the sexes was necessary. This was due to the delicate nature
of 'women's matters'.

> None but Ranters will desire to look into women's matters,

Fox observed, aiming his words at the 'dark spirits' who wanted to keep
all ordering for themselves. Thus it was seemly that from their own
segregated Meetings the women should refer to the men any cases more
'fitting' for them to deal with, just as such referrals should come in the
opposite direction too:

In this we do assist one another in the Spirit and Truth, and are meethelps . . .

read *A Living Testimony from the Womens Meeting in London* of the first of the 4th month 1685. This was signed by Mary Foster, Mary Elson, Ruth Crowch and others on its behalf.

It was also argued that separate Meetings were necessary because of the problem of women's conditioning. This point comes out clearly in a letter from the Cumberland Friend John Banks, in 1674. The letter was entitled *To all the Womens Meetings that Gather in the Name of Jesus*. Banks had witnessed the reticence of women. He had noted their tendencies to self-negation and non-participation. He knew personally women who when they have

> met amongst men, although they have received a measure of the same Spirit and are gather'd by the same power, have been apt to put the service of things from themselves and so . . . have quenched the good notion of the Spirit in themselves by looking out at the men.[40]

He hoped that with the Women's Meetings matters would be improved.

William Penn combined both concerns when he wrote of women

> whose bashfulness will not permit them to say or do as much as to church affairs before the men, when by themselves [they] exercise their gifts of wisdom and understanding in a discreet care for their own sex.[41]

The Yearly Meeting pronouncement of 1675 was confident:

> The rise and practice, setting up and establishment of Mens and Womens Meetings in the Church of Christ . . . is according to the mind and counsel of God,[42]

it declared. More and more Women's Meetings *were* being established and they had as paradigms the London ones which had existed since as early as the late 1650s, before Fox had set about organisation. Had these London Meetings not existed already, it might have proved more difficult still to argue the case for country-wide business Meetings for the women Friends.

A word about Quaker women in London will be in order here. In the winter of 1659 Sarah Blackbury had shared with George Fox her concern about the need for poor relief and the visitation of the sick in London. At very short notice, therefore, and at Fox's behest, she was able to assemble sixty female Quakers to meet with him. The work of these London Friends in the all-female *Box Meeting* (so-called after the receptacle in which its collections were held) and in the Women's *Two Weeks Meeting* (both founded in 1659) became a pattern for other women in the 1670s and later.[43] The *Box Meeting* remained unique, however, in that the women who ran it were never accountable to male Quakers.

It accumulated its capital from gifts. Lady Conway, for example, donated £10 to it. Quaker men made endowments to it, in memory of wives who had loved and served in it. It disbursed loans and gifts too – in 1674 William Penn received £300 and Fox was helped more than once in his imprisonments. The women Friends acted as guarantors when such loans were made and through its officers the *Box Meeting* managed a number of funds. Its assets included property, notably that purchased in Southgate, Middlesex in 1677, which was then run as a going concern.[44] For some years Anne Downer Whitehead was a notable figure in the Meeting and after her death Fox wrote an undated *Epistle of Love to Friends in the Womens Meetings in London*, commiserating with them. He described Anne as 'one of the Lord's worthies'. In 1681 Sarah Fell Meade succeeded the elderly Anne, and thereafter for more than a quarter of a century Sarah's handwriting appeared in the Box Meeting records.

The Women's Meetings which were founded subsequently used the better educated as administrators, clerks, keepers of accounts and so on. The Meetings encouraged the expectation that women should have an education to fit them for such tasks and that each woman's gift was to be used. They offered a structure through which women were assigned to a variety of jobs, depending on their abilities and their calling and it is for this reason that we see that those who travelled as ministers inevitably figured less frequently as activists in their local and regional Meetings. Those who published most for a general readership tended not to be very widely travelled and so on. But they too had parts to play in the local Meetings.[45] Quakerism was offering scope for most women's talents – for the literate and numerate, for the born preacher, the adventurer, the teacher, the counsellor and for the woman whose abilities as succourer and organiser had been nurtured in a lifetime of motherhood and domestic labour. It was not real equality. It was certainly not the promotion of feminism as presently understood, for the realities and the causes of the oppression of *women* were not being analysed and challenged. Nevertheless the changes Quakerism brought for women *are* to be set alongside those other examples of seventeenth-century incipient feminism which many writers have discerned. Quaker women gained a partnership, albeit unequal, at least in 'labouring in the vineyard'.

Women Friends knew that they had to prove themselves. They knew that inside Quakerism, as well as beyond it, there were many waiting for the experiment to fail. Within their limited scope, the segregated Meetings were a success for women. At the same time they were also a success for those Friends who wanted to see *order* prevail. As we shall see in considering marriage, family life and education, *order* was fostered through the Women's Meetings.

The marriages of Friends

Marriage, that most significant rite of passage, was very much the concern of the Men's and Women's business Meetings. George Fox had said that

> We marry none; it is the Lord's work, and we are but witnesses.

Quakers therefore did not 'conduct' marriages and this made them unusual. In other respects they conformed to Protestant pattern. Like radical Puritans in general they did not think of marriage as a sacrament and they also played down its role as a refuge from sin. In 1644 the Presbyterian *Directory for the Public Worship of God* had set down the form for marriage.[46] In 1653, under the Barebones Parliament, the civil registration of marriages in the presence of a Justice of the Peace had become compulsory. The *Marriage Act* of 1656 confirmed that state of affairs. Non-conforming marriages were not necessarily declared invalid thereafter, and in the year 1661 Judge Archer had stated in a ruling that

> Quakers . . . did not go together like brute beasts (as has been said) but as Christians

Indeed an Act was passed following a 1661 case which *ex post facto* validated Friends' marriages.[47] Legal precedents were helpful to Friends in their constant skirmishes with the authorities but still they encountered difficulties. Quaker married couples were readily labelled fornicators and their children bastards so that estates were put in jeopardy.

Civil registration of marriage was abandoned at the Restoration but the church also had its own requirements. The 1662 *Act of Uniformity* was passed to ensure conformity with the Church of England. This part of the infamous Clarendon Code insisted, among much else, that the Book of Common Prayer be used weekly by all parish clergy in churches and that marriages should be solemnised in the presence of clergy. Quakers were intensely anti-clerical and they were not alone in their hatred of the sentiments of the Act of Uniformity. Puritan clergy who felt unable to conform met secretly with their flocks as the subsequent *Five Mile Act* and the first *Conventicle Act* sought to reinforce conformity. For their part the Friends met openly in defiance of the laws, winning the 'convincement' of admirers but ensuring that in terms of numbers Quakers suffered most of all. Persecution was systematised as a result of the Clarendon Code, rather than being localised and sporadic and in these difficult conditions,

> potentially the Quaker crime with the most serious ramifications was their marriage in their own meeting

as a recent writer has observed. When challenged, Quakers appeared with their children unbaptised, their women unpurified after childbirth, their marriages unconventional.[48] Unconvinced and rapacious relatives found cause in these and other things to challenge wills, to seize estates and to cause great misery to Friends. A number of the best known writers published pleas: Philip Swale, Isaac Penington and Robert Barclay among them. The question of what constituted a marriage proper was still being debated years later, for Quakers were still meeting difficulties. In 1679 (i) Meeting for Sufferings asked the attorney Thomas Corbett whether an agreement to lifelong marriage, made without benefit of clergy or Prayer Book, was indeed lawful[49] and (ii) George Fox wrote to Richard Richardson, the schoolmaster Friend, to request that he do some research in libraries and in the works of the Christian Fathers. This was in order to discover what form marriage had taken

before the monkish sort came in in the Britons' time.

At a time when Quaker discipline was only just emerging Friends tried hard not to fall foul of changing legislation while staying true to their principles. This can be seen in their writings about marriage. Margaret Fell's work *To Friends of Mareges* was written in 1656, in the year of the *Marriage Act*. She suggested in it that (men) Friends who were present at a marriage should sign a certificate as witnesses, which should then be taken quickly to a Justice of the Peace. This was not a novel suggestion in Quaker circles, though it is notable that at this early date we see Margaret Fell helping to regulate the Quaker marriage procedure.[50] Fox's own 1661 writing *Concerning Marriage* had contained the advice that marriage proposals should be announced in the couple's own Meeting(s). Time was to be allowed for objections to emerge and to be investigated, before a subsequent Meeting at which the matter would be raised again. The marriage proposal was then to be announced a second time, either in such a Meeting or in the market place, thus testifying publicly against marriage of the worldly kind. Finally the knot would be tied in a Quaker gathering for worship at which at least twelve mature witnesses would sign the certificate. If it was wished, that certificate would then be submitted to a magistrate. It is clear that leading Friends were anxious to ensure that Quaker marriage was a public and not a secret matter. Nevertheless in the 1650s it would have been inconsistent with the Quaker view of things (and it remained inconsistent) to have allowed a Justice or anyone else to 'conduct' a ceremony. Marriage was, indeed, 'the Lord's work' and no one elses.

Marriage, so Fox maintained, was also now 'as it was in the beginning, before sin and defilement was'. Quakers were not to marry for gain and the remarriage of widows was to be looked to, not least to ensure that children of the former marriage did not suffer. In this state of restored perfection (as Fox saw it), it went without saying that there could be no certificate of divorce.

Some of the early converts to Quakerism had had radical ideas about marriage before their convincement. We see this in the case of Mary

Proude Springett, mother of that Gulielma who married William Penn. Mary found Quakerism alongside her second husband, Isaac Penington, but her first marriage had already been unconventional in some respects. Mary had lived in the family of the Springetts since her childhood, and she had longed for a 'god-fearing' person to marry. This unreasonable desire, she was told, would surely mean that she would never find 'a gentleman'! Yet Sir William was just such a man, and close to hand. They determined to be 'joined together in the Lord', without the use of a wedding ring or 'anyone's songs or prayers'. William had arranged that

> many of the usual dark, formal words were left out of the ceremony[51]

and this was before Quakers appeared on the scene.

In mid-seventeenth-century Quaker circles generally, the reality of some marriage arrangements fell short of the ideal as George Fox and Margaret Fell expressed it. Not a few people associated with Friends were ignoring the recommendations. Couples were marrying without parental permission. Meetings were not being kept adequately informed. Magistrates were being disregarded and Friends' practices in their Meetings were being taken advantage of. As Fox noted,

> the loose ones of the world would stand up and take one another in the Friends Meetings . . . to save their money which the priest would ask . . .

One of the objectives in establishing Women's Meetings, therefore, was the closer regulation of marriages. We shall see more of this later.

The Meetings for the women were in some respects reliant upon the good offices of the men and their records are often less full and less colourful than those from some Men's Meetings. Moreover for much of the period we are discussing there were no Women's Meetings in existence in many areas. For such reasons, then, many of the details concerning women in this and other chapters come not from the women's own records, but rather from other sources.

The marriage of Margaret Askew Fell and George Fox

Whatever was happening in some ill-disciplined Quaker settings, the procedures for the marriage of Margaret and George were a model of Quakerly propriety. They were married at Broadmead Meeting House in Bristol in October of 1669, after Margaret had been a widow for eleven years. George had consulted with her children in advance. He had taken the step, remarkable in the seventeenth century, of renouncing all claim to her property and income.[52] Friends had been informed of their intentions, as the marriage discipline required and in a public Meeting for worship they had made their simple declaration and had seen a certificate signed by witnesses. Despite all this the marriage itself caused resentment among some Quakers.

George Fox had presented it in terms of his restorationist theology,

> as a testimony that all might come up into the marriage as was in the beginning . . . out of the wilderness to the marriage of the Lamb . . .[53]

Certain Friends were unconvinced, for George and Margaret had their detractors. There were 'envious and prejudiced reasonings' Bristol Friends recorded. Fox's own *Journal* tells of sneers about marriage being for procreation. Margaret was 55 years old and he was 45.[54] While Fox was likening the union to that of Christ with the Church, Samuel Mucklow, in *The Spirit of the Hat* reckoned it was 'barrenness in the Truth'.

Fox had misjudged his fellow Quakers when a few weeks beforehand he had circulated an epistle referring to his marriage and rich in florid scriptural comparisons. This document was so much resented (Mucklow reported) that it was soon recalled and it was rare to obtain a sight of it.[55]

George and Margaret were married nevertheless, sealing an alliance which had existed since their first meeting. George had had reason to be grateful to her. Her late husband's influence had been of use to him on more than one occasion; her home had been the hub of a lot of Quaker activity. She was a woman after his own heart and there is no doubt that he thought of her with affection. Yet even by Quaker standards theirs was an unusual union. From a total of more than twenty years of marriage they were together little more than a handful. They were separated within a couple of weeks of their wedding and there has been speculation that this marriage was never consummated.[56]

Seventeenth-century critics portrayed Margaret as a nagging woman, easier to tolerate at a distance. She was 'a dreadful scold', wrote Francis Bugg in the margin of his copy of Fox's *Journal*, next to where Fox told of their separations. This was what Francis Bugg had been 'credibly informed' about her, and also that Fox seldom lived with her. Bugg had turned apostate from Quakerism and he debated with, and wrote prolifically about Friends (and they about him). This was done in a colourful and highly personalised way. Formerly clerk to a Monthly Meeting, Bugg had become disenchanted with aspects of the Friends' organisation and he was at odds with individuals. Above all he was a publicist of his discontent and so regarding him as no longer one of them, the Quakers finally disowned him in 1682. The ill-feeling which led him to dub the exceedingly forthright Anne Docwra a 'crazy old piece', 'venomous woman', 'liar' and 'she-goat' (*Jezebel Withstood and her Daughter Anne Docwra*, 1699, 57-62) extended to George Fox and

Margaret too, so his evidence is not altogether to be trusted. Still, it is hard to envisage that Margaret Fell would have been a docile spouse.

The letters between Fox and his wife tell of a caring and affectionate relationship, with each always seeking news of the other as they pursued their different ministries. She was a leader in the North, a debater, writer, an imprisoned Friend and hostess in a home ever open to travelling ministers. He was travelling, visiting Meetings, preaching, on mission overseas, a prisoner and so on. With the exception of George Fell, who never forgave his mother's alliance with the socially inferior and religiously eccentric Fox, Margaret's children willingly addressed George as father. When Margaret travelled to be with her ailing husband in the later years of their marriage, it was proof of her concern about him. But such action, she observed, also helped to dispel rumours about their relationship!

Margaret Fell was never a person to be disregarded by Friends. Even in old age her presence caused a stir, particularly when (as in the 1690s) there were religious and political frictions between the leaders. As Quakerism changed she found herself at odds with her Quarterly Meeting in Lancaster in debates about the extent to which one should 'render unto Caesar', about matters of dress and the growing 'holier-than-thou' outlook of Friends. In 1698 the Quaker John Tomkins was writing in a letter that

> Our ancient Friend M Fox is here about town. I wish she had stayed in Lancashire, or returned back soon after she came. I fear, by reason of her age, that she will be led by her son William [Meade] into something or other, which may not be of the best consequence to Truth, nor the quiet of the Church, nor her own honour.

(Braithwaite, SPQ, 208 n. 1). To the end of her life, then, Margaret Fell Fox was a force to be reckoned with. She could never have been a wife of conventional seventeenth-century expectation.

Unconventionality was the norm for Fox and Fell alike. George was not a man to settle easily into domesticity. He had lived the life of an itinerant since his twenties. In the predominantly female Fell household at Swarthmoor, too, family life had never been strictly patriarchal. Indeed this Fell family has been described as a recognisably modern one, with conjugal mutuality and a great deal of affection within it. At one time six unmarried daughters were occupied with the household economy and all of them married partners of their own choosing.[57] So Margaret and George functioned separately for much of their married lives, but the loyalty of the one to the interests of the other was unswerving. Margaret was her husband's best advocate. Indeed she was probably the catalyst for more of his innovations than has been recognised.

Managing marriages and the lives of women

George Fell, Margaret's son, married outside the Quaker fold. As we shall see, he was a source of great pain to his mother. In well ordered Quakerism, however, endogamous marriage was coming to be carefully controlled and the Women's Meetings played a part in the process. Females who found non-Quaker partners (sometimes due to pressure from their outraged and unconvinced families) would ultimately face 'disownment' and this was regularly a reality in the eighteenth and nineteenth centuries. The Meetings condemned utterly marriages before 'hireling' priests, who were spurious 'mediàtors' of the knowledge of God. Indeed Friends would demand a paper of self-condemnation from the miscreants concerned, which paper was sometimes taken to the hireling clergyman concerned. The growing desire for endogamous marriage, to preserve the purity of the group, was itself evidence of change in Quakerism.

In its early decades it had often been the case that only one partner was convinced. Well-versed in the scriptures as they were, Friends knew that Paul had addressed just such a problem in Corinth, where he had told the Christian partner not to abandon the other (*1 Corinthians* 7:12-16), since the latter might be sanctified by the mate. But as time went on, Paul's other dictum came into play. This was 'be not unequally yoked together with unbelievers' (*2 Corinthians* 6:14). By the end of the seventeenth century, then, Quakers saw themselves as being like the Israelites of old (*Deuteronomy* 7:3) – avoiding partnerships with aliens. This endogamous marriage rule was to cause great soul-searching and heartbreak in families. The Women's Meetings were very familiar with the problems.

Marriages once made suffered strain because of the separations and poverty which Quaker couples had thrust upon them. To alleviate the worst of the difficulties the Women's Meetings organised a great deal of support and relief work. Throughout the 1660s, 70s and 80s Quakers benefited from occasional grants of Pardon – Charles II's *Great Pardon* of 1672, which released some 500 Friends and other Nonconformists for example, and James II's *General Pardon* of 1686. In general, however, legislation weighed heavily upon them. The second *Conventicle Act* of 1670 brought many difficulties:

> In the year 70, which was a time of great suffering . . . we went to our Meetings in the peril of our lives, and our goods they took for a prey,

recorded Elizabeth Stirredge in *Strength in Weakness Manifest* (p. 57). This and the harsh *Test Act* of 1673 ensured that prisoners and needy families were plentiful. It is reckoned that by 1681 there were 1,300 Quakers in gaol so that there was plenty for Monthly Meetings and Meeting for Sufferings to do. There were also widows and orphans to be pensioned and settled and the women and men in their Meetings had to arrange for the placement and education of vulnerable girl children as well as the employment of maidservants. At the same time, of course, they were encouraging female modesty, plainness in dress and speech and they were promoting suitable marriages. A Meeting might even find itself responsible for 'all [Quakers] such as goes to sea', from the highest to the meanest passenger. Should such emigrants dishonour Truth overseas, then on hearing of it the Meeting would require a paper of self-condemnation. Without this, the culprit might face disownment by Friends.[58] Most of all, though, the women saw it as their task 'to help the helpless in all cases'.

These tasks were being fulfilled not just in the face of persecution, with informers at work and amongst those who said killing a Quaker was no worse than louse-killing, but also in the face of the opposition from dissenting Friends. Elizabeth Stirredge claimed that

> The least of our sorrow was loss of goods, beating and hurling to and fro, and dragging out of our meeting house . . . for in the time of suffering, a selfish separating spirit began to break forth amongst us; which added to our affliction more than all our persecutors could do.

(*Strength in Weakness Manifest*, p. 34). She was writing, of course, about the Wilkinson-Storyite schism.

We learn a great deal about these Women's Meetings from a circular letter which was sent out by the Lancashire Quarterly Meeting of women Friends, probably sometime between 1675-80. It may well have been drafted by Sarah Fell. The first half of the work is very reminiscent of the argument in Margaret Fell's *Women's Speaking Justified* of 1666 and of the Bible-based appeals of Fox, Farnworth and others. This surely indicates (i) that it was still necessary to justify women's public religious activity and (ii) that some women themselves needed reassurance about the rightness of what they were doing. The letter tells of discipline for whoever 'walks disorderly'. It suggests that knowledge of a paper of self-condemnation should be circulated as widely as news of the original misdeed. It advised the careful annual assembling and recording of women's refusals to pay tithes. For married women this had to be done quite apart from a husband's statements, for a woman might have an income of her own, from 'pigs and geese, hens and eggs, hemp and flax, wool and lamb'. Though most of the women were not regularly called upon for payment they determined, nevertheless, that if and when the time came they would refuse. These women were not to be regarded simply as appendages of their husbands.

The Lancashire women's epistle advised that receipts should be provided in a Meeting and disbursements recorded with care. Good bookkeeping was to be encouraged. Nevertheless the writers were well aware that in some Meetings it would be hard to find women who were sufficiently literate or experienced for such tasks. There was to be no discouragement. The women should not fight shy of what they were being required to do. It was through such work, the epistle told them, that

> women comes to be coheirs and fellow labourers in the Gospel . . .
> though we be looked upon as the weaker vessels, yet strong and
> powerful is God . . . we can stand our ground.[59]

Proposals for marriage were to be brought twice before the Women's Meetings and twice before the men. The lengthy investigative process involved proved too trying for some couples, who absconded to marry before the 'priests of Baal' instead! The waiting period at least brought the advantage of discouraging too hasty alliances. It allowed for conciliation processes, where families were in dispute or there were uncertainties about obligations to a third person. It brought greater certainty, too, that the man and woman were not within the prohibited degrees of consanguinity. In some cases, of course, ardour did cool all too quickly so that there were 'breach of promise' cases when a Quaker was not true to a public declaration. Thus, for example, in the fourth month of 1704, Chesterfield Monthly Meeting's Minute Book told of the 'disorderly' Joseph Clayton. He had failed to offer it

> satisfactory reasons . . . for his breaking of[f] with Sarah Pixley,
> after his laying before us his intentions of taking her to wife
> afterwards proceeding pretty far . . . to marriage, and at length
> breaking off upon a wordly disagreement, Friends having laboured
> much with him (and his parents, who are found the chief actors
> therein).

Quakers who had avoided the marriage discipline and endogamous marriage appeared before Meetings in quite large numbers. Some of them expressed regrets and offered papers of self-condemnation. Some refused. But within Quakerism, as well as outside it, there were those who continued to think it ludicrous that *women* should have a role in determining both sexes' fitness for marriage. The sole precedent for such autonomous activities amongst women, Francis Bugg observed, was 'the Pope's nunnery' (*The Painted Harlot,* London 1683, Preface).

Some trials of Quaker family life

Since Quaker principles often stood at odds with what 'the world' required, Quaker married life could be troubled. Quaker women, no less than others, knew the agony of child mortality:[60] Katherine Jackson was not untypical. She had married Henry in 1666, during a period of imprisonment in Warwick gaol when Quakers found themselves

thronged up in stinking rooms . . . no straw to lie upon . . .
insomuch that moderate people in the town . . . was stirred up in
tenderness to throw bread over a house top into the dungeon court.

Of their eleven children two died in infancy between the years 1671-73.
These had been born in Warwick, possibly even in prison. Five more did
not survive childhood, with two of them falling victim to smallpox.

The rigours of seventeenth-century travel were great too, and there
was imprisonment and falling into financial straits. 'Go on', wrote Isaac
Penington,

> try it out with the Spirit of the Lord; come forth with your laws and
> prisons and spoiling of our goods and banishment and death . . . and
> see if ye can carry it. For we come not forth against you in our own
> wills, or in any enmity against your persons or government . . . but
> with the Lamb-like nature which the Lord our God hath begotten in
> us . . . and if we cannot thus overcome you . . . and if the Lord our
> God please not to appear for us, we are content to be overcome by
> you.

In such a climate, publicly ministering Friends felt a special obligation
to choose their marriage partners carefully. Romance came a poor second
to other considerations and (like Anne Downer Whitehead in her early
relations with George) they 'had an eye to the Lord'.[61] William Caton,
Swarthmoor Hall Friend, told of his thoughts about marrying Anneken
Dirrix, a Dutch woman. The idea occurred to him while he was in
Germany and he had discussed the matter with 'some of the brethren'
before raising it with her. Then he put the plan to Friends in Holland and in
England before the final decision was made. Several things concerned him
and these he laid before Anneken: (i) his estate was less than hers (ii) she
would have to consider in advance that he expected liberty 'to go abroad in
the service of the Lord', so that when the time came 'it might not seem
strange to her' and (iii) she was to ask herself how she would react to
'trouble' and the attention of magistrates (*Life of William Caton,* London
1689). After a few weeks Anneken replied, though still they 'waited long
in the affair' before publishing an intention of marriage in the Meetings at
Swarthmoor and Amsterdam. Finally it took place in the eighth month of
1662 and it was the first of its disciplined Quaker sort in Holland.

Some women Friends felt free to propose marriage to the men of their
choice, if they believed that God was leading them that way. For their
part, the men felt free to insist that they had experienced no such leading!
Not everyone, it should be said, would have been happy with such
progressive behaviour. In 1666 Francis Howgill wrote a moving letter of
advice to his daughter Abigail. Like quite a lot of Friends' writings it is, for
its age, remarkably gender-inclusive in its language. 'If thou desire to
marry', he advised her,

do not thou seek a husband, but let a husband seek thee . . . above all things choose one (if thou dost marry) that loves and fears the Lord, whose conversation thou knowest, and manner, and course of life well before thou give consent . . .

It happened not infrequently that an unsettled widow caught the eye of an unattached male Friend. His thinking had perhaps strayed to the need to ensure that there was someone to care for him, in the event of imprisonment. The twice-married William Penn, who had quite a lot to say about the wedded state, unromantically toured Meetings in a (successful) search for a second wife, after the death of Gulielma.[62] William was university-educated and patrician but he had learned a great deal from his first marriage to Isaac Penington's step-daughter. Gulielma Springett Penn had been a woman who was erudite, though educated only 'appropriately' for her sex and class. Moreover she was devout and of herself she declared 'I never did to my knowledge a wicked thing in my life'. Gulielma had shared William's joys and trials, just as he had advocated to spouses when he wrote of marriage. She had proved to be an ideal partner.

A prospective bridegroom ought to prefer person before money, virtue before beauty and the mind before the body, William had written in the year which was the one of Gulielma's death. It was not that Gulielma had not had her 'outward' attractions – she had been wooed by others before William Penn – but he had married her (so he wrote to her) more for 'thy inward than thy outward excellencies'. The result had been 'a match of Providence's making'. In Penn's view a 'wife, a friend, a companion, a second self' would not be found by setting one's mind on physical beauty or monetary advantage. For his readers he added, 'use her not as a servant'.[63]

William and Gulielma Penn knew long periods of separation. Gulielma's frail health, exacerbated by pregnancy, had made it impossible for her to join William in the Pennsylvania experiment. Quakers expected such separations and many letters extant between such couples indicate the tenderness of their relationship. William wrote to reassure Gulielma that neither land, sea nor death could extinguish his love for her, and when she did die ('she quietly expired in her husband's arms' wrote the obituarist) his letters to Friends indicate how very distraught he was.[64]

The Quakers' marriage declarations were simple. There was generally no promise to obey on the woman's part (though Edward Milligan reminds me that a few documents *do* preserve reference to it) and each declared in a Meeting their love and fidelity to 'this my Friend John Smith/Mary Jones', until death.[65] When a publicly active Quaker did so, a George Fox, a Margaret Fell, a William Penn or an Anne Downer Whitehead, it would almost certainly be the case that soon the partners

Gulielma Maria Penn
There is a resemblance between this portrait and the one of 'The Fair Quaker', Hannah Middleton Gurney, in that the dresses are identical, but the faces are different. (See Quaker Pictures *by Wilfred Whitten, published 1892).*

would find themselves separated. It was unlikely that the married couple would share precisely the same kinds of ministry and in any case travelling in a married partnership was discouraged. Friends of mature years, like Ann Camm and her husband, sometimes did so, however. For a time some Quakers advocated total celibacy as a norm for Friends but others thought such teaching harmful to the Quaker cause.[66] For practical reasons it was thought preferable that a married couple, both of which were called to public ministry, should be unhampered by children. Though there are cases of women travelling as ministers with a suckling child at the breast it was more often the case that active women ministers were widows and unmarried women. Even among young married couples, however, not everyone concurred with the advice (which *women* rather than men were required to heed, of course) about not combining itinerant ministry with parenthood.

The Kendal Quakers Thomas Holme(s) and Elizabeth Leavens were enthusiastic and somewhat excitable preachers of the Gospel. They had been among the pioneering *First Publishers of Truth* and with the young Elizabeth Fletcher, Elizabeth Leavens had gone to challenge the city and University of Oxford. A battering and torture with pump water met them there.[67] She and Thomas Holme had met while they were preaching in the Welsh border areas of Cheshire and South Lancashire. Thomas was given to fervent outbursts of song, to going 'naked for a sign' and to addressing George Fox and Margaret Fell in extravagant religious language. They married in the autumn of 1654 and after separation Thomas went to join his wife in South Wales.

It was early in the year 1656. Elizabeth Leavens Holme and Alice Burkitt had been ministering with some success in Wales and Thomas brought his considerable powers to the ministry there. Soon, however, Elizabeth became pregnant, and the couple experienced the great ire of Margaret Fell, to whom it seemed that this pregnancy spelt the end of an active ministry. Nor did it seem right to burden newly-convinced Welsh Quakers with the upkeep of an infant. The couple were not people of means. Thomas had been a weaver and before their marriage each of them had been indebted to *The Kendal Fund* for travelling ministers, administered by Margaret Fell and her agents. Thomas had been given shoes and 'britches' to the value of 10s and 6d and Elizabeth had been clothed at the cost of more than a pound. Margaret made her annoyance clear in her letters and in Fox's view Elizabeth should have then returned to her family in the North. Thomas replied to Margaret's letters with respect, pointing to his wife's continued ministry; but Margaret was not to be appeased. He insisted that even before hearing from the matriarch, for even in this first decade of Quakerism Margaret Fell was a figure to be reckoned with, he and his wife had determined an end to 'going together'.

He had said so in a letter of April 30th 1656. Unappeased, however, Margaret Fell continued to be prolific in her advice until at last Thomas observed

Thou might leave her alone. She suffereth all and replies not.

In the event Elizabeth paid no heed to Fox's advice. It was, in any case, too late to return North. She chose the other road open to a ministering female Friend who had children, a road which Fox acknowledged as one which should be open to women. She put the infant in the care of a Cardiff Quaker and continued her work. She and Thomas had two further children.[68]

There were other difficulties for Quaker families. Family loyalties were strained when some were convinced and others not. Well-meaning or devious relatives sometimes paid tithes on behalf of Quakers. It happened occasionally that a wife discovered that an unconverted husband had struck bargains over tithe payment. On his death, of course, she would be confronted with the dilemma of such bargains.[69] Samuel Bownas (1676-1753) ministered as a Friend from the end of the seventeenth century, and according to the *Account of the Travels etc . . . of S. B.* his wife was one such deceived Friend, tricked by her cousin over tithes. Then there were those unconvinced relatives who stole the bodies of deceased Quakers, sometimes even from other family members. This was usually to ensure burial in consecrated ground. The Welsh Quaker Rachel Bowen, for example, had died on the 11th of seventh month 1694 and her body was stolen from Friends for interment 'in Lland[e]ilo Steeple House'. Yet even such traumas were minor when compared to Margaret Fell's experience with her only son George. That was in a class of its own.

Since George Fell was born c. 1638 he must have been in his early teens when Quakers first started to frequent Swarthmoor Hall. In his *Journal* (p. 127) Fox mentions him as a curious lad, who was eager to see what the mob was doing to Fox, on which occasion the young George (Fell) was thrown into a ditch and was threatened with loss of his teeth.[70] The experience may have helped to decide him against the new faith! William Caton, a companion of George in his youth, had lived in the Fell household and had shared a tutor there.[71] George, he recorded, had been 'tender and hopeful' when young, but he fell prey to a love of worldly pleasures. These were open to him in London when he went to study law at Gray's Inn at the age of sixteen. Debt followed. Margaret and his sisters were very concerned about him and there is a ring of desperation in the letter she wrote when he had been in the city two years:

My dear one, I cannot forget thee; my cries to my heavenly Father is for thee and that thou may be kept and that the measure of Him in thee may be preserved.[72]

When his father Thomas Fell died in 1658 he bequeathed George, his only son, his law books and seemingly nothing else. The bulk of the estate was for the daughters. Probably it was George's extravagant lifestyle which had determined that decision. It must have left the young man with a sense of grievance.

In the year of the Restoration George married the non-Friend Hannah Potter. It was a trying year for him, for he was afraid of repercussions from having raised a militia force 'for the service of the Parliament' the year before. At that time he and Antony Pearson (Justice of the Peace and a persecutor of Quakers before he too was convinced) had responded against a revolt being fermented by Sir George Booth in the Royalist cause.[73] Despite his understandable fears, Charles II gave George a warrant of pardon.

The son's decision to marry outside of the Quaker fold was a clear sign of the severance he intended from the Fell family's new-found values. His mother's later marriage to the socially unacceptable Fox was the final seal upon his existing hatred of their commitment. Then his wife's kin abetted him in that hatred. There were attempts to secure the Swarthmoor and Marsh Grange estates in George's hands and one writer has dubbed this prodigal 'emotional, prejudiced, unscrupulous and very difficult to deal with'.[74]

In 1664 Margaret Fell was put on trial for harbouring conventicles at Swarthmoor Hall. She faced the dreaded sentence of *Praemunire*[75] and at the same time 'son' George began proceedings to claim the estate. A kind reader of events (as Margaret's biographer Isabel Ross notes) might think he was attempting to prevent its confiscation, but it was not so. He was collaborating with the Kirkby brothers, Richard and William. Richard Kirkby figures large in Fox's *Journal* as an enemy and in his opinion George Fox was 'not fit to be discoursed with by man'.[76] Kirkby was no friend of Margaret Fell either. His signature is on the petition for the Hall and estate which was produced during Margaret's Lancaster imprisonment. Moreover he took pains to increase her suffering there.[77] Son George's efforts had thus far failed when Margaret was released in 1668, by order of the King and Council. But still he hoped to lay hands on Swarthmoor and the Marsh Grange Estate, Margaret's childhood home, where he now lived with his family. It must have seemed to him that the law's bias towards males would favour the case of an only son. Mary Penington had known relatives conspiring, with success, to gain estates, because they were outraged when Quakers refused to swear oaths (*Experiences*, p. 53). Family conspiracies against Friends were not rare but Friends were incredulous when George Fell went so far as to conspire with his wife's father to have his mother re-imprisoned under *Praemunire*.

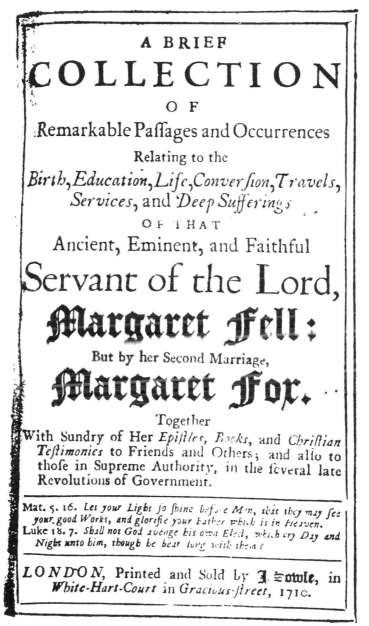

A BRIEF
COLLECTION

OF

Remarkable Paſſages and Occurrences

Relating to the

Birth, Education, Life, Converſion, Travels, Services, and *Deep Sufferings*

OF THAT

Ancient, Eminent, and Faithful

Servant of the Lord,

𝕸𝖆𝖗𝖌𝖆𝖗𝖊𝖙 𝕱𝖊𝖑𝖑:

But by her Second Marriage,

𝕸𝖆𝖗𝖌𝖆𝖗𝖊𝖙 𝕱𝖔𝖝.

Together

With Sundry of Her *Epiſtles, Books,* and *Chriſtian Teſtimonies* to Friends and Others; and alſo to thoſe in Supreme Authority, in the ſeveral late Revolutions of Government.

Mat. 5. 16. *Let your Light ſo ſhine before Men, that they may ſee your good Works, and glorifie your Father which is in Heaven.*
Luke 18. 7. *Shall not God avenge his own Elect, which cry Day and Night unto him, though he bear long with them?*

LONDON, Printed and Sold by J. Sowle, in *White-Hart-Court* in *Gracious-ſtreet*, 1710.

After her death, Margaret Fell's chief writings were included in this 1710 book, which is recommended for further study.

In April 1670, now George Fox's wife, Margaret began another year of imprisonment in Lancaster Castle. Her stolid refusal to abandon Quaker *Testimonies*, combined with the introduction of the second *Conventicle Act* ensured that what might have been a short ordeal became a longer one. Quakers told Hannah Fell, George's wife, that his behaviour was surely 'abominable amongst heathens'. Non-Quakers, too, remarked that it was 'very unnatural' to seek to have one's own mother imprisoned.[78] Elizabeth Hooton, now an old woman, with others approached the King to secure Margaret's release. Margaret had 'suffered more than many have expected'. It was during this second imprisonment that George Fell died.

Hannah Fell however continued the task of destroying her late husband's mother. Elizabeth Hooton remonstrated with her sharply in a letter that nothing so wicked had been known in England than that a woman should 'ruinate' her mother-in-law.[79] But Hannah still remained actively hostile, even after Friends had managed to secure Margaret's release and by good management had placed her portion of the two estates firmly in the Fell daughters' control. After these events members of the Fell family continued to visit Hannah from time to time, still trying to maintain a vestige of civilised family behaviour.

The children of Quakers

Quaker writers varied in their response to the prevailing Christian belief that infants were tainted with original sin. The apologist Robert Barclay summed up one position in the light of Paul's teaching:

> Sin is imputed to none where there is no Law. But to infants there is no Law; therefore sin is not imputed to them.[80]

In his view, the doctrine of original sin was 'unscriptural barbarism' and infant baptism was both unscriptural and unnecessary. Quakers were dismissive of 'water baptism' in general, taken as a conventional rite of passage. They were not dismissive of that true Christian baptism, as they saw it, which was indicative of transformation and incorporation into the Body of Christ.

In his teaching about marriage George Fox had been known to argue that the sinlessness of children resulted from the innocence of parents who were being perfected. Nevertheless the capacity for good and evil was inherent in each person and Quaker parentage was certainly no guarantee of enlightenment. Each individual had to appropriate Truth for herself. Quaker writings extolled the state of infancy. Friends held that it was that very state of innocence which ought to characterise the believer. Women Friends who were 'mothers in Israel', and Margaret Fell in particular, were portrayed as nurturers and so too were Quaker *men* (notably George Fox, of course) but it was *the Word* itself which provided the nourishment. The convinced grew by this: Quaker children were to be nourished with it.

Friends' insistence that children were 'innocent and lamb-like'[81] rather than vessels of sin resulted, then, in Quaker parental and educational practices which were less unpleasant than many in the seventeenth century.

A child's upbringing and education were carefully religious. Parents, teachers, employers, in fact all those Quakers in contact with the young, were exhorted to be good examples at all times. Eventually, it was hoped, the child would also become convinced of the truth of the Christian religion and of the Quaker way of expressing it.[82] So a Quaker childhood was to be a lovingly disciplined one. Robert Barclay advocated that there should not be songs, dancing, plays etc., but 'innocent divertisements' were to be encouraged for a child. These included visiting friends, reading, gardening and 'geometrical and mathematical experiments'. Quaker school books were earnest rather than cheering. Fox's primer and the catechism, created with Ellis Hookes, saw a number of reprintings. The *A for Anathema* standpoint of such works, and the ritual

> [Sarah] was a good woman, Jezebel was a bad woman, who killed the just and turned against the Lord's prophets with her attired head and painted face

would surely have raised few smiles in the classroom. But non-Quaker school material was scarcely more inspiring.

Parents were advised to treat their children with tenderness. Even the very young might prove to have a gift of ministry, for as Stephen Crisp recorded in his *Testimony* to the life of the martyred James Parnall,

> Babes have been his messengers and children have been his ministers,

Parnall, described by Fox as 'a little boy', became a minister at fifteen (though this was not really childhood in seventeenth-century terms). He was dead from ill-use and dreadful prison conditions before he was twenty. Even younger was Mary Fell, who was alleged to have told the local clergyman, priest Lampitt

> the plagues of God shall fall upon thee and the seven vials shall be poured upon thee . . . how can thou escape the damnation of hell . . .

Even by the standards of the assertive Swarthmoor household, such ministry was remarkable. Mary was just eight! Childish insights, then, were not to be quenched.

But Friends' children were certainly not compliant performers, nor were they paragons. Meetings were sometimes of many hours duration and children could be restless and disruptive. In some places the elderly Friends who were appointed as overseers of the boys up in the gallery simply failed to stem the mutterings, shufflings and worse. There were complaints about older youths in the vicinity of Meeting Houses, like this one in Bristol:

> Great complaints being made to this Meeting of the disorders of the youth of our Friends at the time when the Meeting is gathered; in the Friars and places adjacent to the disturbance of the neighbourhood, also that some young men do go out of the Meeting to walk abroad.[83]

Meetings were punctuated by the lusty cries of infants, though one account tells that the zeal and piety of the mothers more than made up for any disturbance. In many families, however, it seems to have been the practice not to take offspring to Meetings until they were well past infancy. They were allowed diversion at home instead.

In certain homes there were more indulgences than 'weighty' Friends approved of. Ellen Coward, for example, who was active in the work of the Women's Meetings in Lancashire, was referred to disapprovingly in the autobiography of William Stout as one who

> took her ease, and took no notice of trade or anything, but indulging her children.

There was certainly no shortage of advice to such a parent. In the closing decades of the seventeenth century there was a plethora of epistles and tracts exhorting parents to nurture their children in the faith and to insist on plain dress and speech as a statement against 'the world'.

> . . . be careful and take heed that you do not stain the testimony of Truth that you have received, by wearing of needless things and following the world's fashions in your clothing and attire, but remember how I have bred you up

Joan Vokins, a Berkshire Friend, wrote earnestly to her children from Dublin in 1686.[84] The fact is, of course, that such copious advice would not have been given had it not also been the case that such *Testimonies* were frequently ignored or diluted by the young.

> . . . the world saith, the Quakers are now like us, they want only lace and ribbons.

read *A Tender and Christian Testimony to the Young People, from the Womens Meeting at the Bull and Mouth,* just the year before Joan Vokins wrote the letter quoted above to her children.

It was hard for a new generation of Quakers to understand the significance of 'the little things' which seemed to loom so large in Quaker life. The very first generation and those who were now fathers and mothers had grown in partnership with the hardships and the *Testimonies*. But in the closing decades of the century those who were now parents themselves still had to be reminded of many things for the sake of the next generation. Thus Elizabeth Stirredge in the autobiography called *Strength in Weakness Manifest* (which she had written for her family) told them:

> Some of these things you know; your eyes have seen this when you were young and tender . . . yet the Lord kept you from the fear of men . . . The way you know; you have been trained in it; and the concern of my spirit is that you may keep in it and be concerned for your children . . . in the beginning we went in a great exercise for that very word thee and thou to one person . . . I could go no further, until I had yielded obedience unto the little things.

Evidently she feared that the importance of such obedience was not being instilled in the next generation.

The Friend from Cork in Ireland, Joseph Pike, had to admit in his *Life* (p. 93) that while some of the Quaker youth he met were insufficiently plain, yet they were

> honest-minded young people who are pretty orderly in their conversation.

Despite this 'orderliness' these young Friends of the last decades of the century often proved quite determined against Testimonies for which they saw no need. Thus, Pike recorded, admonitions and personal approaches had no effect ('though they are not stiff and stubborn as many others are') but rather the young people remained 'glued to the inclination of finery'.

Plainness was a particular trial for the young. It had distinguished Friends from the beginning. When still unconvinced, the young Elizabeth Stirredge had at about twenty years old fallen prey to 'fine clothes' and she remained unsatisfied by them. Still she had wondered in what way she should 'demean' herself to go to listen to John Audland and John Camm, 'hearing of their plainness'. The Friend Barbara Lupton Jackson was not untypical of the next generation. She had been a young Quaker in the closing decades of the seventeenth century and was the child of a Yorkshire Quaker family of means and its heiress apparent. Barbara had taken against plainness in her teens. The girl

> prevailed to get some nippings in her head, cloths and plaits at the ears thereof, tho not to that degree that many now professing truth wears

was one observation made in 1717, the year of her death. There were many young Friends like her but her change of heart also has the ring of Friends' cautionary tales of this time. It was an attack of smallpox at the age of 18, her contemporaries claimed, which had stirred her to return to Quaker plainness.

As time went on this Quaker plainness became not only firmly entrenched but also more rigid. To some of the young the restrictions must have seemed oppressive. To the ageing Margaret Fell, product of the heady first decades of Spirit-governed freedom in Quakerism, such concerns (for uniformity in colour, for example) spoke of a Gospel which was both 'silly' and 'poor'. The Fell household had certainly never been determined in its plainness. Sarah's *Household Account Book* not only spills the beans on such matters but tells us of piety, philanthropy and human warmth which gives the lie to any twentieth century tendency to see these people as dour and charmless.

We learn from this document that little Margery Lower was bought 'a little rattle'. Margaret Lower got to wear specially dyed coloured petticoats, like her Quaker aunts – who also liked blue-green stockings (*Account Book* pp. 17, 65, 321). Aunt Sarah paid 2*d* for gingerbread on the 18th of October 1677 (p. 423), which she gave to the seven year old Charles Fell, son of the late prodigal George, and to William Yeamans, Isabel's son, who was about the same age.[85] There were 'treacle and comfitts', sugar candy, 'liquerice and anniseeds', this last for little Margery again (25, 33, 253) – these things for the ailments of childhood. Margaret Fell's cattle got some of the same from time to time (339, 375). There was closeness and affection in this less-than-plain Swarthmoor household, and William Caton, son George's companion in their early teens, told of the great friendship he had experienced as part of it. It is hard to imagine that dinner with the Fells (unlike dinner with the Peningtons) 'lacked mirth'.

In Quaker thinking religion was one and the same, be it for child or adult. Inevitably the family's religion bore heavily on the children and it is not surprising that in later life some became disaffected or hostile. Yet not a few who have left records also tell of the great love and security they felt in their families, even in times of persecution and hardship. There *was* sometimes very considerable hardship. Other children abused the Quaker young, especially for their plain dress. Youngsters found themselves unceremoniously battered by representatives of the authorities and hauled out of Meetings. They saw their parents taken away and without adult support it fell on them to take on the tasks of housekeeping, farm management, prison visiting and the care of the sick.

During the confusion following the Fifth Monarchist uprising in January 1661 Quaker childen were wandering uncared for on the streets. Mothers took infants into prison with them and nursed them there, as we know from records relating to the Isle of Man, Gloucestershire and elsewhere.[86] Older children, too, found themselves in direct contact with the insanitary conditions and epidemics in prisons. Mary Samm, the twelve year old granddaughter of William Dewsbury, died beside him in Warwick gaol, having fallen ill while she was caring for him in 1680. At that time William was in the relatively comfortable setting of the

Sergeant's Ward – he had known worse conditions, but there Mary died. The *Testimony* to her credits the dying lass with many grave and pious sentiments, as such works tend to do. Records relate that two years later, in 1682, fifteen children from Bristol were incarcerated in the Bridewell. They were between ten and twelve years of age and four of them were girls – Tabitha Jones, Rachel Mears, Martha Watkins and Martha James. In the same period there were eight children in 'The Gallery' in the Bridewell, the youngest eight, the oldest fifteen, kept with eleven women, one of whom was seventy-eight years old.[87]

Many of these children must have nursed painful memories from childhood. Thomas Chalkley never forgot his daily walk of two miles to the house of the schoolmaster Friend Richard Scoryer, a journey he made first when he was eight.

> Many and various were the exercises I went through, my beatings and stonings along the streets, being distinguished to the people by the badge of plainness which my parents put upon me . . . divers telling me, it was no more sin to kill me than it was to kill a dog.[88]

In other families there was poverty and hunger.

In the year 1663–4 Quakers were blamed, erroneously, for involvement with the so-called Kaber-Rigg plot.[89] George Fox himself was prosecuted and imprisoned at Colonel Kirkby's instigation. Given the laws which prohibited gatherings and the requirement to swear an Oath of Allegiance[90] many Friends suffered for the stand they took. In Lancaster some women Friends went to the Justices to demand the release of their husbands. Otherwise, they declared, they would bring along their children for the Justices to maintain! On that occasion a few men were released. Other women Friends were less fortunate. The poverty-stricken wife of William Williams, burdened with many children, applied for relief to Justice Fisher of Wisbech. She received no sympathy but rather he

> more like a cannibal than a Christian, replied if she wanted food she might take her children, fry them for steaks, and eat them.[91]

Fortunately most of the Quaker children seem to have had lovingly supportive parents. Cases of domestic violence are rare in the Meeting records themselves, though perhaps then, as now, such violence was treated as a family secret. It is certainly the case that obituarists and women's own autobiographies sometimes tell how husbands had been harsh, particularly when a woman was first convinced and there were extreme cases too. A Newbury Monthly Meeting Minute for the third month of 1677 does tell of one Humphrey Carter, who

> caused a scandalous report again by striking his wife and causing her to miscarry.

And occasionally we meet a case of child neglect. The inadequate father James Turner appears in the Meeting Book of Chesterfield Monthly Meeting, referred to at a business session which was held at Tupton in the eighth month of 1694. Turner was called

> to the next Monthly meeting that so Friends may have a fuller understanding of his life and conversation and how it is with him, and why he does not take care of his child being he is able as far as we understand to work for his living.

Meanwhile the Monthly Meeting provided money for 'some necessary clothes'. On the 21st of the second month 1696, however, we read again that all was not well. There was further provision and Sarah Storrs was appointed

> to look after them and to bring account to the next Monthly Meeting of the charges.

A parent was more likely to be censured for insufficient strictness than for being severe. Children were the Lord's heritage, as *Psalm 127* proclaimed, and parental authority was God-given. So parental over-indulgence was discouraged. John Banks (who wrote more than once about the welfare of Quaker children and family life) deplored the parent who did nothing when faced with a determined 'I will not', though violence towards children was no answer. The Friends' writings show that good parental example was thought preferable to beating, for as John Banks observed,

> Wrath, anger and passion beget their own likeness in children, and rather make them more stubborn.[92]

It was not that the rod was taboo for Quaker parents or teachers, but rather that less negative approaches were preferable. Thus the educationist John Bellers noted in his *College of Industry* proposals that

> A rebellious temper must be subdued by correction, but such will not make ingenious scholars; stripes weakening that presence of mind which is needful to a ready learning . . . grief hurting the memory . . . Raise a child's love to what he should learn, by rewards and emulation.[93]

Nevertheless Quakers knew that the use of the rod had been sanctioned by the scriptures.[94]

As Quaker children approached adulthood and marriageable age the question of endogamous marriage had to be addressed. There were of course 'arrangements' between Quaker families but the marriage discipline insisted on the full consent of both partners. The system was imperfect, for as Quakerism grew to set more store by respectability and prosperity there were even occasional financial wrangles. Even some Friends' marriages, it was observed, were 'like Smithfield bargains'.[95]

Young Quakers often became acquainted through Meetings. It is not surprising, then, that knots of young Quaker men sometimes toured Meetings for reasons not entirely spiritual. Social contacts beyond Quakerism were not curtailed rigidly. Had that been the case, there would have been fewer disciplinary hearings relating to marriages with non-Friends before priests. Quakers lived and worked *in* the world, even if they felt themselves not entirely of it, and it was not every young Quaker who operated under the watchful eye of convinced parents. So Quakers met and made friends with non-Quakers, with the depth of such friendships depending on an individual's loyalty to the group and the efficiency of the local group's encouragement of intramural relationships. A Quaker couple's decision to marry, they were told, should be determined by spiritual considerations and not worldly ones. It is clear that the advice was sometimes taken very much to heart. Some courtships were very tentative and plagued by soul-searchings.[96] Once the decision for marriage was made, however, the next steps were appearances before the Meetings of the man and the woman, in order to obtain 'clearness'. While some prospective spouses probably feared the spiteful or over-rigorous interjection which would ruin their wedding plans, for others the appearances must have been a not-unpleasant formality in an interim period of preparation for a Quaker family life of their own.

For the parents of the young Friends concerned, some of which would have been married before their own convincement or before the advent of the marriage discipline, such alliances and the discipline itself must have seemed proof of a continuity for which, at times, they had never dared to hope. These parents were the women and men who had been rebellious offspring in the 1650s, who had refused to honour their own parents in conventional ways, who had left their homes and sometimes made public spectacles of themselves. By the 1680s they were expecting obedience and respect from their own children and grandchildren. They looked for a new conformity now – to the mores of Quakerism and where *Quaker* belief and practice were concerned there was little talk of 'freedom of conscience'. It is a pattern familiar to students of religion and of sectarianism. As Keith Thomas observed in his study of women and the civil war sects, it was 'completely in accordance with their stated principles' that once institutionalisation set in, even the most radical sects became conservative as regards the organisation and discipline of the family and 'Quakers were notoriously patriarchal'.

Some family members dissented. But despite the many peculiarities of their Quaker childhoods, not a few of the second and third generation Friends paid glowing tributes to such parents. While all around there had been hostility and uncertainty (albeit partly self-imposed, by virtue of embracing Quakerism), *inside* the family circle there had been an atmosphere of love, hospitality and prayer – of private prayer, family prayer and the prayer encountered in the gathered Meeting. The clear, if to us inflexible, framework of Quaker belief and practice was in its way a bastion of certainty in a troubled world.

Both the present chapter and the preceding ones have shown that life for a seventeenth-century Quaker was not one of ease. Quaker children

> grew up in an environment likely to develop in their characters sturdiness bordering on stubbornness, if they could survive the grim struggle.[97]

Their parents faced the consequences of their choice of religion as well as all the usual hardships of seventeenth-century family life. All things considered, therefore, the carefully formalised Quaker concern about their parenting seems understandable and it would surely have been construed as supportive by many families. There is evidence, however, that some who thought of themselves as Friends also thought Quakerly visitation was officious and interfering.

Joseph Pike, again, the Irish linen-draper and serge merchant, was a great advocate of 'family visits' and he was not tolerant of parents who thought that a lovingly unoppressive atmosphere ('bear with them and draw them by love') was more conducive to their children's convincement. There were many 'godly elders', he observed, who agreed with his own more rigorous point of view. It is clear from the account in his *Life* that some families did not welcome the visitations of the likes of Joseph Pike and the 'godly elders'!:

> I have known some Friends, who have gone under a religious concern to such parents, to give them advice, who instead of taking it well have been so blind and stupid as to have returned undue reflections . . .[98]

For whatever reason, the Quaker publications about children became more and more prolific after 1680, so as to become 'a corporate preoccupation' by the middle of the eighteenth century.[99]

At this point it may be helpful to recall what has been shown thus far. I have tried to illustrate how and why, through their Meetings for worship and business, Friends had evolved an impressive network of ministry, philanthropy and mutual support. They did this in just a few decades, in the face of opposition and it was very demanding of the time and commitment of members. These early Friends believed themselves to be both a Gospel-type 'old-believer' movement and a group in which the activity of the Spirit was much in evidence. Hence individual Quakers, be they called upon to be public ministers or employers, conciliators, prison overseers, administrators, teachers (though these were hard to come by, as we shall see), providers for the welfare of the poor or whatever, believed

The Quaker Meeting (Engraving by Egbert van Heemskirk).

themselves to be acting in response to a living, motivating divine presence and imperative. Their 'leadings' were tested against the experience of the group and as the century passed, against its code of discipline. Some of the early Friends did not stay the course of persecution. Some fell foul of the discipline which accompanied developing organisation while others were resentful of what seemed its oppressive all-pervasiveness. Many had cause to be grateful to Friends for financial, moral and prayerful support and for a familial solidarity which replaced the one they had left behind on becoming Quakers, against the judgement of their own relatives. But there were others still – in the seventeenth century fewer than is usually assumed – who suffered the fate of being disowned by the group. Disownment will be considered next.

From discipline to disownment

There were many people whose associations with Quakerism were tenuous but fairly public nevertheless. Friends' Meetings were open to all, even the most 'profane' so there was the danger that an occasional attender of Quaker gatherings would do something outrageous, or merely unQuakerly, and so bring Friends into disrepute. On the fringes of Quakerism were to be found some who had been attracted by aspects of its radical message. There were those who were, in a limited way at least, bound to Meetings because they had become pensioners of them and those whose relatives were more surely aligned to Quakerism than they were themselves. Such 'fringe' Friends were often among those who were reprimanded in the Women's Meetings.

Sexual morality was of particular concern and the seventeenth-century 'double standard' is sometimes observable in Friends' discipline. Women might find themselves more roundly censured than their partners.[100] Quakers were clear about pre-marital co-habitation. The London *Six Weeks Meeting* had condemned it in 1672. Yet they did not necessarily advocate the marriage of those concerned as a remedy. Occasionally, indeed, couples were refused 'clearness' precisely because they had had 'too intimate' a relationship beforehand. However, men who had fathered children were not allowed simply to abrogate their responsibilities without Friends trying to gain redress for the woman and her child. The language of Minutes about such matters is sometimes remarkably opaque, with only a line or two on a topic over several months of Meetings. The following extracts from Chesterfield Monthly Meeting records is typical.

For the 17th of the first month 1701/2 and the 23rd of the second month 1702 there were records concerning

> Isaac Kirk . . . and the miscarriage betwixt himself and Eliz. Haslem.

Elizabeth had been an active member of her Monthly Meeting and Isaac, it would seem, was not discharging his new responsibilities as a father to the satisfaction of the Meeting. He was called on

> [to] give further security for future maintenance of the child, such as shall be satisfactory to the Parish and Friends.

As for the 'wicked actions' between them, the Meeting observed that Quaker Truth had been dishonoured. Still it had 'tenderness' for Elizabeth, who was showing signs of 'godly sorrow' and she was still in its midst. The unregenerate Isaac Kirk, however, was in 'a stubborn unreconciled state'.

'Clearness' for marriage might be denied because of other sexual misdemeanours too. The twentieth-century reader, blessed with new insights on dysfunctional families and the abuse of children, may feel ill at ease with some decisions, but in the tenth month of 1677, for example, Upperside Monthly Meeting (Bucks) refused 'clearness' to a woman because in the past she had 'behaved herself immodestly with her father'.[101]

Meetings went to considerable length to deal fairly with miscreants. They appointed aribitrators and conciliators where there were disagreements.[102] Those accused were invited to speak for themselves and repentance (if the 'crime' were established) and reconciliation were desired, rather than condemnation and estrangement. Still if the reputation of the group were at risk, Friends' Meetings did not shirk disownment as a last resort. Months and even years passed in some cases, before that final step was taken and even in disownment there were not the theological implications of excommunication.[103] Offenders were not 'cast out' or 'delivered to Satan'. Indeed Fox had allegedly once said that

> We . . . cast out none, but they cast themselves out. For we do not receive them in, therefore we cannot cast them out.[104]

Despite the Quakers' best efforts there were disownments. These tended to be for failures of orthopraxis (disorderly behaviour) rather than for failures in orthodoxy (unacceptable beliefs), though the two were not obviously separable in Friends' thinking. Sometimes it was persistently uncharitable behaviour that was the cause, for Quaker women had all the human failings. A few of them were involved in long-running disputes with other members of a Meeting and there were occasionally serious cases of injustice and unreasonable behaviour which called for rebuke from a Monthly Meeting. Two examples in the Norwich region are cited below, years apart in date, for it is not generally the case that much of a Meeting's time was taken up with internecine disputes.

1684 was a time of persecution again. Monthly Meetings were sometimes held in prisons as the most convenient settings and in Norwich

113

two women Friends, Mary Defrance and Anne Weymer, were seriously at odds. The matter was raised in an already burdened Monthly Meeting, since the women's behaviour was creating difficulties for it. That Meeting, therefore, appointed visitors to speak with them, to try to resolve the matter. This was the normal procedure. Visitors might be men or women, depending on the nature and seriousness of the difficulty, the availability of suitable Friends as visitors and the existence or otherwise of a Meeting for women in the region. More serious still in the Norwich area, but in the time of toleration (1698), the widow Elizabeth Sheltram and Christian Neppa were arguing violently over a house. Evidently Neppa was determined that the widow had to vacate it and when the matter had been discussed with her, the Friends had failed to get Neppa to agree on a reasonable passage of time in which widow Sheltram should leave. Instead she had taken over the house when Sheltram was out. She had had the locks changed and had kept the evicted woman's belongings. Month by month, according to the Minutes, Neppa was 'very high' and the matter remained unresolved. Eventually, therefore, the Meeting felt obliged to reject her.[105]

Where Women's Meetings were not established, it was still the case that women Friends would be called upon by the men to act as representatives, especially in the delicate task of counselling or reasoning with other women. But more stereotypically *male* misdemeanours were coming to the fore by the end of the seventeenth century, with the Men's Meetings dealing with cases of drunkenness, debt and business failure. This last came to be regarded as a disgrace. Quaker men as non conformists were denied access to university education and so they had been turning their energies more and more to business. In response Quakerism had come to emphasise the importance of honest dealing, of sobriety and of sound business practice. Even as early as the 1680s, then, *financial* imprudence might bring disownment.[106] The wives, sisters and daughters of businessmen, and those women who were themselves in trade, therefore added the fear of financial instability and possible disownment to those they already had. In the early nineteenth century it was a fear which haunted Elizabeth Fry constantly.

It seems to me that despite their obvious concern with discipline and good order, the Women's Meetings were places where a woman might expect a degree of understanding of her difficulties. Certainly this was tempered with a firm belief in the possibility of self-improvement and self-help was advocated. But there was also willingness to provide support, financial and otherwise, sometimes over a long period, sometimes as an interim measure. The Women's Meetings showed little willingness to sanction the self-assertions of men, where these impinged on the welfare of vulnerable women and children. Neither would they accept vulnerability as an excuse for what they regarded as wrong doing on a woman's part. Toughness and tenderness combined in the ranks of seventeenth-century women Friends. Thanks to their segregated Meetings women found outlets for their energy and opportunities to learn and use skills, opportunities which would otherwise have been denied them. They found a solidarity in sisterhood and friendship through the Meetings and many of the young women found safe, relatively unexploitative employment and a modicum of education too. Employment and education are my final concerns in this chapter.

'Placing' and educating Quaker girls

Though the proverb quoted in the previous chapter said 'beware a young wench, a prophetess and a Latin woman', very few seventeenth-century women were fortunate enough to enjoy an education in Latin. Learning was not thought to make a girl marriageable[107] and even for the very few who studied at the grammar schools their curriculum was different. It avoided the heavy concentration on Latin grammar. Just such study was the key of access, however, to the universities, to theological study and to a reputation for learning. Such things were closed to all but the most exceptionally fortunate girls, i.e. to those whose family contacts gave them access to the influence of the universities they were not allowed to enter.[108] Matters had not always been so bleak.

> I found a late ingenious author . . . speaking of the repute that learning was in about 150 years ago. It was very modish (says he) that the fair sex seemed to believe that Greek and Latin added to their charms . . . One would think by the effects, that it was a proper way of educating them, since there are no accounts in history of so many great women in any one age, as are to be found between the years 15 and 1600.

So Mary Bell wrote in *A Serious Proposal to the Ladies* (1694-97).[109] But by contrast, and throughout the seventeenth century, the standard of education provided for girls of good family was generally in decline. That for boys was improving. The gap was sadly apparent to women writers with an eye for injustice:

> The God-like Virgil and great Homer's verse
> Like divine Mysteries are concealed from us,

complained Aphra Behn.[110] It is true, of course, that all but the most basic education was largely a mystery to the great mass of the population of both sexes but women writers (who were not themselves of the poorest and least articulate levels of society) were scathing of the educational double standard which they had experienced. Hannah Woolley, formerly a governess and schoolmistress, was dismissive of parents who catered for 'the barren noddles of their sons' while it was enough that a woman should know her husband's bed from another's.[111] Mary Astell wrote succinctly of the gender divide:

> Boys have much time and pains, care and cost bestowed on their education, girls have little or none. The former are early initiated in the sciences, are made acquainted with ancient and modern discoveries, they study books and men, have all imaginable encouragement . . . the latter are restrained, frowned upon, and beat, nor for but from the Tree of Knowledge.[112]

Some women discerned that it was not just families but indeed the whole nation which suffered because of this waste of potential.[113] Unfavourable comparisons were made with the more progressive Dutch:

> I have often heard some of our considerable merchants blame the conduct of our country-men . . . that they breed our women so ignorant of business; whereas were they taught arithmetic, and other arts which require not much bodily strength, they might supply the places of abundance of lusty men now employed in sedentary business . . .

remarked the late seventeenth-century author (perhaps Judith Drake) of *An Essay in Defence of the Female Sex*.[114]

In reality the kind of 'education' open to the daughters of the prosperous was one which encouraged 'gentle' accomplishments – some painting and 'japanning', embroidery and decorative shell work, a little music, dancing, preserving, reading, this last often not at the head of the list of proferred subjects. Reading allowed a girl to imbibe the scriptures (though many girls turned to romances for solace), and the form of shorthand which was taught in some establishments allowed her more easily to take sermon notes, to keep a Journal and so on. The 'presumptious' women who wanted more, who wrote and desired recognition, like Anne, Countess of Winchelsea (b. 1661), were advised that writing, thinking etc. 'would cloud our beauty'. Anne herself refused to succumb to the hours of monotony and embroidery of 'safe' subjects – nature, the royal family and biblical scenes:

> Nor will in fading silks compose
> Faintly the inimitable Rose.
> Fill up an ill-drawn bird, or paint on glass
> the Sovereign's blurr'd and undistinguished face,
> The threatening angel and the speaking ass.[115]

She represented the exception rather than the rule.

It was the learned Bathsua Pell Makin's great desire to persuade rich women to scorn their 'toys and trifles' and to turn to the study of arts, languages and religion instead. Bluntly she wrote of time wasted in dressing and trimming themselves like Bartholomew-babies, in painting, dancing, in making flowers of coloured straw, and building houses of stained paper . . .

and of parents' preferences for schools for girls where 'the less any thing of solidity is taught the more such places are frequented'.[116]

Such were the time-filling activities of the leisured classes. Women of the poorest sort were occupied with the challenges of daily survival and those of the middle sort with household economy, business affairs and the oversight of family and employees. Women of this last type, if they were averagely literate (products of a tutor, a local schoolteacher or of schooling in some clergyman's house) could make use of the manuals on household management which were published, also guides to medications, book-keeping and so on. Soundness in home economics, at least, was esteemed in such women, appropriate as it was to their class and sex.[117]

We find few women of the most leisured kind associated with seventeenth-century Quakerism and in any case all Quaker women were discouraged from 'trimming themselves'. The Quaker fold was no place for the idle as we may see from the following examples of quite privileged Quaker women.

Gulielma Springett Penn was the product of thoughtful parents. They (her mother Mary and stepfather Penington) had seen to it that as well as being tutored, Gulielma had benefited from family accomplishments. She had learned both her mother's organisational skills and her grandmother's knowledge of 'physic':

> oils, salves, balsams, drawing out of spirits, distilling of waters, making syrups and conserves, lozenges and pills.[118]

Ann Audland Camm, 'of a family of good repute' and one of the first ministers, was described (according to the *Piety Promoted* series of *Testimonies*, pp. i, 355) as 'well educated in learning proper for her sex'. Anne Downer later Whitehead, daughter of an Oxfordshire clergyman, had a knowledge of shorthand which made her a useful amanuensis for George Fox in the 1650s, when she made a 200 mile journey to Launceston to the prison to be with him. But Anne had more than the ability to be a useful secretary for George Fox. She had 'readiness in accounts and disposing of it more than many, for abilities therein exceeded most', recorded one testifier after her death. She was a woman of formidable energy and organising skills, who gave great service in time of plague and fire in London in the 1660s.

Mary Mollineux of Liverpool was exceptionally fortunate in her learning. 'Much afflicted with weak eyes' in her childhood (recorded, again, in the *Piety Promoted* series i, 164 seq.), she was therefore unfit for 'the usual employment of girls'. Instead her father ensured her 'more learning than is commonly bestowed upon her sex'. The learning included Latin, Greek, 'several useful arts' and knowledge of 'several hands', physic, surgery and mathematics too. While imprisoned in Lancaster Castle in 1684 Mary wrote religious poetry, though she was reticent about publishing it. Then there was Ann Waldegrave Docwra. This benefactress of Cambridge Friends was well-born and she had married into a landed family with several estates. While she was in her teens her enlightened father had pointed to the great Statute Book which lay on the parlour window, instructing her to read that. Since women as well as men had to live under the laws, he observed, it was proper that they should understand them. The experience was beneficial, she said later, 'to myself and others in the time of persecution'.

For years Sarah Fell kept the Swarthmoor Hall *Household Account Book* with meticulous care and when (in 1680) her sister Rachel succeeded her as clerk to the Women's Meeting there (some months before Sarah married William Meade) Rachel's spelling and punctuation were markedly inferior. Yet Sarah, it seems, was not entirely confident of her own skills. Page 113 of the *Account Book* records that she had purchased, through Thomas Lawson, a book called *The Young Clerks Tutor*.

Sarah Fell may indeed have been an example of what the Quaker experience did for the educational aspirations of some women. The Dutch writer Gerard Croese claimed that Sarah had set about teaching herself Hebrew. Although academic theological training was not held in high esteem among Friends, the purpose, Croese reported, was so that this considerable ('ravishing') preacher might confound her critics.[119]

By contrast many of the women converts to Quakerism were of the servant class, such as had been dependent on the good offices of a pious mistress who would teach them to read the scriptures. The vast majority of them did not take up writing as a significant element in their ministries. In fact only 82 out of 650 early writing Friends were female, and the majority of these published just one item. Quite a number of the early *male* ministers would probably have had a grammar school education.[120] Some men Friends (William Penn, Thomas Lawson, Robert Barclay [who attended the Scots Theological College], Samuel Fisher, Thomas Taylor, George Keith [later apostate] among them), had attended universities. But for most women in the seventeenth century the ability even to write one's own name, and certainly to read the Bible, were matters of good fortune rather than widespread provision.

It is notable that when Beatrice Carré made her study of Quaker women in Lancaster and Lancashire, she was able to record that

> work in the ministry reflects the degree of education of women Quakers. This was often quite high, when compared with the generally dismal level of educational attainment of the majority of early-modern English women.[121]

It goes without saying that the women Friends would have chosen the most appropriately gifted among them to keep these comprehensive records but at the same time the Quaker concept of women's ministry had also raised expectations. A woman was expected to be knowledgeable in the scriptures, and hence able to read them. She should not stand 'idle out of the vineyard' but rather she should participate actively and intelligently in the life of her Meeting and in its administration. Girls needed to be educated accordingly. So in practice even former (and presently serving) household servants occasionally published tracts. More of them penned letters and yet more such women were able at least to add their names to petitions. To achieve this level of female education which was 'often quite high', albeit in comparison with a disappointing norm, Friends sometimes had to go to great lengths.

Quakers were not aiming for the kind of education Bathsua Pell Makin had in mind for the rich, though like her they thought it should befit social status:

> Beyond reading and writing, a multitude of scholars is not so useful to the public as some think,

the Quaker John Bellers observed in his recommendations for the *College of Industry*

> Learning is useful, yet a virtuous, industrious education tends more to happiness here and hereafter . . .

Industry was to be promoted. There were Quakerly principles to be taken into account too:

> education of them in seamstry of a nicer sort tends rather to destroy the end

was Bellers' view of one skill in which training should be offered. But reading and writing, at least, were important, and preferably the learning of an occupation which allowed one to be 'useful'.

The burden of providing a modicum of education and training for the Quaker poor fell at first on those masters and mistresses to which apprentices and servants were assigned. Quaker families did not necessarily welcome the task of taking on a young girl and not all girls were happy with a Meeting's choice of employer. In 1670 in Norwich Monthly Meeting, for example, two Friends were delegated to speak with Dorothy Teate and Elizabeth True. They had not complied with that Meeting's suggestion of

> . . . the place of a servant, to such one as Friends judge would not oppress them.

Such placements were sometimes matters of urgency. The unemployed and unsupported poor might find themselves in a House of Correction.

Yet servant girls sometimes proved to be troublesome and a liability, consuming of a family's time and resources. Margaret Fell Fox and the Swarthmoor Women's Meeting knew this well, for they had encountered girls like Mary Benson. Mary had been orphaned in 1679 and the Meeting had worked to protect her small legacy. She had then been placed in the households of several Friends ('instruct and correct her and see that she keeps her reading and knitting or rather improves it'), had been kept clothed and shod through allowances and on one occasion had been sent to Manchester 'to better herself', with 3s 11d travelling expenses and new stockings. Eventually in 1686 the now elderly Margaret Fell Fox agreed to take her to Swarthmoor for a year. The Meeting held out no great hopes:

> . . . she hath the character of a very stubborn forward child, so that it is an exercise to meddle with her.

Meetings often gave very much time and energy to the care of such young people. There was no shortage of orphaned children of Friends, poor children whose parents were unable to support them adequately and sick children. The Meeting in the immediate locality had direct oversight of their affairs, but it was the Monthly Meeting which provided reimbursements and nominated individual Friends to take on caring tasks.

We see this clearly in the *Minutes of Gainsborough Monthly Meeting 1669-1719* as they relate to the case of Mary Codd. The amounts of money involved in these disbursements and the many other disbursements recorded in the Minutes indicate just how deep into their pockets committed Friends must have been digging, and at regular intervals, to keep up the Monthly Meeting's work. More important still, however, they show an unflagging loyalty to the welfare of the child of a deceased Friend, even when she has grown and would normally be expected to be self-supporting.

When I noticed her name in the three volume collection of the Minutes which H. W. Brace edited for the Lincoln Record Society between 1948-51, Mary Codd seemed just another orphaned girl dependent on Friends. However as her name reappeared year by year I wondered more and more about her. Was Mary Codd a pious Friend or perhaps one who would not freely have associated with Quakerism had she not been so dependent on it? What was the truth of her situation – had she been sickly since childhood or was she perhaps of limited intellectual ability as well as physically weak? Were her several masters and mistresses good to her? The Minutes are silent on all such matters, for Mary Codd was one of that large body of women which was discussed and legislated for but whose voices were never heard. There was no Women's Meeting in her area at the time, although discussions were in progress about establishing one (as we see in the Minute of the 8th of the 8th month 1689). Here then, little abbreviated but with some of my own comments added, is the story of Mary Codd as Gainborough Monthly Meeting Friends' Minutes record it:

14th of the 10 month 1670 Friends were being reminded of the need to relieve the 'present necessity' of one Christopher Codd, who was a poor man with children to care for. In 1670 the Monthly Meeting noted that Gainsborough Meeting was paying him weekly maintenance and his rent. He was probably a widower and indeed his wife may have died in giving birth to their last child, Mary.

Then Christopher Codd died.

4th month 1672 the care of his children was relegated to Gainsborough Meeting. Four months later Rebekah Codd was placed with William West of Gate Burton, apprenticed for ten years. Mary Codd was probably under three years old at this time.

12th, 4th month 1678 3s 3d came from Monthly Meeting, 'towards the nursing of Mary Codd and apparel'.

11th, 7th month 1678 another £1 is disbursed 'towards nursing of Christopher Codd's child'.

11th, 4th month 1679 Anne Rechett is approached about the tuition of Mary.

9th, 5th month 1679 they

> recount . . . that Anne Rechett demandeth £7 with Mary Codd, in consideration whereof she is willing to acquit Friends from all further charge and take the child in the condition she is at present and keep her eight years or till she be aged eighteen year.

Mary Codd was ten years old. The Monthly Meeting was to pay by installments and the agreement was that Mary would have

> sufficient meat, drink and apparel with lodging and all other things necessary both for life and health

(Minute of 8th, 8th month 1679).

In May of 1681 Anne Rechett signified her intent to the Meeting of marrying John Potter. At much the same time, the payment of instalments came to an end and Anne appeared before the Meeting to ratify it (so *Minute of 11th, 3rd month 1681*). Anne Rechett was not an educated woman, for she left her mark only in agreement. We do not hear of Mary Codd for some years.

8th, 2nd month 1687 it was noted that Mary had been 'put forth as an apprentice until she came to eighteen years old' and that the time was almost expired. 'She is still left to Friends' care'.

8th, 5th month 1687:

> It is desired that some care be taken about the disposing of her, to some place against the next Monthly Meeting, and search the register when her time with John Potter is expired.

<u>7th month 1687</u> in September it was determined that 'Mary Codd be brought to Jane Davis of Belton'. Gainsborough Meeting still had oversight and the Monthly Meeting reimbursed it 4*s* and 6*d* in December, for its outlay regarding Mary Codd. Perhaps all was not well, however, especially where the provision of food and drink was concerned, for on <u>11th, 3rd month 1688</u> we read

> it is ordered by this Meeting that care be taken for the tabling of Mary Codd, who is at present with Jane Davis of Belton.

<u>8th, 12th month 1688</u> seven months later Mary received 2*s* 0*d* for shoes and two months later again Jane Davis got £1, partly as payment in arrears for service given.

<u>In 1690 Mary Codd would have been twenty-one years old.</u> Volume 2 of the records tells of payment of 30*s* to Jane Davis for 'tabling' Mary and <u>9th, 3rd month 1690</u> it was recorded that Joseph Pilsworth of Epworth had agreed to 'table' Mary Codd for one year, by arrangement with Jane Davis, and £3 5*s* was made in disbursement.

<u>The following month</u> Pilsworth received 7*s* 10*d* for Mary and 7*s* 9*d* given four months later to Jane Davis 'clears of for Mary Codd'. Yet still there was £1 12*s* 6*d* due to Friend Pilsworth for half a year's provision.

<u>13th, 1st month 1691</u> Mary was twenty-two and her clothing was in disrepair. Joseph Pilsworth was delegated to organise the repairs and bring account to the Meeting.

<u>Two months later</u> he got the sum of £1 12*s* and 6*d* owed to him. Similar sums were being paid out to the Potter family in 'tabling' fees.

<u>13th, 3rd month 1692</u>: more urgently needed repairs were paid for, with Thomas Potter (father of Joseph) receiving the 10*s* 11*d* concerned.

<u>9th, 12th month 1692</u> another £1 12*s* 6*d* for tabling and 4*s* for repairs.

<u>9th, 4th month 1693</u>: to Peter Naylor went £1 12*s* 6*d* for half a year's provision and a reminder to Gainsborough Meeting that it was responsible for the 'necessities' of Mary Codd.

<u>Another such reminder is in the Minutes of 14. 5. 1693.</u>

<u>14th, 5th month 1693</u> Mary Berier was asked to take Mary Codd into her house and was granted leave until the following Monthly Meeting, to discuss the matter with her husband.

<u>11th, 6th month 1693</u> Mary Berier reported back and the answer was negative. 'She is still left to Friends' care' the Minute recorded.

<u>7th month 1693</u> George Atkinson of Roxby came into the Minutes. He was willing, he said, to take Mary. Two disbursements of 10*s* 6*d* and 3*s* 9*d* followed, for repairs and for shoes and stockings.

<u>10th, 9th month 1693</u> George Atkinson came again before the Meeting and signified his unwillingness to continue Mary Codd for a year, according to a former contract with Friends, and therefore desires that Friends should take care to dispose of her, and in the meantime

he is willing she should continue with him till a convenient place be found out.

The search was unnecessary.

From the Minutes of the Monthly Meeting held at Brigg(e) on 12th, 11th month 1693 we learn that

> This day an account was made with George Atkinson for Mary Codd table and burial . . . there remains yet owing George Atkinson the sum of 12s 2d.

He didn't get his money until the first month of 1694, and Robert Colyer was given her clothes to dispose of. She was twenty-four years old.

8th, 4th month 1694 at a Meeting held in Garthrop it was noted that Robert Colyer brought into the Meeting, 'for clothes he sold of Mary Codd's', the sum of 7s 0d.

Formal schooling was an even more difficult matter. Quakers wanted to provide schools for their own, not least because they feared the contamination of young minds by the conventional 'worldly' sort. In 1690, following the *Act of Toleration*, Yearly Meeting advised that parents should not send their children

> to such schools where they are taught the corrupt ways, manners, fashions and languages of the world, and of the heathen in their authors, and names of the heathenish gods and goddesses

(Friends avoided such 'heathenish' names by reference to 'fifth day', 'eighth month', etc.). But it was hard to provide such Quaker schooling. In the early decades there had been other concerns, and even as the century moved on and there *had* been moves to provide teachers and to found schools, such provision had been very patchy. Difficulties remained even after the passing of the Act of Toleration which had given Quakers the confidence to insist on provision of schooling in their midst, so that it was only in the eighteenth century that Friends' schooling became properly established. The fact was that schoolteacher Friends were very hard to come by, as indeed was the money with which to pay them. Few of the converts had been teachers or clergy (the other class which usually provided tuition). Therefore Monthly and General Meetings had had to make a careful appraisal of the 'conversation' of what applicants there were for teaching posts.

Fox had written in his *Warning to all Teachers of Children* . . . (London 1657) that teachers had to be beyond reproach. Meetings rejected many applicants as unsuitable, and we are not always told why:

> Friends on enquiry do think fit to wave making use of him.

reads a cryptic Minute on the interviewing of a prospective master for the Friends' school at Sidcot. Sometimes the reason for rejection is clear. Applicants were simply deficient in basic learning. At other times they withdrew their applications on discovery that funds were insufficient to ensure them an income after a short period. Not a few schools were of short duration.[122]

Bristol Friends were being optimistic when they declared that their school for boys should provide

> useful learning, as reading, writing, arithmetic, with other profitable parts of knowledge and such tongues as may be beneficial and not for ostentation.

Yet they seemed to have found a good candidate in John Silkfield, who offered his services in Bristol. Here was a man who could teach Greek, Latin and handwriting. Nevertheless, according to the Minutes of the Men's Meeting (p. 101) Silkfield was rejected. At twenty-two he was considered too young. The Bristol Quakers wanted a man who would teach mathematics, a person of maturity and of tested sobriety. Moreover they wanted a *married* man –

> his wife a good motherly woman, fit to table and cherish up lads.

Schoolmistresses were even more at a premium. Usually they taught girls and small children. Occasionally one would offer her services in a hard-pressed Meeting or region, but frequently those who did were not even moderately educated women. They tended to leave, too, to marry or to answer a call to minister (as did the men) but at least, and unlike the male teachers, they were not required to have an episcopal licence to teach, after the 1662 *Act of Uniformity*, and so the women were not hauled before Quarter Sessions on that account. D. G. B. Hubbard's University of London Master's thesis on *Early Quaker Education* (1940), recorded in an appendix that there were twenty-eight prosecutions before 1700 of Quaker men for teaching. Among those so prosecuted were Richard Scoryer, Joseph Besse, George Keith and Ambrose Rigge. A woman Friend was prosecuted too, one Sarah Carlisle, and she shared the fate of other such illicit teachers in being imprisoned.

Derbyshire was a poor county, for which there were no Yearly Meeting returns about Quaker education until the 1690s. In 1697 Esther Storrs volunteered her services as a teacher there. Chesterfield Monthly Meeting recorded that she would teach children (presumably girls) to 'read, knit and sew' (not write).[123] Nearly twenty years earlier the Quarterly Meeting for Edinburgh had determined in the twelfth month of 1678 that a 'public school' would be established in Aberdeen for the teaching of Friends' children by a Friend. Margaret Ker was the schoolmistress there from at least 1682. The Quarterly Meeting was concerned that the school should increase its numbers of pupils. Poor take-up of places was a problem in a number of schools, including in the one for 'young lasses and maidens' at Shacklewell from 1668 (they were to be taught things 'civil and useful') and at Patrick Logan's school at the Friars Meeting House in Bristol in 1690-91.[124] Patrick Logan, as his name suggests, was an Irishman. In 1690 he reported that just twelve children had been sent to him and his son James recorded later that though his father had found the wages good, he had been unable to tolerate

> the mothers taking upon them to direct his treatment of their children.

In some cases it was the inadequacy of the teachers which was to blame for the poor take-up of school places. In Edinburgh, however, a Meeting sent two women Friends, Lilias Skene and Isabell Gerard, to talk with the teacher Margaret Ker. She was to be encouraged to improve her own standards.

> to accomplish herself in arithmetic and writing for the education of the children,[125]

because parents had indeed been withdrawing them from the school. In the twelfth month of 1682 the Quarterly Meeting deplored the parents' actions.

Quaker benefactresses made donations towards the pay of such teachers and the provision of places for the poor. Elizabeth Dickson gave £50 to this Aberdeen school (but £100 for the engagement of a schoolmaster elsewhere![126]). Her £50 was for

> a schoolmistress to teach three girls in the art of reading their mother tongue and sewing and making plain work

and the Aberdeen Friend Mary Dannerman gave more than £5.

Other schools were in existence. Fox had first mooted the Waltham Abbey school in 1668. Children of the Fell, Penington and Penn dynasties studied there. Anne Travers and her daughter ran a school in Chiswick from 1685 and John and Margaret Rous (née Fell) sent their daughter Ann there, not long after its establishment.[127] She would have been in her fourteenth year at the time. In the same letter which tells us of this we also get an insight into the conditions in some Friends' schoolrooms. Ann's older brother Nathaniel had for several weeks attended Richard Scoryer's 'writing school' in Southwark. This was the one to which the harassed Thomas Chalkely walked as a child. But it had proved to be

> a nasty stinking place, the air did not agree with him

and Nathaniel, thinner and feverish, was sent home by coach. The child succumbed to smallpox not long after. Bridget Anstell was teaching in Tottenham in the late 1680s. We know of a girls' school in Warrington, of an establishment in Ramsey, Huntingdon and of another in Brighton.[128] There were many smaller schools of which we know next to nothing and presumably others to which all reference has been lost. It is known, for example, that there was a school in Pennington. William Yeamans, who had previously been tutored at Swarthmoor Hall by Richard Gawith (Gowth) was there at one point. There is an entry in the *Household Account Book* which records a payment of 2*s* to Jane Marshall (another 'motherly woman'?) for giving William his dinner over a sixteen day period. Beyond the fact of its existence nothing is known of this school. Yearly Meeting Minutes of 1691 mention several other Friends' schools, including ones at Thornbury near Bristol, at Brighthelmstone in Sussex and at Bradley in Yorkshire.

Elizabeth Couldam was teaching in Norwich in 1677. Here was another teacher who met opposition from parents and as usual she received support from her (Norwich) Monthly Meeting. Like all such Meetings it was anxious to safeguard its hard-won, if imperfect, schools and teachers. In her case it was (in part at least) the school discipline which had alienated parents. The Minute of the eighth of the eighth month, 1677 declared that Thomas Buddery and Edward Monk were delegated to speak

> to those Friends who have taken their children from Elizabeth Couldam, to know wherefore they did so, to the great discouraging the said Elizabeth . . . it being the sense of this Meeting, that she ought to reprove and correct them in moderation for words and actions contrary to the truth, and be encouraged for so doing.

As Patrick Logan and Elizabeth Couldam had discovered, Quaker parents felt free to involve themselves closely with the educational process! In the Penketh school, near Warrington however (founded 1687), the gifted and much prosecuted Gilbert Thompson ('eminently qualified for the instruction of youth'), was producing scholars who would be teachers of the next generation:

> being imbued with wisdom and skill to govern them by mild and gentle means.[129]

After 1670 quite a few Friends' schools existed,[130] serving boys more than girls. Indeed by 1671 there were at least seventeen boarding establishments, some co-educational. 'The private tutor had almost disappeared from Quaker families by the end of the century', Stroud claimed, for the policy was to send children to Friends' own boarding or day schools. The reality was different in some areas and provision was inadequate for those who would never have had a tutor in the first place. As Ralph Randles observed in his study of the early years of the Friends' school at Lancaster (in Mullet [ed.] *Early Lancaster Friends*),

> the major determinant of the creation of Quaker education was the ebb and flow of religous persecution and toleration between the emergence of Quakerism and the Toleration Act of 1689.

Since the purpose of repression was to eliminate the influence of Puritan radical ideas, the environment was not conducive to the widespread establishment of Friends' schools! Pre 1690, then, the general provision of education by Quakers for Quaker children was more hope than reality, more formulated theory than practice, even though a growing number of small schools of Quaker foundation *were* to be found. There had been few serious attempts to see that *all* Quaker children, rich and poor alike in a region, were given a formal Quaker education. Some areas were better provided for than others by the 1690s. In Lancashire in 1692, for example, the Women's Quarterly Meeting wanted

> that due care be taken in every Meeting to get schoolmasters and mistresses that are Friends to teach and train up children[131]

and in that county the response was good. It was reported in 1703 that there was 'not one Friend's child but what goes to Friends schools' in the region.[132] It was not so in other places.

Although they found it hard to make provision, Friends *were* conscious of the need to educate the poor. In 1662, Quakers imprisoned in the Ilchester Friary had started a school for poor, non-Quaker boys, where they might learn the rudiments of reading, writing and accounts. As early as 1659 a General Meeting in Durham had determined

> to help such parents for the education of their children as have more than they can maintain that there be not a beggar among us.

When *Six Weeks Meeting* in 1674 set up a schoolroom in a lower room of Devonshire House, Bishopsgate in London, the terms of its contract with the master, Richard Richardson, included a guaranteed payment of £20 from the Meeting, *provided that he taught free* the children who were referred to him by Monthly Meetings. The Women's Meeting offered to help defray expenses. He was allowed to agree payment privately with the parents of other children (and this was an often-repeated pattern). The school was short-lived. Yearly Meeting was very aware of the need to establish more schools which would cater for all and in 1697 the Joint Committee of the *Morning Meeting* and of *Meeting for Sufferings* issued a Minute which called for

> schools in your respective counties; wherein your children may not only be instructed in language and sciences, in the way of Truth, but likewise in some profitable and commendable labour, with literature, both to rich and poor; which may also contribute to the poor children's maintenance, and take away the reflection of the Dutch proverb on our English, viz. 'that they keep their children to work to make things for ours to play withall'.[133]

Education, it said, should be free to those who were in need of it. The cost of boarding education should be subsidised. (Already childless Friends had been known to complain of the cross of supporting and educating the orphaned and poor, though they got little sympathy from George Fox.) Moreover, the Minute read, 'weighty, suitable Friends' from Monthly and Quarterly Meetings should be appointed to inspect schools, just as they visited families. The scene was set for eighteenth-century developments in Quaker education, such as had not been mustered in the seventeenth.

Several Quaker theorists were at work when it came to determining the curriculum of schools. None was so worldly or daring as to advocate a Bathsua Makin-type education for girls, with half the time devoted to music, dancing, singing, writing and accountancy, the rest given over to languages (including Greek, Latin, Hebrew and French) with options on preserving and 'experimental philosophy' for those not linguistically inclined. The music and dancing would not have been considered fitting for Quaker children, and in any case the double standard was at work. William Penn advocated that Gulielma should encourage their boys in 'navigation, the building of ships and houses', with some knowledge of agriculture, while the girls were to learn housewifely arts and crafts: 'spin, sew, knit, weave, garden, preserve . . . helping others', never neglecting 'secret and steady meditations on the divine life'.[134] Education, he believed, was best when practical. 'We press the memory too soon' he wrote in his *Fruits of Solitude*, loading (boys') minds with rules of grammar and rhetoric. 'Natural knowledge' remained uncultivated and neglected. In his view

> Children had rather be making tools and instruments of play, shaping, drawing, framing and building . . . than getting some rules of propriety and speech by heart . . . it were happy if we studied nature more . . . the creation would be no longer a riddle to us.

When Francis Howgill wrote his letter of advice to his daughter Abigail in 1666 he included sewing, reading, writing and knitting among the 'points of good labour that belongeth to a maid'. As she grew, however, she was also to

> labour in the affairs of the country, and beware of pride and riotessness and curiosity.[135]

These writers were certainly discouraging the leisurely female vanities, just as George Fox had done in his *Warning to all Schoolteachers* (p. 2). In that work he had condemned education 'to play of instruments and music of all kinds . . . teaching them to dance . . .' as well as condemning the teaching of fencing to boys. But on the other hand Friends were not advocating a broadly-based education for girls, nor one which would produce great scholars.

Quakers wanted to see greater simplicity in education. There should be less emphasis on classical languages (which were a means to the powerful retaining control, as William Salt observed[136]), the abandonment of 'courtly style' and provision for the study of those practical things which would enable the individual, especially the less-privileged individual, to be self-supporting. The practicality in the Quaker vision of education was shown in the former clergyman and botanist Thomas Lawson's hope for the setting up of gardens (including a 'physic-garden') and for the study of plants. Careful observation of nature, he believed, should be part of the curriculum.[137] John Bellers hoped that from a young age scholars would learn to read, knit and spin, with older boys learning 'turning' etc. In practice, and after a lot of debate on the subejct (not least concerning the violent and 'heathenish' content of Latin textbooks) some Quaker offspring *were* even taught Latin. Among them was Nathaniel Meade, Margaret Fell's grandson. Latin had a practical use, some Friends acknowledged, *viz.* that knowledge of it allowed a Quaker 'to read a writ and other law process'.[138] Given the Friends' history of being at odds with the law, that was no mean consideration! So Latin came to be introduced into Friends' boarding schools. John Bellers' imaginative hope that children would imbibe foreign languages through contact and working alongside their immigrant teachers never blossomed into reality, but the picture is a pleasant one:

> all languages . . . may be learned there, by having some of all nations (tradesmen) who may teach their mother-tongue to the youth, as they teach it to their own children.[139]

Above all, however, the language and sentiments of the Bible pervaded the Quaker classroom.

> I would suggest that you read the Scriptures daily; the Old Testament for history, chiefly; the psalms for meditation and devotion; the prophets for comfort and hope; but especially the New Testament for doctrine, faith and worship

wrote William Penn in his *Advice to Children*. Sarah Fell Meade recorded the purchase of a Bible in 1683, which Susannah Fell sent to little Margery (she would have been about eight years old). On this occasion Sarah mentioned her misgivings, that she

> feared it was too small a print, but several tell us it's fittest for a child having young eyes, and should learn all prints, both small and great.

From 'those first heady days' through the 'calmer, politer Quakerism of the end of the century', the Bible held its place.[140]

It is evident that in the seventeenth century Quaker education did not reach fruition. Its innovations and achievements came later. Yet even in the first half century of the Friends' existence they showed a desire (often thwarted) to meet the needs of children of all classes of society, to encourage reading and writing in girls as well as boys, and the study of arithmetic by those deemed suitable (and where a teacher was available). They made provision, sporadically and patchily, for the passing on of skills which might rescue some, at least, from impoverishment. Through their Meetings they set up Friends in business, providing 'bridging-loans' and meeting initial costs, and such provisions applied to women as well as men. We read in record books of occasional arrangements by hard-pressed Meetings to give a girl at least *one* year's schooling, where no more could be provided, and whereas the number of girls' schools in the nation declined in the post-Restoration years, the Quakers were beginning to establish them.

Yet in this respect (i.e. in education), just as in other aspects of the Quaker treatment of women, there was only a tilting, rather than an upturning of the prevailing order. It was still assumed that the educational *needs* of girl students were in some respects different from those of the boys and that girls needed to be fitted for the domestic role. Nevertheless there *was* a pushing back of boundaries. The fact that the standard of literacy among women Friends seems to have been higher than was the norm among women in wider society does indicate an expectation in Quaker circles which was not shared elsewhere. The requirements of Quaker ministry would have fueled such an expectation.

Final remarks

By 1700 the formalism which had entered into Quakerism had sapped (or as some see it necessarily modified) spontaneity. 'Presumptious prophesying against a nation, town or person' was discouraged and ministry was carefully regulated. Writing of the 1690s Braithwaite (*Second Period,* p. 179) observed:

> The Quaker Church, effectively organised as a state within the State, was now mainly concerned with preserving its own quiet way of life; and, driven in on itself by storms of persecution and by the growth of a narrowing discipline, was no longer aflame with a mission to the world . . . The yearning expressed itself in a letter, issued by Stephen Crisp and George Whitehead with the Printed Epistle from the Yearly Meeting in 1692: . . . 'let all study to be quiet and mind their own business'.

Yet in the preceding five decades the variety of services women Friends had rendered had managed to survive and indeed to increase. This was so despite both the shifts internal to Quakerism and the many pressures from outside it. The emphases of Quakerism helped to ensure that even while formalism and patriarchy became firmly entrenched, no Quaker woman or girl was to be regarded simply as an appendage or property of a husband or father. The tenet about the spiritual equality of the sexes, which had been held among Quakers from the outset, retained enough of its vigour to ensure that the worst excesses of other churches were avoided.

Women Friends, it was decided, had a right to 'labour in the vineyard', according to their calling. Despite some of the aberrant views of the Wilkinson-Storyites and their like, a woman Friend had an obligation to respond to such a calling and a reasonable expectation to be 'freed' and fitted to do the job. This had been part of the initial vision and it had not been destroyed at the end of the century. Yet in the five decades of the seventeenth century in which Quakerism existed there had been no single or simple set of male-female relationships within the group, no easily carved niche into which a Quaker woman fitted neatly. The Quaker woman, then, was constantly asserting and re-negotiating her position, both within the group of Friends and in relation to the wider world. Nevertheless certain things were 'given' as certainty, not least that no Quaker woman was to surrender to others the responsibility for her own spirituality and its expression. George Fox had said as much in 1676, when writing *To All The Faithful Womens Meetings*. Echoing *Luke's* parable (15:8-9) he had written:

> . . . must not every woman light her own candle at the light of Jesus Christ, and sweep her own house with the power of God, before she finds God's treasure? And then for joy that they have found it, go and declare it unto their friends and neighbours?

The women themselves said as much.

> every member hath its office in the body . . . we have a garden to weed, a house to keep clean, inward as well as outward

(Deborah Winn, Sarah English and six others on behalf of the *Womens Yearly Meeting at York,* 10th of 6th month 1690, p. 4)

> and so we are not to put our candles under a bushel, nor to hide our talents in a napkin . . . but we are to have oil in our lamps, like wise virgins to the Lord.

(*A Living Testimony from the Womens Meeting in London,* 1685, p. 2).

In an age when women were believed to be beset by moral and physical weaknesses, by ignorance and love of frivolity, when they were linked in the minds of Christian men with carnality, Nature in need of control and with defective biology, the task of these women Friends was not one which was accomplished lightly. The preceding chapters have shown some of the hardships associated with being a Quaker and the struggles of the women themselves. Their doggedness, joyfulness, humour and certainty were the products of a theology and a faith which were derided and legislated against, and of a sisterly solidarity which the structures of Quakerism promoted. Their philosophy was summed up in the letter already quoted from the women Friends of Lancashire to those elsewhere:

> though we be looked upon as the weaker vessels, yet strong and powerful is God . . . we can stand our ground.

131

Notes

'NO MORE THAN A GOOSE'

[1] Puritanism forms the background for any study of this period. *See* C. Hill *Society and Puritanism in Pre-Revolutionary England,* Harmondsworth 1984; *Puritanism and Revolution,* London 1965; W. Hunt, *The Puritan Movement: the Coming of Revolution in an English County,* Cambridge Mass. 1983; A. L. Rowse, *Reflections on the Puritan Revolution,* London 1986 (a contentious and stimulating reappraisal); R. T. Vann, *SDEQ*; H. Barbour, *QPE.*

[2] R. T. Davies, *Four Centuries of Witch Beliefs with Special Reference to the Great Rebellion,* London 1947; B. Rosen, *Witchcraft in Tudor and Stuart England,* London 1970; K. Thomas, *RDM*; A. Fraser. *TWV,* 110-131; A. Anderson and R. Gordon, 'Witchcraft and the Status of Women – the Case of England', *British Journal of Sociology* 29 (1978), 171-184.

[3] Thomas in *RDM* illustrates the interest in alchemy, astrology, magic, physiognomy, geomancy, etc. Changes of outlook were evident by the end of the seventeenth century. See also Hill, *TWTUD,* 87-91, chp. 14; *Reformation to Industrial Revolution,* Harmondsworth 1967, 115, seq.; G. Scarre, *Witchcraft and Magic in Sixteenth and Seventeenth Century Europe,* London 1988; H. Rusche, 'Merlini Anglici: Astrology and Propaganda from 1644-1651', *EHR* 80 (1966), 322-333. Ralph Gardiner's *England's Grievance Discovered,* London 1655, 107 seq. has a good account of a spurious 'witch-finder' and of growing public distaste for such abuse.

[4] On the religious and political groups of this period and on gender-related issues see the works of Christopher Hill; A. L. Morton, *The World of the Ranters,* London 1970; B. S. Capp, *The Fifth Monarchy Men,* London 1972; H. N. Brailsford, *The Levellers and the English Revolution,* Nottingham 1976; M. R. Watts, *The Dissenters from the Reformation to the French Revolution,* Oxford 1978 (esp. chp. 2); W. M. Lamont, *Richard Baxter and the Millenium* Totowa NJ 1979; *Godly Rule: Politics and Religion 1603-1660,* London 1969; M. A. Mullett, *Radical Religious Movements in Early Modern Europe,* London 1980; A. Hamilton, *The Family of Love,* Cambridge 1951; N. Smith (ed.), *A collection of Ranter writings from the Seventeenth Century,* London 1980; B. Reay, J. F. McGregor (eds.) *Radical Religion in the English Revolution,* Oxford 1984; see also D. Underdown, *Revel, Riot and Rebellion: Popular Politics and Culture in England 1603-1660,* Oxford 1985; S. D. Amussen,

An Ordered Society: Gender and Class in Early Modern England, Oxford 1988;
P. Collinson, *The Birthpangs of Protestant England: Religious and Cultural
Change in the Sixteenth and Seventeenth Centuries*, London 1988.

[5] C. Hill, W. Lamont, B. Reay, *The World of the Muggletonians*, London 1983.

[6] Hill, *Antichrist in Seventeenth Century England*, Oxford 1971; B. Manning, *The
English People and the English Revolution*, London 1976 (esp. chp. 9); K. Firth,
The Apocalyptic Tradition in Reformation Britain 1530-1645, Oxford 1979;
C. A. Patrides, J. Wittreich (eds.), *The Apocalypse in English Renaissance
Thought and Literature*, Manchester 1984; A. Hamilton, 'The Apocalypse
Within: Some Inward Interpretations of the Book of Revelation . . .' in
J. W. van Henten *et al.* (eds.), *Tradition and Re-interpretation in Jewish and Early
Christian Literature* (essays in hon. J. C. H. Lebram), Leiden 1986, 269-283;
H. Popkin, *Millenarianism and Messianism in English Literature and Thought
1650-1800*, Leiden 1988.

[7] Hill, *Antichrist* (n.6), 104; *TWTUD*, 33 seq., 92f; Underdown, *Revel, Riot*,
140 seq.

[8] Hill, *TWTUD*, 107 n.2; 'The Agrarian Legislation of the Revolution' and
'William Perkins and the Poor' in *Puritanism and Revolution* (n. 1 above),
153-196, 215-238; *Reformation to Industrial Revolution* (n. 3, esp. chps. 3-4);
B. Manning, *The English People* (n. 6. useful material on agrarian
grievances, exploitation of the poor, etc.); M. James, *Social Problems and
Policy During the Puritan Revolution*, London 1930 (esp. chp. 2).

[9] Hill, *TWTUD*, 63 seq.

[10] Morton, *Ranters*, 20-26; J. Morrill, 'The Church in England 1642-1649', in
Morrill (ed.), *Reactions to the English Civil War 1642-1649*, London 1982,
chp. 4; M. L. Schwarz, 'Some Thoughts on the Development of a Lay
Religious Consciousness in Pre-Civil War England' in G. J. Cuming and
D. Baker (eds.), *Studies in Church History: Popular Belief and Practice*,
Cambridge 1972, 171-178; D. P. Walker, *The Decline of Hell*, London 1964;
Hill, *A Turbulent, Seditious and Factious People: John Bunyan and his Church
1628-1688*, Oxford 1989.

[11] See R. R. Ruether, E. C. McLaughlin (eds.), *Religion and Sexism*, New York
1974; E. Clark, H. Richardson (eds.), *Women and Religion*, New York 1977;
J. O'Faolain, L. Martines, *Not in God's Image*, London 1979.

[12] See G. Leff, *Heresy in the Later Middle Ages*, Manchester 1966; E. McLaughlin,
'Women, Power and the Pursuit of Holiness . . .' in Ruether and
McLaughlin (eds.), *Women of Spirit: Female Leadership in the Jewish and
Christian traditions*, New York 1979, 99-130; N. Cohn, *The Pursuit of the
Millenium*, London 1970, 148-186; E. Boulding, *The Underside of History:
a View of Women Through Time*, Boulder Colorado 1976, 445-453; K. O.
Sprunger, 'God's powerful army of the weak: the Anabaptist women . . .'
in R. L. Greaves (ed.), *Triumph Over Silence: Women in Protestant History*,
London 1985, 45-74.

[13] Cohn, *The Pursuit of the Millenium* (n. 12), 287 seq.; E. M. Williams, 'Women
Preachers in the Civil War Sects' *Journal of Modern History* 1 (1929), 561-569;
K. Thomas, 'Women and the Civil War Sects' *PP* 13 (1958), 42-62;
R. L. Greaves, 'The Ordination Controversy and the Spirit of Reform in
Puritan England', *JEH* 21 (1970), 225-41; C. Cross, '"He-goats before the

flocks". . .', in Cuming and Baker (eds.) *Studies in Church History* (n. 10 above), 195-202; E. C. Huber, 'A Woman Must Not Speak: Quaker Women in the English Left Wing', in Ruether and McLaughlin (eds.), *Women of Spirit*, 153-182; J. L. Irwin, *Womanhood in Radical Protestantism 1525-1675*, Toronto 1979. See also the studies by R. L. Greaves and D. P. Ludlow in Greaves (ed.) *Triumph over Silence*, 75-92, 93-123; C. Berg and P. Berry ('Spiritual Whoredom: an Essay on Female Prophets . . .') in F. Barker, J. Bernstein *et al.* (eds.), *1642: Literature and Power in the Seventeenth Century*, Colchester, University of Essex 1981, 37-54.

[14] Fraser, *TWV*, 65-85; L. Stone, *FSM*, 60, 77 seq. *et passim.*

[15] A. Clark, *WLW*, 86; Cf. Thomas, *RDM*, 6-7.

[16] A. Clark, *WLW*, 86.

[17] D. V. Glass, 'John Graunt and his *Natural and Political Observations*', in *Notes and Records of the Royal Society* 19 (1964), 75. Cf. also the editors' introduction in the 1982 edition of Clark's *WLW* and the literature cited in M. Ferguson (ed.), *FF*, 37 seq.

[18] J. Nohl, *The Black Death*, London (Unwin books), 1961, 25 seq., 34 seq., 43 seq.; W. H. McNeill, *Plagues and Peoples*, Harmondsworth 1979, 161 seq. *et passim*; J. F. D. Shrewsbury, *A History of Bubonic Plague in the British Isles*, Cambridge 1971; H. Zinsser, *Rats, Lice and History*, New York 1934.

[19] J. Brewer, J. Styles (eds.), *An Ungovernable People: the English and Their Law . . .*, London 1980 (esp. chps. 1-2); C. B. Herrup, *The Common Peace: Participation and the Criminal Law in Seventeenth Century England*, Cambridge 1987; L. Kaplan, *Politics and Religion During the English Revolution: the Scots and the Long Parliament 1643-45*, New York 1976; J. Morrill and J. D. Walter, 'Order and Disorder in the English Revolution' in A. Fletcher, J. Stevenson (eds.), *Order and Disorder in Early Modern England*, Cambridge 1985, 137-165; C. Russell, 'The British Problem and the English Civil War', *History* 72 (1987), 395-415.

[20] See Fraser, *TWV*, 155-207; Clark, *WLW*, 161-170, 243-89; Boulding, *The Underside of History* (n. 12), 558-576 and P. Higgins, 'The reactions of women, with special reference to women petitioners' in B. Manning (ed.), *Politics, Religion and the English Civil War*, London 1973, 177-222; B. Ehrenreich, D. English, *For Her Own Good: 150 years of the experts' advice to women*, London 1979 chp. 2.

[21] R. P. Leibowitz, 'Virgins in the service of Christ: the Dispute Over an Active Apostolate . . .' in Ruether and McLaughlin (eds.), *Women of Spirit*, 131-152; Fraser, *TWV*, 137-142, 161 seq.; J. Morris, *The Lady was a Bishop*, New York 1973.

[22] Antonia Fraser's chapter on midwifery makes chilling reading (see *TWV* 497-523 cf. 65-88). I cheerily shared some of its contents with a midwife I was chatting to at an ante-natal clinic. I was advised to read something else.

[23] These women cannot be considered adequately here but there is a growing body of literature on them. As well as Fraser, *TWV* and Keith Thomas's work see also Berg and Berry, 'Spiritual Whoredom'; D. P. Ludlow, 'Shaking Patriarchy's Foundations', in *Triumph over silence*; A. Cohen, 'The Fifth Monarchy Mind: Mary Cary and the Origins of Totalitarianism',

Social Research 31 (1964), 195-213; 'Prophecy and Madness: Women Visionaries During the Puritan Revolution', *Journal of Psychohistory* 11 (1984), 411, 426; C. Burrage, 'Anna Trapnel's Prophecies', *EHR* 26 (1911); T. Spencer, 'The History of an Unfortunate lady' (on Lady Eleanor), *Harvard Studies and Notes in Philology* 20 (1938); P. Mack, 'Women as Prophets During the English Civil War', *Feminist Studies* 8 (1982), 20-45; B. R. Dailey, 'The Visitation of Sarah Wight: Holy Carnival and the Revolution of the Saints in Civil War London', *Church History* 55 (1986), 438-455; N. Smith, *Perfection Proclaimed: Language and Literature in English Radical Religion 1640-1660,* Oxford 1989, 45-53, 83-95 *et passim*; Rosemary Radford Ruether, 'Prophets and Humanists: Types of Religious Feminism in Stuart England', *Journal of Religion* 70 (1990), 1-18.

[24] Anna Trapnel, *Report and Plea* (also a narrative of her journey into Cornwall), 1654. In the same year she wrote *A Legacy for the Saints and The Cry of a Stone.* See also Cohen, 'Prophecy and Madness' and M. MacDonald, *Mystical Bedlam: Madness Anxiety and Healing in Seventeenth Century England,* Cambridge 1982.

[25] Eusebius *Ecclesiastical History* v. 16, 17. Ammia the early second century Asian prophetess was appealed to by the catholics and the Montanists alike, as were the four daughters of Philip (Acts 21:9).

[26] 'The work of middle-class women' (Fraser, *TWV*, 253); 'in practice John Taylor' was the author (C. Belsey, *The Subject of Tragedy*, London and New York 1985, 219). Taylor had penned the 1639 Juniper lecture to which these works were 'replies'.

[27] *Swetnam the Woman-Hater* was the title of a play of 1619, in which women drove him out of the land. The work reflects the views of Speght and Mundi, according to Simon Shepherd in *Amazons and Warrior Women,* Brighton (Harvester Press), 1981, 206f. See also K. Rogers, *The Troublesome Helpmate: a history of misogyny in literature,* Seattle 1966; C. Crandall, *Swetnam the Woman-Hater: the controversy and the play,* Lafayette Ind. 1969.

[28] Shepherd, *Amazons* (n. 27), 1. Cf. H. L. Smith, *Reason's Disciples: seventeenth century English feminists,* Chicago and London 1982; S. Shepherd (ed.), *The Women's Sharp Revenge,* London 1985; Ruether, 'Prophets and Humanists' (n. 23). In a paper I read at the 16th Congress of the *International Association for the History of Religions* in Rome, September 1990 ('Christian Prophecy and Gender: Some Aspects of the Struggle for Female Emancipation in Seventeenth Century England') I suggested that the experience of women in these sects, as in other groups throughout Christian history, was of a shortlived and partial 'breakthrough', with no lasting improvement in the lot of women. Even in Quakerism, which survived the Restoration, there came the marginalisation of women's charismatic authority which (or even worse suppression) is common with the onset of institutionalisation.

[29] See S. M. Gilbert, S. Gubar (eds.), *Shakespeare's Sisters: Feminist Essays on Women Poets,* Bloomington and London 1979, xv; Fraser, *TWV* 388-391, 451 seq.; J. Goulianos (ed.), *By a Woman Writ: Literature from Six Centuries By and About Women,* London 1974, 71 seq.

[30] See S. Findlay, E. Hobby, 'Seventeenth Century Women's Autobiography' in *1642: Literature and Power,* 11-36; C. F. Smith, 'Jane Lead: Mysticism and

the Woman Cloathed with the Sun', in *Shakespeare's Sisters* (n. 28), 3-18 and (in the same volume) W. Martin, 'Anne Bradstreet's Poetry: A Study of Subversive Piety', 19-31; K. Rogers, 'Anne Finch, Countess of Winchelsea: an Augustan woman poet', 32-46; C. E. Hambrick-Stowe (ed.) *New England Meditative Poetry: Anne Bradstreet and Edward Tayloe,* New York 1988; see also C. F. Smith, 'Jane Lead: the Feminist Mind and Art of a Seventeenth Century Protestant Mystic', in Ruether and McLaughlin (eds.) *Women of Spirit* (n. 12), 184-203.

[31] On Margaret Cavendish see Fraser, *TWV,* 34 seq., 133 seq., 183 seq., 444 seq. *passim*; Findlay and Hobby, 'Seventeenth Century Women's Autobiography'; Goulianos, *By a Woman Writ,* 55 seq.; D. Palamo, 'Margaret Cavendish: defining the Female Self', *Women's Studies* 6 (1979), 411-422; Smith, *Reason's Disciples,* 75-95.

[32] Selections from her writings and from those of Esther Sowernam, Anne Finch, Bathsua Makin, Margaret Fell and others are in *FF,* esp. pp. 85-101.

[33] Belsey, *The Subject of Tragedy,* 160. See also C. L. Powell, *English Domestic Relations 1487-1653,* New York 1917, 160-169, 192-206.

[34] Cf. S. W. Hull, *Chaste, Silent and Obedient, English Books for Women 1475-1640,* San Marino (Huntingdon library edn.), 1982; Irwin, *Womanhood in Radical Protestantism,* 70-105; Powell, *English Domestic Relations* (n. 33), 134-146, 160 seq.

[35] It was common to find disclaimers in the writings of such women. Elizabeth Warren (*Spiritual Thrift or Meditations,* London 1647, 81) was 'conscious to my mental and sex deficiency' and she acknowledged that women were susceptible to error.

[36] Fraser (*TWV,* 51 seq.) writes of Elizabeth Walker, married in 1650, who rose at four a.m. or earlier, lit her own fire, was a fine baker, cheesemaker, wine and cidermaker, looked to her husband's business affairs, cared for the physical and spiritual welfare of her family, her servants, labourers and the neighbouring poor and was a woman of liberal sentiments.

[37] E. C. McLaughlin, 'Equality of Souls, Inequality of Sexes: Women in Medieval Theology' in *Religion and Sexism,* 213-266.

[38] Hill, *TWTUD,* 311.

[39] U. King, 'Towards an Integral Spirituality: Sexual Differences and the Christian Doctrine of Man', *Vidyajyoti, Journal of Theological Reflection* (Delhi), September 1981, 348-371.

[40] See O'Faolain and Martines, *Not in God's Image,* chp. 8; R. Ruether and B. P. Prusak, in *Religion and Sexism,* 150-183, 89-116.

[41] B. Reay, *QER,* 26; M. M. Dunn, 'Saints and Sisters' *American Quarterly* 30 (1980), 595-601.

[42] L. Eeg-Olofsson, *The Conception of the Inner Light in Robert Barclay's Theology* (Studia Theologica Lundensia 5), Lund 1954; L. Grubb, *Authority and the Light Within,* London 1908; A. N. Brayshaw, *The Quakers: Their Story and Message* (3rd. rev. edn.), London 1969, chp. 3; R. Hadley King, *George Fox and the Light Within,* Philadelphia 1940; G. H. Boobyer, *The Bible and the Light Within* (Quaker Home Service Study in Fellowship Booklet 34), London 1973; M. B. Endy, *William Penn and early Quakerism,* Princeton 1973. There was in each person, heathen or not, male or female, 'a principle

of God which, as it was heeded, would lead to salvation' (Brayshaw, p. 45).
In his *Journal* (p. 33) Fox wrote that

> The Lord God opened to me by his invisible power that every man
> was enlightened by the divine Light of Christ, and I saw it shine
> through all.

[43] P. C. Atkinson, 'The Montanist interpretation of Joel 2:28, 29 (LXX 3:1, 2)',
Studia Evangelica (= Texte und Untersuchungen series, 126), Berlin 1982,
11-15.

[44] Cf. John Vicars (sometimes Vickars), *The Schismatick Sifted,* London 1646, 34:

> Is it a miracle or a wonder . . . to see young saucy boys . . . bold
> botching tailors and other most audacious illiterate mechanics . . . run
> rashly and unsent for too into a pulpit· To see bold impudent
> housewives, without all womanly modesty, to take upon them (in the
> natural volubility of their tongues and quick wits or strong memories
> only) to prate (not preach or prophesy) after a narrative or discoursing
> manner, an hour or more, and that most directly contrary to the
> Apostle's inhibitions. But where I say is their extraordinary Spirit
> poured out upon them . . .

Where, asked Vicars, were the gifts of tongues or of healing? Cf. also
Edwards, *Gangraena,* 30 seq., 50 seq., 84 seq. *et passim.*

[45] Hill, *TWTUD,* 373 seq.; R. Knox, *Enthusiasm,* Oxford 1950, 168 seq.;
C. W. Horle, 'Quakers and Baptists 1647-1660', *Baptist Quarterly* 26 (1976),
344-362; D. Durnbaugh, 'Baptists and Quakers: left-wing Puritans?' *QH*
62 (1973), 67-82.

[46] Pagitt, *Heresiography* 5th edn. 1654, 136.

[47] See Braithwaite, *BQ,* 44.

[48] So G. Croese, *The General History of the Quakers,* 1696, I, 37. See also
E. Manners, *Elizabeth Hooton. First Quaker Woman Preacher (1600-1672),*
London 1914, 1-5.

[49]
> I Jane Withers, was moved of the Lord to go to the steeple-house
> of Kellit to speak to priest Moor . . . 'thou art the Beast that all the
> world worships . . . the plagues of God must be poured upon thee'

recorded James Nayler in *A Discovery of the Man of Sin,* London 1656, 45. She
had felt 'bound about my body above the middle as if with chains . . . I was
forced to go'. Interestingly Jane insisted (despite the accusation) that she had
been lucid and not in a trance at the time – 'as sensible all the while as ever I
was' (p. 45). Such language was typical. Ann Blaykling called a priest
'hireling and deceiver, greedy dumb dog'; the Yorkshire Friend Margaret
Killam, in a publication to the people of Plymouth, declared (in God's name)
'I have spread dung on your faces already'. Phyllis Mack suggests, however,
that the language of Quaker women from the *south* of England was less
aggressive and of a 'gentler, more mystical and introspective tone' ('Gender
and Spirituality', in E. Potts Brown, S. Mosher Stuard (eds.) *WFC,* 1989,
45-46). On Quaker speech see R. Bauman, *Let Your Words Be Few,*
Cambridge 1983; 'Speaking in the Light: the Role of the Quaker Minister' in
R. Bauman, J. Shezer (eds.), *Explorations in the Ethnography of Speaking,*
Cambridge 1974; R. Darnell, 'The Second Person Singular Pronoun in
English: the Society of Friends', *Western Canadian Journal of Anthropology* 1

(1970), 1-11 and cf. M. Graves, 'Functions of Key Metaphors in Early Quaker Sermons 1671-1700', *Quarterly Journal of Speech* 69 (1983), 364-378.

50 See Besse, *Sufferings,* e.g. i, 137; Manners, *Elizabeth Hooton* (n. 48), 6. On legislation affecting Friends (the 1650 *Blasphemy Act,* Cromwell's *Proclamation Against the Disturbing of Ministry* 1654, new vagrancy laws, etc.) see Thomas, *RDM,* 69 seq.; Reay, *QER,* chp. 3; Hill, *TWTUD,* 27, 35, 140 seq. *et passim.*

51 J. Scheffler, 'Prison Writings of Early Quaker Women', *QH* 73 (1984), 25-37, esp. p. 28; Besse, *Sufferings* i, 137; ii, 89.

52 The version signed by Elizabeth is in Swarthmoor MSS ii, 43. Cf. also Fox, *Journal,* 55; H. Barbour, A. Roberts, *EQW,* 381 seq.

53 Quoted by Manners, *Elizabeth Hooton,* 10. Cf. Huber, 'A woman must not speak', 165 seq. Barbour, *QPE,* 229 succinctly describes prison conditions.

54 Scheffler, 'Prison writings' (n. 49), 29; Brailsford, *QW,* 333.

55 See also J. M. Chu, *Neighbors, Friends or Madmen: the Puritan Adjustment to Quakerism in Seventeenth Century Massachusetts,* Westport 1985; L. Koehler, *A Search for Power: the 'Weaker Vessel' in Seventeenth Century New England,* University of Illinois Press 1980, esp. chapter 9 and pp. 248ff with a Table showing the increase in criminal offences committed by Anabaptist and Quaker women. On Mary Dyer's fate and her earlier association with Anne Hutchinson and the American Antinomians see E. C. Huber, *Women and the Authority of Inspiration,* New York and London 1985, 65-122, esp. 106-116.

56 The first such *Act* proscribed worship other than that of the Anglican Prayer Book. 700 Quakers were freed from prison at the time of Charles II's coronation but in 1664 400 Friends were seized from one spot in London on just two successive Sundays. Quakers continued to meet openly, which made opposition inevitable and easy. Fines, distraint on goods and imprisonments were commonplace. Transportation for a third offence was possible. See Barbour, *QPE,* 225; Reay, *QER,* 105 seq.; 'The Quakers, 1659 and the Restoration of the Monarchy', *History* 63 (1978), 193-213; 'The Authorities and Early Restoration Quakerism', *JEH* 34 (1983), 69-84; Braithwaite, *SPQ,* 5-54.

57 Braithwaite, *SPQ* chps 2-4; Brailsford, *QW,* 29 seq.

58 E. Stirredge, *Strength in Weakness Manifest* London 1711.

59 See H. J. Cadbury (ed.), *George Fox's Book of Miracles,* Cambridge 1948; K. L. Carroll, 'Quaker attitudes towards signs and wonders', *JFHS* 54 (1977), 74 seq.; H. E. Collier, 'Then and Now, Miracles and Healings During the First Period of Quakerism', *Friends Quarterly Examiner* 78 (1944), 280-288. Collier and Cadbury tell of the suppression of the 'miracles' book during Fox's lifetime.

60 'Filthy bewitched stuff' commented the leading Quaker James Nayler. See Reay, *QER,* 136 n. 26; Knox, *Enthusiasm,* 124; Fox, *Journal,* 229 (Toldervy temporarily 'run out', he observed). In fact Toldervy more than once passed in and out of the Quaker fold.

61 Braithwaite, *BQ,* 192 n. 4, 148 seq.; N. Penney, *FPT,* 259; Mack, 'Gender and Spirituality' in *WFC,* 42 seq., 51.

62 Elizabeth Fletcher was a lone female missionary in Dublin before Smith joined her in 1657. 'I suffer for her', Edward Burrough wrote to Margaret Fell, 'she

being as it were alone . . . in this ruinous nation, where it is very bad travelling' (see Ross, *MF* 53 seq.).

63 'The early Quakers reproduce some of the more disconcerting characteristics of Anabaptist prosphesying' (Knox, *Enthusiasm,* 136 *et passim*). Cf. also K. L. Carroll, 'The Early Quakers and "Going Naked as a Sign"', *QH* 67 (1978), 69-87; Bauman, *Let Your Words Be Few*, chp. 6.

64 See Greaves and Zaller, *BDBR, in loc.*; Cohn, *Pursuit of the Millenium*, 298 seq.; Mack, 'Women Prophets'; Thomas, *RDM*, 125 seq.; Cohen, 'Prophecy and Madness'; Mary Adams, condemned for Ranter libertinism, was said to have committed suicide by disembowelling. John Robins, husband of Joan, appears later in this chapter. Cohen in the article cited and Thomas *RDM* discuss such 'holy family' groups and their likeness to some of the Middle Ages.

65 T. L. Underwood, 'Early Quaker Eschatology' in P. Toon (ed.), *Puritans, the Millenium . . .*; C. L. Cherry, 'Enthusiasm and Madness: Anti-Quakerism in the Seventeenth Century', *QH* 73 (1984), 1-24, R. S. Mortimer, 'Warnings and Prophecies', *JFHS* 44 (1952), 13-20.

66 On the Assize records see Reay, *QER*, 69, 77. See also E. E. Taylor, 'On the Great Revival at Malton in 1652', *JFHS* 33 (1936), 29 seq.; Braithwaite, *BQ*, 71 seq.; J. W. Spargo, *Juridical Folklore in England Illustrated by the Cucking-Stool*, Durham NC 1944; also Reay, 'Popular Hostility Towards Quakers in Mid Seventeenth Century England', *Social History* 5 (1980), 387-407; Underdown, 'The Taming of the Scold'.

67 Brailsford, *QW*, 110 seq.; Reay, *QER*, 68-72; J. M. Douglas, 'Early Quakerism in Ireland', *JFHS* 48 (1956), 3-32. John Bunyan took seriously accusations of witchcraft against Quakers, as W. Y. Tindall noted in his 1934 study *John Bunyan, Mechanick Preacher*, 221 seq.

68 *Strange and Terrible News from Cambridge*, anonymous writing of 1659. See also E. Porter, *Cambridgeshire Customs and Folklore*, London 1969, 169 seq.; N. Penney, 'The Early Quakers in East Anglia: Cambridgeshire' in *East Anglia Notes and Queries* NS 10 (1903), 65-68; L. Phillipson, *Quakerism in Cambridge Before the Act of Toleration* (= reprint of *Proceedings of the Cambridge Antiquarian Society* 76 [1987], 10 scq.).

69 Fox, *Journal*, 148 seq. for 1654 also pp. 101, 201; Braithwaite, *BQ*, 181; A. Neave Brayshaw, *The Personality of George Fox*, London 1933, 70 and nn. Pepys had heard similar tales about Quakers and the anonymous *The Quakers Fiery Beacon* of 1655 tells of Friends' 'inchanted potions, ribbons and bracelets'.

70 *An account of the Travels of Barbara Blaugdone*, London 1691, 22. She travelled in the Quaker cause for half a century, and her Irish relatives feared she might indeed be a witch. See Besse, *Sufferings* ii, 459; Braithwaite, *BQ*, 171, 217 seq.; Brailsford, *QW*, 159-176; Scheffler, 'Prison Writings', 29 seq.; Elizabeth Bathurst, *Truth Vindicated,* London 1691, 132.

71 Trances, fasting and vomiting too are recurring features in the accounts of seventeenth century women prophets.

72 Mary Fisher will be discussed more fully in Chapter Two.

73 Braithwaite, *BQ*, 72 seq.; Brailsford, *QW*, 22. Jane Holmes, Mary Fisher and Elizabeth Hooton are signatories of the 1652 prison writing *False Prophets and False Teachers*. See Barbour and Roberts, *EQW* 358 seq.

74 Historians debate whether some of these women were in fact mad. Though prophecy (the product of the Spirit's direct inspiration) was a less assailable religious activity for women than teaching and preaching, prophets, in particular, were suspected of madness. The case *for* mental disturbance is put by Cohen in 'Women Visionaries' (n. 22) while Hill, Thomas and others point to method in such 'madness', e.g. as 'a deliberate form of self-advertisement' (*TWTUD*, 280, 286).

75 Like the Ranter Mary Gadbury in Winchester John Robins seems to have been associated with small, self-sufficient (but unconnected) groups in which there was a female 'Mary' (Messiah-bearer) figure. See Morton, *Ranters*, 92; Hill, *TWTUD*, 226 seq.; Thomas, *RDM*, 136.

76 On Robins see R. L. Greaves in *BDBR* iii, 100 seq.

77 Braithwaite, *BQ*, 391, 575 n.3.

78 From J. Smith, *Bibliotheca Antiquakeriana*, New York 1968, 10. See also Baxter, *Reliquiae Baxterianae* 1696 (ed. M. Sylvester), i, 77; Cadbury, *Book of Miracles*, 13 seq. and for condemnation of Quaker 'signs', demonic possession, drugging, etc., see Richard Blome, *The Fanatick History*, London 1660.

79 Besse, *Sufferings*, i, 61 seq., 66.

80 Knox, *Enthusiasm*, 360, 370; Thomas, *RDM*, 128 seq.

81 G. Nuttall, *James Nayler: a Fresh approach*, Suppl. 26, *JFHS* 1954, 9 seq.

82 See especially M. Brailsford, *A Quaker from Cromwell's Army*, New York and London 1927; E. Fogelklou, *James Nayler the Rebel Saint*, London 1931.

83 James Nayler, *Works*, 1716. See also W. G. Bittle, *James Nayler: the Quaker Indicted by Parliament*, York 1986, chps. 1-2.

84 Cf. Hill, *TWTUD*, 205, seq.

85 M. H. Nicholson (ed.), *The Conway Letters: the Correspondence of Anne Viscountess Conway, Henry More and their Friends 1642-1684*, London 1930, 407 seq.

86 Ross, *MF*, 101 seq.; Fox, *Journal*, 220, 223; Bittle, *James Nayler*, chp. 4.

87 The former Baptist Rice Jones and 'the proud Quakers' had earlier caused a rift among Friends. Nayler had tried to conciliate between Jones and Fox. See Braithwaite, *BQ*, 45 seq.; Bittle, *James Nayler*, 61 seq.

88 Letter of Francis Howgill to Margaret Fell. See Brailsford, *QW*, 252 seq.; Braithwaite, *BQ*, 244 seq.

89 For the letters referred to in these paragraphs see Ross, *MF*, 101 seq., 105, Appendix 9, 396 seq. Cf. also Fogelklou, *James Nayler*, 130.

90 The second century Montanists were accused of producing their own literature, including 'general epistles' when catholic churchmen were doing no less. See also n. 94 and the associated text.

91 See Brailsford, *QW*, 258 seq. and the letters from Andrew Parker to Margaret Fell in A. R. Barclay, *Letters of Early Friends*, London 1841, 57; Barbour and Roberts, *EQW*, 480-485.

92 A letter to Martha from Thomas Simmonds made reference to Nayler and events with the Levellers at Burford. Some sources suggest that Thomas was not involved in the Bristol entry and that he had decried the course of things. Other sources suggest he was so involved. See R. Farmer, *Satan Inthron'd in his Chair of Pestilence*, London 1657, 20.

[93] See Hill, *TWTUD*, 248 seq. and Knox, *Enthusiasm*, 164:
> There was some affectation . . . of treating Naylerism as an independent sect . . . denying that the Scriptures are the word of God, and esteeming their own speakings to be of as great authority . . . that Jesus Christ inhabits their flesh as man . . . *All that is only, at worst, an unfriendly interpretation of early Quaker language,* unchecked as it was by any tradition of authority, any system of theology (emphasis mine).

[94] For the same expressions in other letters by Friends see Braithwaite, *BQ* 249 n.4; 105 n.1. Bittle's study shows that leading Friends secreted such letters at the time of Nayler's arrest. See also Mack, 'Gender and Spirituality', 42, on erotic and maternal, holding and feeding' imagery in correspondence with Fell and Fox.

[95] Cf. Nuttall's appendix 'Messianic Language in Early Quakerism' in *The Holy Spirit in Puritan Faith and Experience,* Oxford 1946 181 seq.

[96] On Bristol Friends disowning Nayler see Barbour and Roberts, *EQW,* 184. Farmer's *Satan Inthron'd* (1657), the anonymous works *A True Relation of the Life, Conversation, Examination . . . of James Naylor* (1657) and *The Quakers Quaking* as also William Grigge's *The Quakers Jesus* (1658) were among many descriptions of the events.

[97] The literature on this topic is vast and varies in its slant. See as introduction Reay, *QER,* 54 seq.; Bittle, 'The Trial of James Nayler and Religious Toleration in England', *QH* 73 (1984), 29-33 and *James Nayler,* final chapters; A. Fraser, *Cromwell, Our Chief of Men,* St. Albans 1975, 591 seq., 598.

[98] Fraser, *Cromwell,* 592; Braithwaite, *BQ,* 264 seq.

[99] Other sources tell of John Stranger in the lead, Dorcas Erbury and an Isle of Ely man (Samuel Cater) in the rear. Ely, according to Edwards in *Gangraena* was the 'island of errors and sectaries' and had its share of preaching women (p. 84). *The Quakers Quaking* (see n. 96) tells of
> The most just and deserved punishment . . . of James Nayler, together with the confessions of his associates who were
>
> | | |
> |---|---|
> | Timothy Wedlock | Hannah Stranger |
> | Thomas Symons | Martha Symons |
> | John Stranger | Dorcas Erbury |

[100] John Deacon also wrote *The Grand Imposter Examined* (1656), which was translated into Dutch. Such translations account for the damage done to Quakerism's reputation abroad, and British Friends received adverse reports from Holland and Barbados.

[101] Fogelklou, *James Nayler,* 220. Ann Cargill (Gargill) was alleged to have knelt before Fox when he first went to London and to have called him 'son of the living God' (so Daniel Phillips, *Vindiciae Veritatis,* London 1703, 41). She was allegedly Ranterish in spirit and later it was claimed she had infiltrated herself into the Friends' Meetings. She published several works in 1656 and came to be disowned by the Friends.

[102] In 1678 Robert Rich published *Hidden Things Come to Light.* On this, on Rich's religion and his later activities see Bittle, *James Nayler,* 99 seq.; Smith, *Perfection Proclaimed,* 149, 347; Nuttall, 'The Last of James Nayler, Robert Rich and "The Church of the First Born"', *FQ* 60 (1985), 527-534.

103 See also Maureen Bell, 'Mary Westwood Quaker Publisher', *Publishing History* 23 (1988), 36 seq.

104 Bell also writes of Mary Westwood (p. 31) that 'some of her publishing
✳   concerned the very elements within Quakerism which Fox and his supporters tended to want to suppress'.

105 Bell, 'Mary Westwood', p. 36 referring to the findings of Kenneth Carroll in particular and see also his study of *John Perrot, Early Quaker Schismatic, JFHS* Suppl. 33, 1970.

106 Cherry, 'Enthusiasm and Madness', 9.

107 Carroll, 'Elizabeth Harris,' in *QH* 57 (1968), 110. He also noted George Fox's silence about this Elizabeth, concerning whom there are hints that she became a Perrotonian. In a conversation with Kenneth Carroll on 2.8.'89 he told me that he would now modify his reference to 'evidence' of Fox's mistrust of women, but that subsequent events did suggest that some shift had occurred. On this period see also J. F. Maclear, 'Quakerism and the End of the Interregnum', *Church History* 19 (1950), 240-270.

108 Knox, *Enthusiasm*, 161. Cf. Braithwaite, *BQ*, 243-251.

109 This is also the view of Maureen Bell. Her study of Mary Westwood was published before my own article on 'The women around James Nayler, Quaker: a matter of emphasis' appeared in print (*Religion*, 1990), but after I had completed the study.

110 On Mildred as 'Ranter' see Fogelklou, *James Nayler*, 233, 429; Braithwaite, *Beginnings*, 269 seq.; Kenneth Carroll (*John Perrot*, 42) suggests that John Perrot's 1660 epistle *To all which wander from the true Order* was directed at Judy and Mildred.

111 Mack, 'Gender and Spirituality', 51. The final quotation is from S. M. Wyntjes, 'Women in the Reformation Era' in R. Bridenthal, C. Koonz (eds.), *Becoming Visible: Women in European History*, Boston 1977, 165.

Chapter II   *(pages 43-74)*

'WOMEN'S SPEAKING JUSTIFIED'

1 J. Denham, *News from Colchester*, 1659; 'The Four-Legg'd Quaker' in H. Playford (ed.), *Wit and Wisdom*, 1682; T. H. Banks (ed.), *Poetical Works of Sir John Denham*, New Haven 1928, 91 seq.; W. de Sola Pinta and A. E. Rodway (eds.), *The Common Muse: An Anthology of Popular British Ballad Poetry, 15th-20th Century*, Harmondsworth 1965, 167 seq.; Smith, *Antiquakeriana*, 147; D. Blamires, 'Quakers Observed in Verse and Prose' in *A Quaker Miscellany for Edward Milligan*, 18 seq. See also Fraser, *TWV*, 419 on the 1680s chapbook *Loves Masterpiece*, where a Quaker bids his mistress retire with him to the coal hole: 'There only the light within will shine'.

2 Knox, *Enthusiasm*, 462.

3 Dorothy Ludlow, 'Shaking Patriarchy's Foundations', 113, 99. The Friend Mary Howgill was branded 'distracted' and Ann Blaykling (once described as 'no woman but a man') tried to organise Sunday working and the payment of tithes (but refusal of taxes). She was pronounced 'out of unity'.

Of the fifteen 'chided' women Phyllis Mack refers to (*WFC*, 51) most
originated from the south of England.

[4] Cf. Ralph Farmer, *Satan Enthron'd*, 10 seq. and K. L. Carroll's balanced
assessment of Martha in 'Martha Simmonds: A Quaker Enigma', *JFHS* 53
(1972), 31-52; H. J. Cadbury (ed.), *Letters to William Dewsbury and Others*,
Suppl. to *JFHS* 22, London 1948, 41.

[5] John Knox, *First Blast Against the Monstrous Regiment of Women*, Geneva 1558.
For similar works of the period see K. Rogers, *The Troublesome Helpmate*,
136 seq.; Greaves, 'Foundation-builders', in *Triumph Over Silence*, 75 seq.;
D. Underdown, 'The Taming of the Scold' = chp. 4 of A. Fletcher, J. Stevenson
(eds.), *Order and Disorder in Early Modern England*, Cambridge 1984.

[6] *Jane Anger Her Protection for Women to Defend Them Against the Scandalous
Reportes of a Late Surfeiting Lover*, London 1589. This was probably a reply to
Thomas Orwin's *Surfeit in Love* of the year before. Anger's points were
echoed in Joan Sharpe's Postcript to Sowernam's *Esther Hath Hang'd Haman*
1617), in Henricus Cornelius Agrippa's *The Glorie of Women*, London 1652,
1-9, by the Quaker Elizabeth Bathurst and many others.

[7] *Mouzel*, 1617, 2.

[8] Mary Astell in the 1670 work *Some Reflections on Marriage*.

[9] John Robinson, *A Justification of Separation from the Church of England*, 1610,
pp. 150, 206, 237. On women's lack of freedom in religious groups at this
time see Irwin, *Womanhood*, 162 seq.; Greaves, *Triumph Over Silence*, 7 seq.,
83 seq.; Sprunger, 'God's Powerful Army', 51 seq.

[10] Richard Mather, *Church Government and Church Covenant Discussed*, London
1643, 60.

[11] Baillie, *A Dissuasive from the Errours of the Time*, London 1645, 110 seq. John
Cotton responded in *The Way of the Congregational Churches Cleared*, London
1648, 11, 19:

> God hath expressly forbidden them all place, speech and power in the
> Church . . . the female sex, and nonage fall short of some powers,
> which Christ hath given to the brotherhood.

[12] Writing on the education of a daughter, Sir Ralph Verney maintained that
St Paul would have regarded a woman with literary pretensions as being just
as shameful as one who spoke in the Church. See F. F. Verney, *Memoirs of the
Verney Family During the Civil War*, 4 vols., 1892, vol. iii, 72.

[13] Brathwaite, *The English Gentlewoman*, 82.

[14] Makin, *An Essay to Revive the Antient Education of Gentlewomen*, London 1673.
Cf. also Mary Astell's *A Serious Proposal to the Ladies*, 1694 (Ferguson, *FF*,
187 seq.).

[15] Fox, *Journal*, 24 seq.

[16] Irwin, *Womanhood*, 202.

[17] Thomas Edwards, *Gangraena*, 1646, 85.

[18] The passage occurs in writings by Fox of 1658 and 1671, in Farnworth's *A
Woman Forbidden to Speak* of 1655, in Fell's *Womens Speaking Justified*, in
Livingstone and Dewsbury's *Truth Owned and Deceit Denyed* of 1667, in
Thomas Camm's *The Fulfilling of the Promise* of 1689, Barclay's *Apology for
the True Christian Divinity* . . . (x. 27) of 1678 and in other Quaker writings.

[19] George Herbert listed this among proverbs. See Fraser, *TWV*, 136 n. 10.

[20] *FPT*, 87; Fox, *The Great Mistery of the Whore* . . ., 187 seq.; Barbour, *QPE*, 132 seq.

[21] P. Toon (ed.), *Puritans, the Millenium and the Future of Israel*; D. S. Katz, *Philo-Semitism and the Re-admission of the Jews to England 1603-1655*, Oxford 1982, chps. 3-4; N. I. Matar, 'The Idea of the Restoration of the Jews in English Protestant Thought, 1661-1701', *Harvard Theological Review* 78 (1985), 115-148; H. J. Cadbury, 'Hebraica and the Jews in Early Quaker Interest' in E. H. Brinton (ed.), *Children of Life*, London 1938, 155 seq. Margaret Fell wrote an open letter *For Rabbi Manasseth-ben-Israel* (1656) and *A Loving Salutation to the Seed of Abraham*. The Hebrew translation (1658) of the latter may have been by Spinoza, and his earliest publication.

✳ [22] Even John Bunyan doubted this of women. The inference, it seems, was from 1 Corinthians 11:7.

[23] The debate about women and souls interested Pepys (against), John Donne and Ben Jonson (for). See H. J. Cadbury, *Friendly Heritage*, Friends Publ. Co., 1972, 244-5. I am indebted to Malcolm Thomas, librarian at Friends House, for drawing my attention to this book. See also Mack, 'Gender and Spirituality' on the nature of personhood in Quaker understanding, on the expression of male and female characteristics in *both* sexes and in the private and public spheres.

[24] I have used the 1667 version, with Postscript. See Trevett (ed.), *Womens Speaking Justified and Other Seventeenth Century Quaker Writings About Women*, Invicta Press, Ashford, Kent, 1989.

[25] Before Margaret Fell there were many examples of women using scripture against those who used scripture against women. Her own work did so more thoroughly than others, however. I cannot agree with Isabel Ross (*MF*, 201) who saw in *Womens Speaking* the first post-Reformation work by a woman to plead for the spiritual equality of women.

[26] Brailsford (*QW*, 46-7) quotes Thomas Holme(s) who wrote of Margaret as a nursing mother and one

> who feeds the hungry with good things but the fat with judgement, who kills and slays the living and raises the dead . . . judgement is committed to thy hands . . . Power in heaven and earth is given to thee.

The epithet 'a mother in Israel' was also applied to married, middle-aged Quaker women. Its biblical origins show it could have overtones of assertiveness as well as of comfort and nurturing – cf. Judges 5:7 of the prophet, judge and stirrer-up of armies Deborah. See also B. R. Dailey, 'The Husbands of Margaret Fell: An Essay on Religious Metaphor and Social Change', *The Seventeenth Century*, 2 (1987), 55-71 and Mack, 'Gender and Spirituality' in *WFC*, 53-56.

[27] R. A. Houlbrooke, *The English Family 1450-1700*, London 1983, 23.

[28] In 1657 she requested Gerard Roberts to send her writing abroad to thwart Thomas Fell, 'lest he light of it and prevent the service of it'.

[29] Bonnelyn Young Kunze, *The Family, Social and Religious Life of Margaret Fell*, unpublished D.Phil. study, University of Rochester, New York, 1986, 7, 392.

30 This was a common observation. Cf. Richard Ferrer, *The Worth of Women*, London 1662, 11-12 and John Milton on Adam's culpability in *Paradise Lost*, x.

31 *Womens Speaking Justified*, 3, 6-7.

32 Elizabeth Bathurst, *The Sayings of Women* . . ., 1683. Cf. Livingstone and Dewsbury *Truth Owned and Deceit Denyed*, 1667.

33 Fox, Nayler, William James and others published advice to merchants. Thomas Lawson in 1660 issued *An Appeal to the Parliament . . . that there may not be a Beggar in England*, calling for the establishment of labour offices in every parish. John Bellers deplored the exploitation of the poor and set up workhouses. Karl Marx (*Das Kapital*[2], i, 515) paid tribute to Bellers.

34 Reay, *QER*, 20-26; Barbour *QPE* chp. 3; Punshon, *A Portrait in Grey* chp. 5; A. Cole, 'The Social Origins of the Early Friends', *JFHS* 38 (1957), 99-118; R. T. Vann, 'Quakerism and the Social Structure in the Interregnum', *PP* 43 (1969), 71-91; J. J. Hurwick, 'The Social Origins of the Early Quakers', *PP* 48 (1970), 156-162 and Vann's reply, *idem.* pp. 162 seq. Elizabeth Hooton hoped the King would arrange return of some of her property, 'that I may have a horse to ride in my old age' (Manners, *Elizabeth Hooton*, 60).

35 W. Crouch, *Posthuma Christiana*, 1660, 23. Cf. Braithwaite, *BQ*, 320 and Barclay, *Letters of Early Friends*, 299.

36 Hubberthorne, *Works*, 219. Minute Books of Meetings do record disapprovingly that some Friends applied for parish relief or begged abroad. Cf. Braithwaite, *SPQ*, 560, 566.

37 Fox, *Epistle to the Governor and Assembly of Barbadoes*, 1671 and *To the Ministers, Teachers and Priests . . . in Barbadoes*, 1672. In later centuries Quaker women were much involved in the struggle against slavery. See M. Hope Bacon, *Mothers of Feminism* and F. B. Tolles (ed.), *Slavery and 'The Woman Question'. Lucretia Mott's Diary*, Suppl. to *JFHS* 23, 1952.

38 *Journal*. 598 seq. and an epistle of 1673.

39 These Minutes were published in *JFHS* 37 (1940), 22-24, after discovery among Munster Quarterly Meeting papers.

40 Jane Sharp was the first woman to publish a textbook in English on midwifery (*The Midwives Book of the Whole Art of Midwifery Discover'd*, 1671) and in 1687 the Roman Catholic midwife Elizabeth Marshall Cellier (tried for high treason during her colourful life) advocated *A Scheme for the Foundation of a Royal Hospital . . . a Corporation of Skilful Midwives*. *The Midwife Unmask'd* (1680) was one of a number of works written against this 'she-champion and midwife'.

41 By contrast, the Hertford County Records show that a midwife might be paid 1s 6d from parish funds for her services (Clark, *WLW*, 279).

42 Grateful families of means gave gifts and often substantial sums to midwives and wet nurses. The Fell family made such gifts. See N. Penney (ed.), *The Household Account Book of Sarah Fell*, Cambridge 1920, 241, 259, 439, 473, 675 *et passim*.

43 *Testimony to the Life and Death of Mary Batt*, 1683, 1-3.

44 *JFHS* 33 (1936), 32 seq. Rapparees (spelt rapperies in the original text) were Irish irregular soldiers. For examples of sexual assault suffered by women Friends see Craig Horle, *The Quakers and the English Legal System*, 127 seq.

[45] T. Mardy Rees, *History of the Quakers in Wales,* Carmarthen 1925, 46.
[46] *The Journal of John Banks,* 1684, 101. Imprisonments after *The Quaker Act* of 1662 fully stretched the Friends' system of oversight and care in prisons.
[47] See Scheffler, 'Prison Writings'; Besse, *Sufferings* ii 399-420; Braithwaite, *Beginnings,* 428 seq. Fox was displeased at the extent of Perrot's generosity. See Carroll, *John Perrot,* 19, 52.
[48] On Bridget Fell's letter to her mother see I. Ross, 'Bridget Draper née Fell', *JFHS* 35 (1938), 43 seq.
[49] B. Carré, 'Early Quaker Women in Lancaster and Lancashire', 45, 49 in Mullett [ed.], *Early Lancaster Friends.*
[50] *The History of the Life of Thomas Ellwood,* London 1714, 126-7. The 'motherly woman' in early Quakerism is surely a phenomenon deserving of research! An Anne Travers later kept a Friends' 'woman's school' at Chiswick, to which Margaret Fell Rous was minded to send her daughter.
[51] *An Account of the Travels, Sufferings and Persecutions of Barbara Blaugdone,* 1691, 97, 12, 27 seq.
[52] Brailsford, *QW,* 115-131; Braithwaite, *BQ* 420 seq.; Fraser, *TWV,* 412-417; F. A. Budge, *Annals of the Early Friends,* London 1877, 188 seq.
[53] Braithwaite, *BQ,* 423.
[54] Bayly was formerly a Baptist. As a Friend he ministered and travelled extensively. After his death Mary married John Cross in 1678. They settled in South Carolina. Her will indicates that like other Friends of this period Mary was a slave owner.
[55] Braithwaite, *BQ,* 401, 575; *SPQ,* 45 seq.; L. Rickman, 'Esther Biddle and her Mission to Louis xiv', *JFHS* 47 (1955), 38-45. See also Elaine Hobby in S. Sellars (ed.), *Feminist Criticism,* Wheatsheaf Press 1991 (forthcoming).
[56] Charles Tyzack gives an account of later and more successful Friends' contacts there, in *Friends to China,* York 1988.
[57] J. M. Douglas in *JFHS* 48 (1956). Mary Westwood published such petitions for the Friends, and herself signed them. See Bell, 'Mary Westwood', 5, 24, 41.
[58] *The Conway Letters* (see Chp. 1 n. 81), 412-3. Anne Finch was related to the Countess of Winchelsea of the same name. See also T. L. Underwood, 'Quakers and the Royal Society of London in the Seventeenth Century', *Notes and Records of the Royal Society of London* 31 (1976), pp. 136-8.
[59] Maria Webb, *The Penns and Peningtons of the Seventeenth Century,* London 1867, 2-3. The earnest Quaker woman figures in later literature, such as the neatly suicidal Quakeress of George Borrow's *Lavengro,* who allowed her blood to issue into a bucket laid by for the purpose. See Blamires, 'Quakers Observed', 18 seq.
[60] W. Sewel, *History of the Rise . . . ,* 71-2. Reay, *QER,* 53; Ross, *MF,* 52, 60, 67, 100. Miles was certainly often away from home.
[61] Braithwaite, *SPQ,* 552. Born in the seventeenth century, Luke Cock flourished in the eighteenth.
[62] *A Short Account of Alice Hayes* in *The Friends Library* series vol. 2, Philadelphia 1838, pp. 68 seq. especially p. 74; C. La Courreye Blecki, 'Alice Hayes and Mary Penington: Personal Identity Within the Traditions of Quaker Spiritual Autobiography', *Quaker History* 65 (1976), 24. Alice wrote *A Legacy: or Widows Mite* and she led a protest against tithes.

63 *Piety Promoted* i, 631-2.

64 Clark, *WLW,* 33; Fraser, *TWV,* 426; H. T. Mennell, *The Charitable Trusts of Joan Dant, William Seaton and Joseph Smith,* London n.d. After the disbursement of £3425 in legacies, the rest was given into a Trust.

65 Lloyd, *Social History,* 146; Barbour and Roberts, *EQW,* 27 seq. and David Runyon's Appendix, 567-76; L. M. Wright, *The Literary Life of the Early Friends 1650-1725,* New York 1932; Bell, 'Mary Westwood'.

66 It was not unusual for a woman to take over her father's or husband's business. See M. Bell, 'Hannah Allen and the Development of a Puritan Publishing Business, 1646-51', *Publishing History* 26 (1989) 5 seq., 44 seq.; Clark, *WLW,* 161-167. On Giles Calvert, the brother of Martha Simmonds, see A. E. Terry, 'Giles Calvert: Mid Seventeenth Century English Bookseller and Publisher', *JFHS* 35 (1938), 45-49; R. S. Mortimer, 'First Century of Quaker Printers', *JFHS* 40 (1948), 37-49; T. P. O'Mally, 'The Press and Quakerism 1653-1659', *JFHS* 54 (1979), 169-184; Bell, 'Mary Westwood'. Despite her activities on the Friends' behalf it is possible that Westwood herself was not a Quaker. Just as possible (as Bell observed) is the 'disappearance' of Mary from the Friends' record of their history, when this was 'cleaned up' in the last decade of the seventeenth century.

67 *Piety Promoted . . . Testimonies to Anne Downer Whitehead,* 1686, 8. Mary Moore, daughter of Thomas Camm, was also anxious not to disrupt male ministry. She would not have her father summoned to her sick bed (*Piety Promoted* i, 441).

68 Braithwaite, *SPQ,* 360 seq.; Barbour and Roberts, *EQW* 469. There were some common Meetings from 1890, but men and women did not transact Yearly Meeting business together until 1896. It was in that year, too, that women first functioned in *Meeting for Sufferings,* which had been a representative body since 1677 and became the parent body of Quakerism. See E. Isichei, *Victorian Quakers,* Oxford 1970, 107-110, 167.

69 Braithwaite, *SPQ,* 541.

70 We find such language in Fox's *Concerning Sons and Daughters and Prophetesses Speaking* of 1661, in Fell's *Womens Speaking Justified* and elsewhere. Cf. also the ongoing defence of women's ministries in Daniel Phillips *Vindiciae Veritatis* and Ann Docwra's *An Epistle of Love and Good Advice to . . . the Old Royalists,* London 1683.

Chapter III   *(pages 75-131)*
'THIS MY FRIEND'

1 L. Stone, *The Family, Sex and Marriage in England 1500-1800,* 217. For criticism of Stone's method see M. Anderson, *Approaches to the History of the Western Family 1500-1914,* London 1980, 39-45. There is disagreement about when exactly patriarchy decayed, companionate marriage emerged and individualism developed. See also C. Durston, *The Family and the English Revolution,* London 1989; R. Houlbrooke (ed.), *English Family Life (1576-1716),* London 1989; P. Earle, *The Making of the English Middle Class,*

London 1989; Underdown, *Revel, Riot and Rebellion*, 10 seq., 38 seq., 98-102 *et passim*; K. M. Davies, 'The Sacred Condition of Spirituality. How Original were Puritan Doctrines of Marriage?' *Social History* 5 (1977), 563-580.

2 See C. Bridenbaugh, *Vexed and Troubled Englishmen 1590-1642*, Oxford 1967, 62. On marriage, divorce, domestic conduct books, misogyny, etc., see C. L. Powell, *English Domestic Relations*; K. M. Rogers, *The Troublesome Helpmate*; A. B. and C. M. Wallis Chapman, *The Status of Women Under the English Law*, London 1909; C. S. Kenney, *The History of the Law of England as to the Effects of Marriage on Property and on the Wife's Legal Capacity*, London 1879; P. Laslett (ed.), *Family Life and Illicit Love in Earlier Generations*, Cambridge 1977; Thompson, *Women in Stuart England*, 162-169; D. Underdown, 'The Taming of the Scold' in A. Fletcher, J. Stevenson (eds.), *Order and Disorder in Early Modern England*, Cambridge 1984, chp. 4. See also M. Todd, 'Humanists, Puritans and the Spiritualized Household', *Church History* 49 (1980), 18-34. In his *Two Treatises of Government* (1689) John Locke challenged some prevailing views on the relation between family and state patriarchy.

3 Gouge, *Of Domesticall Duties* 1626, 160.

4 P. Aries, *Centuries of Childhood*, Harmondsworth 1962, 390. Parts of Stone's work (e.g. pp. 79-80) on the century pre 1740 show a distinct *lack* of sociability.

5 J. O'Faolain, L. Martines, *Not in God's Image: Women in History*, 208-212 on Luther and Calvin.

6 John Milton, *Prose Works* i, 367. Milton argued in his *Doctrine and Discipline of Divorce Restored to the Good of Both Sexes* (1643) that incompatibility of minds should be taken into account.

7 Irwin, *Womanhood in Radical Protestantism*, 105-111; Powell, *English Domestic Relations*, 61-100. Ecclesiastically granted annulments of marriage were available in some cases. There was debate about polygamy (*A Dialogue of Polygamy*, London 1657) and about the prohibited degrees of consanguinity too (*Little Nonsuch*, London 1646).

8 See the works cited in nn. 2-3; Fraser, *TWV*, 12.

9 Fraser, *TWV* chapters 1-3; Thompson, *Women in Stuart England*, 116-120.

10 Francis (writing in 1656) is quoted in M. Ashley, *The Stuarts in Love*, London 1963, 19 and Dorothy in Thompson, *Women in Stuart England*, 116.

11 Hannah Woolley, *The Gentlewomans Companion . . . wherunto is added a Guide for Cook-Maids and all others that go into Service*, 1675, 104.

12 See O. C. Feucht *et al.*, *Sex and the Church* (on the Lutheran Tradition), St Louis 1961, 84. I owe the reference to R. E. and R. Dobash, *Violence Against Wives*, London 1980, 226 n. 35. In the opinions of Dobash the position of married women was at its lowest in the sixteenth and seventeenth centuries. Contrast R. Hamilton, *The Liberation of Women: A Study of Patriarchy and Capitalism*, London 1978, 64-75 on the effects of the rise of Protestantism on women.

13 Cf. Gouge, *Of Domesticall Duties,³* 1634, 220 seq.

14 From *Poems on Several Occasions*, London 1703. Cf. also M. Slater, 'Marriage: the female perspective' in *Family Life in Seventeenth Century England: the Verneys*, London 1984, 78 seq.

[15] Ferguson, *FF*, 84–101.

[16] In *The Underside of History* (p. 604) the American Elise Boulding (who happens also to be a Quaker) wrote of the 19th century that 'the delights of family life were all very well for Quaker women . . . [they] had other spheres of action too'.

[17] *Esther Hath Hang'd Haman*, 24. See also John Addy, *Sin and Society in the Seventeenth Century*, London 1989, and the rise of post-Restoration 'bawdy-courts'.

[18] See Fox, *Journal*, 524 seq. (for 1668) and Braithwaite *SPQ* chps. 9 and 13 for the 'settling' of Monthly Meetings.

[19] See K. L. Carroll, 'John Perrot, Early Quaker Schismatic', Suppl. 33 to *JFHS*, 1970 and Lloyd, *QSH*, 21 seq. 'Hat-honour' figured in the controversy and the Perrot-Fox divisions have echoes in Samuel Mucklow's *The Spirit of the Hat* (London 1673) which triggered much of the later Wilkinson-Story debate.

[20] John Wilkinson and John Story lent their names to the controversy and schism which emerged in the 1670s. It will be referred to later. See Lloyd *QSH* chapter 2 and Baumann, *Let Your Words Be Few*, chapter 9.

[21] Robert Barclay, *The Anarchy of the Ranters* 1676, 68. This work discussed the power of Quaker assemblies to examine and make decisions (pp. 18–31, 66–74) and it castigated those arrogant spirits who

> rather than give up their own wills, will study to make rents and divisions, not sparing the flock.

[22] William Penn, *Select Works*, London 1971, iv, 439. See also L. Ford, 'William Penn's Views on Women: Subjects of Friendship', *QH* 72 (1983), 75–102. Quakerism's opponents seized on the Wilkinson-Story opposition to the women and the Friends' 'excommunication' of the two. But as Daniel Phillips observed, that opposition was not the simple cause of the Friends' disfavour (*Vindiciae Veritatis*, 164–168).

[23] Bauman, *Let Your Words Be Few*, chps. 8–9; Vann, *SDEQ*, 99–101.

[24] Mortimer, 'Warnings and Prophecies', *JFHS* 44 (1952), 17 seq.; Barbour, *QPE*, 234 seq.

[25] Vann, *SDEQ*, 104; Lloyd, *QSH* chp. 4; Reay, *QER*, 88 who observes:

> If we were to concentrate on the political impact of the Quaker movement during the Interregnum, the crucial names would be Hubberthorne, Burrough, George Fox the younger, and George Bishop, not that of George Fox. But most of these men would be dead a decade later. George Fox lived on.

[26] Reay, *QER* chp. 6; Braithwaite, *SPQ*, chps. 9–10; Vann, *SDEQ*, 116, 125–200.

[27] *SPQ*, 273. Cf. M. M. Dunn, 'Women of Light' in C. R. Bekin and M. B. Morton (eds.), *Women of America*, Boston 1979, 121:

> Some historians have assumed that women's meetings were established to give women enough authority to keep them happy but not enough to make them powerful.

[28] In 1677 in London 'unreasoned persons and forward lasses' were invading the women's gallery at Gracechurch Street Meeting while down below 'forward young lads and apprentices' were imposing themselves 'among

some young maids which commonly sits on that side too'. The *Six Weeks Meeting* therefore recommended that the sexes be seated separately. See I. L. Edwards, 'The Women Friends of London: the Two Weeks and Box Meetings' *JFHS* 47 (1955), 12.

[29] B. Carré, 'Early Quaker Women . . .', 45 seq.

[30] One had existed in Ireland since 1679.

[31] See also Isichei, 'Organisation and Power in the Society of Friends', 186, n.1; Dunn, 'Women of Light', 121.

[32] In *An Epistle for True Love* . . . (see n. 38 below) Anne Goddard Whithead insisted that 'a marriage hath an equal concern in the woman as in the man' and Mary Elson countered the grudging concession that Women's Meetings might perhaps be justifiable in London, but not elsewhere (pp. 6, 13). Feeling beyond the Society is illustrated in the *Novelty or a Government of Women distinct from Men* (c. 1694) by the now disaffected former Quaker William Mather. This pointed to precedents like the Amazons.

[33] Vann, *SDEQ*, 104; Braithwaite, *SPQ*, 274. It was difficult to establish Women's Meetings in some areas.

[34] 'Arbitrary commands' was one of its themes (pp. 17-18). Many more publications from both sides followed in the 1670s. See Braithwaite, *SPQ*, 293-295.

[35] *Strength in Weakness Manifest: the Life* . . . *[of] Elizabeth Stirredge*, London 1711, 77, 84, 196. Elizabeth came from Thornbury near Bristol.

[36] *Strength in Weakness Manifest*, 70 seq. Seventeenth century women, not least Quaker ones, were familiar with such comments. Sarah Tims had appeared at Banbury Assizes in 1655, after eleven weeks of imprisonment, beatings and abuse. Arguing that she had broken no law she refused to give sureties of good behaviour, though the result would be re-imprisonment:

> John Austine, called Mayor answered, that sweeping the house and washing the dishes was the first point of law to her (or words to that effect), so sent her back to the prison again, she not being charged with breach of any law

(Richard Farnworth, Ann Audland, Jane Waugh *et al.*, *The Saints Testimony Finishing through Sufferings*, 1655, 8).

[37] Fox, *Journal*, 667. It was in areas like Slaughterford, known for clothing manufacture and where there was a history of religous radicalism, that Quakerism had found success. See Underdown, *Revel, Riot and Rebellion*, 250.

[38] Bonnelyn Young Kunze, *op. cit.*, Abstract p. v and chp. 4.

[39] *An Epistle for True Love, Unity and Order*, London 1680, 5, 11-13. Women Friends continued to write tracts and epistles for the remainder of the century. Among later writers were Abigail Fisher, Theophila Townsend and Dorcas Dole. Quaker women's writing has great flashes of wit and insight, but like Dorothy Ludlow I would have to concede that much of the corpus is 'monotonous in style, unimaginative in content, incoherent in syntax' ('Shaking Patriarchy's Foundations', 112), indeed much of it is as little inspiring as the work of most of the male writers. It is important, nevertheless, for understanding female Quaker piety in this period.

[40] Banks, *To all the Womens Meetings*, 181-82. See also *The Life of John Banks*, 1712, 182 seq.

[41] Penn, 'Just Measures in an Epistle of Peace and Love', in *Select Works* vii, 591.

[42] It reprimanded any who would 'discountenance' such Meetings. In 1691, 1707 and 1744, however, Yearly Meeting was still expressing support for Women's Meetings. See Mullett, *Radical Religious Movements*, 120 seq; Braithwaite, *SPQ* 274.

[43] See I. L. Edwards, 'The Women Friends of London', *JFHS* 47 (1955), 3-4; Braithwaite, *SPQ*, 272; Mary Elson, *An Epistle for True Love*, 9-10. In an address *From the Womens Meeting at the Bull and Mouthe*, 1685, Mary Elson, Martha Fisher, Anne Goddard Whitehead and others wrote a spirited, scripture-based defence of women as teachers of women and doers of good works, directed against those who thought their Meetings 'an idol and an image'.

[44] On Lady Conway see chapter 1 and index. The last portion of this estate was not sold until 1923.

[45] H. Barbour, 'Quaker Prophetesses and Mothers in Israel' in C. and J. Stoneburner (eds.), *The Influence of Quaker Women in American History* (Studies in Women and Religion 21), New York 1986, 57-80. The majority of early Quaker women writers produced just one tract or prophetic 'proclamation' of c. 8pp in length. Only 8% of the writings by women debated theology, while 21% of those by men did so (Barbour, p. 63). Margaret Fell excepted,

> the nine Quaker women who published five or more tracts were little known as preachers or leaders.

Sarah Blackbury (Blackberry, Blackborrow), Ann Docwra, Esther Biddle and Rebecca Travers were among the other women writers.

[46] Published in London in 1644: see pp. 58-64. The essence of its 1644-5 form of 'mutual declaration' was used by the Friends.

[47] For precedents in support of Quaker practice see W. Horle, *The Quakers and the English Legal System 1660-1688*, Philadelphia 1988, 234-5; Lloyd, *QSH*, 51; Braithwaite, *BQ*, 144 seq.

[48] Horle, *The Quakers and the English Legal System*, 234, 237-8 on appearances before ecclesiastical courts. For examples of other difficulties see I. Edwards, 'Early Discipline', *JFHS* 31 (1934), 71-76.

[49] On Corbett as legal counsel for the Friends see Horle, *op. cit.*, 190-195, 236.

[50] See Lloyd, *QSH* 50 seq. and n. 15.

[51] N. Penney (ed.), *Experiences in the Life of Mary Penington*, Philadelphia and London, 1911, 25-28 *et passim*. See also R. Hamilton *The Liberation of Women*, 64-75.

[52] See Ross, *MF*, 213.

[53] See Ross, *MF*, 219; Brailsford, *QW*, 58; B. R. Dailey, 'The Husbands of Margaret Fell; an Essay on Religious Metaphor and Social Change', *The Seventeenth Century* 2 (1987), 55-71.

[54] *Journal*, 557. Anne Downer Whitehead was fifteen years the senior of George Whitehead, who was effectively successor to Fox.

[55] *The Spirit of the Hat*, 42-43.

[56] See J. H. Cadbury, 'Interrupted Correspondence of William Penn', *Pennsylvania Magazine of History and Biography* 70 (1946), 354-356. But cf. Kunze's discussion in her thesis of a possible late pregnancy and miscarriage for Margaret (pp. 78-81).

[57] Kunze, *op. cit.*, 13, 26 seq.; A. Clark in the Introduction to N. Penney (ed.), *The Household Account Book of Sarah Fell*, xxviii-xxxii.

[58] Brailsford, *QW*, 286 seq.

[59] Isabel Ross *MF*, 290, 298-9, suggested the probable date for this epistle *From Our Country Womens Meeting in Lancashire to be Dispersed Abroad*. It has been published by M. D. Speizman and J. C. Kronick as 'A Seventeenth Century Quaker Women's Declaration' in *Signs: Journal of Women in Culture and Society* 1 (1975), 231-245 and again in S. Mosher Stuard's 'Womens Witnessing: A New Departure' in *WFC*, 25-28.

[60] Not untypical was the Friend Grace Brown, whose husband Thomas 'buried her decently'. She died aged forty-eight, after thirty years of marriage, in the year 1682. Five of their eight children had preceded her to the grave.

[61] For the examples I've quoted see D. Bower, J. Knight (eds.), *Plain Country Friends: the Quakers of Wooldale*, 13 on Henry and Catherine Jackson; Isaac Penington, *Works*, 1681, i, 406 and *Piety Promoted, Testimonies to Ann Whitehead*, 1686, 9. Anne had had a previous marriage to Benjamin Greenwell. Cf. also Thomas Ellwood's statement about his marriage day, which stands today in the document *Church Government* of the Religious Society of Friends (section 882 on marriage):

> We sensibly felt the Lord with us joining us, the sense whereof remained with us all our lifetime, and was of good service and very comfortable to us on all occasions.

[62] *See* L. Ford, 'William Penn's Views on Women: Subjects of Friendship', *QH* 72 (1983), 98-100. A Minute of the Bristol Men's Meeting for November 1695 discusses 'clearness' for the marriage of the sixty-one year old William Penn and the twenty-four year old heiress Hannah Callowhill (*Minute Book of the Men's Meetings of the Society of Friends in Bristol 1686-1704*, Bristol Record Society xxx, 1977, 101). Hannah bore him seven further children, not all of which survived. She was much loved in Pennsylvania. Hannah took care of his affairs and was given responsibilities never accorded to Gulielma. See also H. J. Cadbury, 'Hannah Callowhill and Penn's Second Marriage', *The Pennsylvania Magazine of History and Biography* 81 (1957), 76-82.

[63] Penn, *Some Fruits of Solitude*, 1693 in *Select Works* iii, 362:

> The satisfaction of our senses is low, short and transient. But the mind gives a more raised and extended pleasure, and is capable of a happiness founded upon reason.

Cf. also Jacques Tual, 'Sexual Equality and Conjugal Harmony: the Way to Celestial Bliss. A view of Early Quaker Matrimony', *JFHS* 55 (1988), 161-174, esp. pp. 165 seq. On Gulielma Penn see *Piety Promoted* i, 117 seq.

[64] Penn's legacy to women was a mixed one, as Linda Ford reminds us. He was very much the patriarch and a stern Puritan (as some of his legislation indicated), but his Quakerism and his marriage to Gulielma nevertheless led him to further 'a new sort of Protestant marriage . . . new attitudes towards wives and women in general' (pp. 101 seq.). Gulielma had at least eight pregnancies.

[65] The declaration presently used by the woman Friend on marriage is (or is similar to) the following:

Friends, I take this my Friend XY to be my husband, promising with God's help to be unto him a loving and faithful wife, so long as we both on earth shall live.

It was not the custom of the Friends to exchange or wear rings.

66 Dorothy Waugh (Vaugh), formerly a servant in the Camm household and Mary Clark had been among those advocating greater asceticism. In the 1650s such views were well received by some New England Friends but not so by many others. See Brailsford *QW*, 146-7; Braithwaite, *BQ*, 236; and M. M. Dunn, 'Latest Light on Women of Light', *WFC*, 71-85, esp. 83 notes increased celibacy in eighteenth century U.S. Quakerism.

67 Ross, *MF*, 64; Croese, *The General History of the Quakers*, London 1696, i, 108 (Croese has the name as *Havens*). Little Elizabeth Fletcher, her former companion, had died from accumulated ill-treatment and exposure before she reached twenty.

68 Their children were left with others while they ministered. They did not emulate their parents. Elizabeth died in 1665. She had been troublesome to the authorities in South Wales and was imprisoned there. See M. F. Williams, 'Glamorgan Quakers 1654-1900', *Morgannwg* 5 (1961), esp. 49-59; F. Gawler, *A Record of Some Persecutions in South Wales*, London 1659, 6; R. Jones, *Crynwyr Bore Cymru*, Abermaw 1931, 19-25; Besse, *Sufferings* i, 737 seq., 747 seq.

69 B. Carré, 'Early Quaker Women', 44, 49.

70 See Ross, *MF*, 22.

71 On Samuel Bownas see *An Account of the Travels . . . of Samuel Bownas*, London 1759, 142 seq., and on George Fell see *Life of William Caton*, 8. He had studied alongside George from the age of fourteen, first at Swarthmoor Hall, then at Hawkshead Grammar School near Windermere.

72 A letter of 1657, quoted by Ross, *MF*, 23.

73 Booth, later Lord Delaware, led a Royalist uprising in Cheshire, allegedly to suppress a rising of Quakers. On the political and military activity of Pearson while a Quaker see Braithwaite, *BQ*, 457 seq., 461 seq., 480.

74 See Ross, *MF* chapters 3, 9, 13, 14 and 16. On these London Meetings see W. Beck and T. F. Ball, *The London Friends Meetings*, London 1869.

75 *Praemunire* or 'forewarning' made an outlaw of its victim, putting her 'out of the king's protection'. An estate was forfeit to the crown with the possibility of imprisonment for life or at the monarch's pleasure. Here was (as Braithwaite observed)

a readier instrument of persecution than the express laws against Quakers and seditious conventicles.

(*BQ*, 15). See also n. 90 below.

76 *Journal*, pp. 456, 463, 476 *et passim*, but especially 488, 534-37, 572. On Colonel Richard Kirkby's hostility towards the Swarthmoor household see Ross, *MF*, 142 seq., 164 seq.

77 'Colonel Kirkby causes our bonds to be renewed . . . more and more' she wrote to her daughter Margaret and son-in-law John Rous.

78 Quoted in Ross, *MF*, 222.

79 Ross, *MF*, 226.

80 Robert Barclay, *Apology* iv, 4.

81 Humphrey Smith, *To All Parents of Children*, London 1660, 3-4.

82 Vann, *SDEQ*, 168-173.

83 Recorded in the autumn of 1699, *Minutes . . .* , Bristol Record Society xxx, 1977.

84 *Joan Vokin's Works*, Cockermouth 1871, 105.

85 The Yeamans' first child, also called William, had died in infancy. On Barbara Lupton Jackson see D. Bower, J. Knight (eds.), *Plain Country Friends*, 165.

86 Jane Waugh Whitehead, for example, was imprisoned with an infant for five months (*Piety Promoted* i, 69). See also Besse, *Sufferings* (1753), i, 227, 271 *et passim*. on the hardships children faced and their gathering to worship together while parents were absent in prison (following the *Quaker Act*). Dorcas Dole's *A Salutation and Seasonable Exhortation to Children* (London 1700 but original from the Bridewell in 1682) has a postscript to children who maintained the Meeting.

87 Besse, *Sufferings* i, 66 seq. See also Fraser, *TWV*, 80-85; L. Hugh Doncaster, 'Quaker Children in the Seventeenth Century', *FQ* 3 (1949), 48-55; Besse, *Sufferings* i, pp. 15, 19, 27, 32, 66, 89, 368 seq. *et passim*.

88 Thomas Chalkley, *Journal*, London 1751, 1-2. This seems to have been a common sentiment expressed to Quakers, cf. Besse, *Sufferings,* i, 219.

89 Kaber Rigg is in Westmorland. The 'plot' involved a small number of Parliamentarians, none of them Quakers.

90 The swearing was demanded of suspicious persons who met together, for example after the Fifth Monarchist rising in 1661. Those over eighteen might be required to swear before a Justice, on pain of immediate imprisonment and with *Praemunire* to follow (though not for married women) if refusal were repeated.

91 Besse *Sufferings* i, 92. For the Lancaster incident and another involving a letter to Justice Fleming see Fox, *Journal* 464, 470.

92 John Banks, *Journal*, 342-3.

93 *See* Barbour and Roberts *EQW*, 458.

94 *See* John Banks, *An Epistle to Friends Shewing . . . Converted Estate*, London 1692 and *A Rebuke to Unfaithful Parents and a Rod for Stubborn Children*, London 1710. However, the following eighteenth century instance was probably exceptional:

> In the year 1778, I was one morning opening the door of a highly respected Friend at Bristol who was then correcting his daughter . . . upon seeing me he desisted . . . I shut the door and went away with feelings of disgust, and surprise, and wondering how a man of amiable character could horse-whip a female.

(J. W. Frost [ed.], *The Records and Recollections of James Jenkins (1753-1831)*, Texts and Studies in Religion 18, New York and Toronto 1984, 14).

95 Lloyd, *QSH*, 61. Cf. also (on the mercantile classes and the bourgeoisie) Stone, *FSM*, 98 seq.; M. Slater, 'Marriage: the Male Perspective' in *Family Life in the Seventeenth Century*, 60-77; A. MacFarlane, *Marriage and Love in England: modes of reproduction 1300-1840*, London 1986, 263-290.

96 J. Tual, 'Sexual Equality and Conjugal Harmony', 167-69; Brailsford, *QW*, 144 seq.; J. W. Frost, *The Quaker Family in Colonial America*, New York 1873, 152 seq. Robert Weaver, for example, worried about his own motives in being attracted to a young woman – 'being her mother kept a shop'.

97 Doncaster, 'Quaker Children', 52. See also B. Levy, *Quakers and the American Family: British Settlement in the Delaware Valley* (c. 1660-1750), Oxford 1988.

98 *Life of Joseph Pike* (John Barclay Select Edition vol. v), London 1837, 15-16, 86. On the topic of children see also W. J. Homan's rather sentimental account in *Children and Quakerism*, Berkely Ca., 1939.

99 Vann, *SDEQ*, 167.

100 See Mullett, *Early Lancaster Friends*, 15 seq. and Ford, 'William Penn's Views on Women', 88, for examples. On rates of pre-nuptual pregnancy and illigitimate births see Stone, *FSM*, 385-95.

101 The prospective husband, however, had also 'done wrong to a maid'.

102 The same names may appear many times in these roles in the records of Meetings.

103 Vann, *SDEQ*, 130.

104 See the hostile source Nathaniel Smith, *The Quakers Spiritual Court Proclaimed*, London 1669, 31 and cf. C. Hill, *Society and Puritanism in Pre-Revolutionary England*, London 1964, 354-381.

105 A. J. Eddington (ed.), *The First Fifty Years of Quakerism in Norwich*, published Friends' Home Service 1932, 131 seq.

106 Lloyd, *QSH*, 71 seq.; Mullett, *Radical Religious Movements*, 127 seq.

107 Thompson, *Women in Stuart England*, 192 seq.; Fraser, chapter 'unlearned virgins' in *TWV* and pp. 367 seq. Bathsua Pell Makin acknowledged that silly men who thought themselves wise would not welcome the competition which marriage to a wise woman would bring, but a learned man might well prefer his like and a relatively unlearned one might not only be improved but 'glory in her' (*An Essay to Revive the Antient Education of Gentlewomen*, excerpted in Ferguson *FF*, 140).

108 Fraser, *TWV*, 152, 156 seq., 377 seq. Bathsua Makin mentioned a number of such exceptional women in her *Essay* (Ferguson, *FF*, 132-3)

109 Ferguson, *FF*, 188. Cf. Fraser's chapters on 'unlearned virgins' and 'benefiting by accomplishments'.

110 See A. Goreau, *Reconstructing Aphra – A Social Biography of Aphra Behn*, Oxford 1980, 31.

111 Quoted by Fraser, *TWV*, 360 seq.

112 Mary Astell, *Some Reflections upon Marriage*, 1670, in Ferguson, *FF*, 194 seq.

113 Bathsua Pell Makin, *An Essay*, 129.

114 Excerpted in Ferguson, *FF*, 209. Makin, too, commented on the care of the Dutch for the education of women.

115 *FF*, 248, 254.

116 *FF*, 139-140. John Locke, Jonathan Swift and Daniel Defoe were among seventeenth and eighteenth century male advocates of improved female education.

117 The number of schools (mostly for boys) varied from region to region. In *QPE* Barbour estimated that before 1660 there were only 44 schools in the whole of the North of England. Corporal punishment of a brutal and degrading kind was the norm in them. See Stone, *FSM*, 116-122, 274 seq, 278-82.

118 *Experiences in the Life of Mary Penington*, 74 seq., in a letter to Mary's grandson Springet Penn. Mary (née Proude) had been born in 1623.

119 On Sarah Fell see Ross, *MF*, 313 seq. For Mary Mollineux's poetry see *Fruits of Retirement: or Miscellaneous Poems Moral and Divine*, London 1702 (several

reprints thereafter and the first American edn. in 1776). On Ann Docwra see E. T. and T. Backhouse, T. Mounsey, *Biographical Memoirs: Ann Docwra* (kept in Friends' House Library), pp. 63 seq.

[120] It goes without saying, however, that such a level of education was untypical of men Friends. See also T. L. Underwood, 'Quakers and the Royal Society of London in the Seventeenth Century' in *Notes and Records of the Royal Society of London* 31 (1976), 133-150.

[121] Carré, 'Early Quaker Women', 121. On levels of literacy and the education of girls see H. L. Smith, *Reason's Disciples,* 24 seq.; M. Slater, *Family Life in the Seventeenth Century*, 134-136; Stone, 'Literacy and Education in England 1640-1900', *PP* 42 (1969), 69-139 (dealing almost exclusively with male literacy); D. Cressy, 'Levels of Illiteracy in England 1530-1730', *Historical Journal* 20 (1977), 1-23; 'Literacy in Seventeenth Century England: More Evidence', *Journal of Interdisciplinary History* 8 (1977), 141-150. Mack remarks that

> Quaker women preachers were more educated and powerful than many of their contemporaries, or our received wisdom about marriage and family life in early modern England needs to be reconsidered and revised.

('Religion and Gender' in *WFC*, 45).

[122] *See* J. Stroud's Master's degree thesis, *The History of Quaker Education in England 1677-1903*, University of Leeds 1944, 17.

[123] *See* the University of Leicester PhD thesis *Derbyshire Quakers 1650-1761* by H. Forde, 189 seq. It was only in 1695 that Yearly Meeting gave detailed consideration to education, though some regions had started provision earlier.

[124] On the Aberdeen school see W. F. Miller, 'A Note on Early Friends Schools in Scotland', *JFHS* 7 (1910), 105; The Shacklewell school was being run by Jane Bullock when the *Six Weeks Meeting* recorded a Minute about shortage of pupils in it, in the eleventh month of 1677. Beck and Ball (*The London Friends Meetings,* 360) claim that Mary Stott was its first headteacher but I can not confirm this. Regarding loans to this school see Hubbard, *Early Quaker Education,* 42 and on Patrick Logan see Braithwaite, *SPQ,* 530.

[125] W. F. Millar, 'A Note on Early Friends Schools in Scotland', 110.

[126] The year was 1700. Elizabeth was a London Friend of Scottish origin.

[127] See Ross, *MF* 342 for a letter to grandmother Margaret on the subject.

[128] Stroud, *History,* 17. We know more of Richard Scoryer than of other Quaker teachers. He was respected as a pedagogue and offered to train up other willing Quaker men in his method. In 1693 he moved to Wandsworth.

[129] See Ralph Randles, 'Faithful Friends and Well Qualified' in Mullett (ed.), *Early Lancaster Friends,* 33-42 citing also M. Mullett, 'A Note on the Origins of the George Fox School, Lancaster', *JFHS* 53, 256 seq.

[130] Stroud, *History,* Appendix 2, 178 seq.; A. J. Eddington, *The First Fifty Years of Quakerism in Norwich,* 134.

[131] Carré, 'Early Quaker Women', 48.

[132] Vann, *SDEQ,* 180-81, noting also that neither Norfolk nor Buckinghamshire had a Friends' boarding school at that time and that schoolteachers were an 'intermittent presence'.

[133] Stroud, *History,* Appendix 3, 182 seq. See also the note 'A School in Ilchester Jail 1662', in *JFHS* 8 (1911), 16–19. On Richard Richardson and the Devonshire House school see Hubbard, *Early Quaker Education,* 45 seq.

[134] L. Ford, 'William Penn's Views on Women', 85, 90; Braithwaite, *SPQ,* 529.

[135] Quoted in Sewel, *History of the Rise . . .,* 484.

[136] Salt, *The Light, the Way that Children ought to be trained up in . . .,* London 1660, 3.

[137] *See* E. J. Whittaker, *Thomas Lawson,* York 1986.

[138] Minute from the *Six Weeks Meeting* in 1675. See Braithwaite, *SPQ,* 526.

[139] Barbour and Roberts, *EQW,* 458 seq.

[140] G. Nuttall, '"Nothing Else Would Do"; Early Friends and the Bible', *FQ* April 1982, 651.

Select Bibliography

Addy, John, *Sin and Society in the Seventeenth Century,* London 1989.

Amussen, S. D., *An Ordered Society: Gender and Class in Early Modern England,* Oxford 1988.

Bacon, Margaret Hope, *Mothers of Feminism: the Story of Quaker Women in America,* San Francisco 1986.

Barbour, H., *The Quakers in Puritan England,* New Haven Conn. 1964 and Friends United Press 1985; 'Quaker Prophetesses and Mothers in Israel' in C. and J. Stoneburner (eds.), *The Influence of Quaker Women in American History,* New York 1986, 57-80.

Barbour, H. and Roberts, A. O. (eds.), *Early Quaker Writings 1650-1700,* Grand Rapids 1973.

Barclay, A. R. (ed.), *Letters of Early Friends,* London 1841.

Bauman, R., *Let Your Words Be Few: Symbolism of Speaking and Silence Among Seventeenth Century Quakers,* Cambridge 1983.

Berg, C. and Berry, P., 'Spiritual Whoredom: an essay on female prophets' in F. Barker and J. Bernstein (eds.), *1642: Literature and Power in the Seventeenth Century,* Colchester University of Essex 1981, 37-54.

Besse, J., *A Collection of the Sufferings of the People Called Quakers from 1650-1689,* 2 vols. London 1753.

Bittle, W. G., *James Nayler: the Quaker Indicted by Parliament,* York 1986.

Boulding, Elise, *The Underside of History: a View of Women Through Time,* Boulder Colorado, 1976.

Brailsford, M., *Quaker Women 1650-1690,* London 1915; *A Quaker from Cromwell's Army,* New York and London 1927.

Braithwaite, W. C., *The Beginnings of Quakerism to 1660,* and *The Second Period of Quakerism,* 2nd. edns. (ed. H. J. Cadbury), York 1981, 1979.

Brown, E. Potts and Stuard, S. Mosher, *Witnesses for Change: Quaker Women Over Three Centuries,* New Brunswick and London 1989.

Carré, Beatrice, 'Early Quaker Women in Lancaster and Lancashire' in M. Mullett (ed.), *Early Lancaster Friends* (Centre for North West Regional Studies Occasional Paper 5), University of Lancaster 1978, 43-54.

Carroll, K. L., 'Quaker Attitudes Towards Signs and Wonders' *Journal of the Friends Historical Society* 54 (1977); 'The Early Quakers and "going naked as a sign"', *Quaker History* 67 (1978).

Cherry, C. L., 'Enthusiasm and Madness: Anti-Quakerism in the Seventeenth Century', *Quaker History* 73 (1984), 1-24.

Chu, J. M., *Neighbors, Friends or Madmen: the Puritan Adjustment to Quakerism in Seventeenth Century New England,* Westport Conn. 1985.

Clark, A., *The Working Life of Women in the Seventeenth Century*, original 1919 now ed. M. Chaytor, J. Lewis, London 1982 reissue.

Cohen, A., 'The Fifth Monarchy Mind: Mary Cary and the Origins of Totalitarianism', *Social Research* 31 (1964), 195-213; 'Prophecy and Madness: Women Visionaries During the Puritan Revolution', *Journal of Psychohistory* 11 (1984), 411 seq.

Cole, A., 'Quakers and the English Revolution', *Past and Present* 10 (1956), 39-54; 'The Social Origins of Early Friends', *Journal of the Friends Historical Society* 48 (1957), 99-118.

Cross, C., '"He goats before the flocks": a Note on the Part Played by Women in the Founding of Some Civil War Churches' in G. J. Cuming and D. Baker (eds.), *Studies in Church History 8: Popular Belief and Practice*, Cambridge 1972, 195-202.

Dailey, B. R., 'The Visitation of Sarah Wight: Holy Carnival and the Revolution of the Saints . . .', *Church History* 55 (1986), 438-455; 'The Husbands of Margaret Fell: an Essay on Religious Metaphor and Social Change', *The Seventeenth Century* 2 (1987), 55-71.

Davies, K. M., 'The Sacred Condition of Equality. How original were Puritan Doctrines of Marriage?' *Social History* 5 (1977), 563-580.

Durston, C., *The Family and the English Revolution*, London 1989.

Ferguson, M. (ed.), *First Feminists: British Women Writers 1578-1799*, Bloomington Ind. 1985.

Fogelklou, E., *James Nayler the Rebel Saint*, London 1931.

Fraser, Antonia, *The Weaker Vessel: Woman's Lot in Seventeenth Century England*, London 1985.

Greaves, R. L. (ed.), *Triumph Over Silence: Women in Protestant History*, Westport Conn. and London 1985, 45-74.

Greaves, R. L. and Zaller, R., *The Biographical Dictionary of British Radicals in the Seventeenth Century* 3 vols., Brighton 1982-84.

Higgins, P., 'The Reactions of Women, with Special Reference to Women Petitioners . . .' in B. Manning (ed.), *Politics, Religion and the English Civil War*, London 1973, 177-222.

Hill, Christopher, *Puritanism and Revolution: Studies in Interpretation of the English Revolution of the 17th Century*, London 1965; *The World Turned Upside Down: Radical Ideas During the English Revolution*, Harmondsworth 1975; *Antichrist in Seventeenth Century England*, Oxford 1971.

Horle, W., *The Quakers and the English Legal System 1660-1688*, Philadelphia 1988.

Houlbrooke, R. A., *The English Family 1450-1700*, London 1983; (ed.) *English Family Life (1576-1716)*, London 1989.

Hubbard, D. G. B., *Early Quaker Education*, unpublished M.A. thesis, University of London 1940.

Huber, E. C., 'A Woman Must Not Speak: Quaker Women in the English Left Wing' in R. R. Ruether and E. McLaughlin (eds.), *Women of Spirit: Female Leadership in the Jewish and Christian Traditions*, New York 1979, 153-182.

Irwin, J. L., *Womanhood in Radical Protestantism 1525-1675*, New York 1979.

Isichei, E., 'From Sect to Denomination among English Quakers' in B. R. Wilson (ed.), *Patterns of Sectarianism*, London 1967.

Jones, Marcia Bell, *The Shaping Spirit: the Autobiographies of Early Women Friends*, unpublished undated typescript in the library of Friends House, London.

Knox, Ronald, *Enthusiasm: A Chapter in the History of Religion*, Oxford 1950.

Koehler, L., *A Search for Power: the 'Weaker Vessel' in Seventeenth Century New England*, Urbana University of Illinois Press 1980; 'The Case of the American Jezebels: Anne Hutchinson and Female Agitation During the Years of the Antinomian Turmoil, 1636-1641', *William and Mary Quarterly* 31 (1974), 55-78.

Kunze, Bonnelyn Young, *The Family, Social and Religious Life of Margaret Fell*, unpublished D.Phil. dissertation University of Rochester, New York, 1986.

Lamont, W. M., *Godly Rule: Politics and Religion 1603-1660*, London 1969.

Lloyd, A., *Quaker Social History 1669-1738*, London 1950.

Ludlow, D. P., 'Shaking Patriarchy's Foundations' in R. L. Greaves (ed.) *Triumph Over Silence*, 1985, 93-123.

MacDonald, M., *Mystical Bedlam: Madness, Anxiety and Healing in Seventeenth Century England*, Cambridge 1982.

Mack, P., 'Women as Prophets During the English Civil War', *Feminist Studies* 8 (1982), 20-45. 'Gender and Spirituality in Early English Quakerism' in E. Potts Brown and S. Mosher Stuard *Witnesses for Change*, New Brunswick and London 1989.

Manners, E., *Elizabeth Hooton: First Quaker Woman Preacher (1600-1672)*, *Journal of the Friends Historical Society* Supplement Series 12, London 1914.

Manning, B., *The English People and the English Revolution*, London 1976.

Mason, G., *Quaker Women and Education 1642-1840*, unpublished dissertation in partial requirement for the M.A. degree, University of Lancaster 1987.

Morton, A. L., *The World of the Ranters: Religious Radicalism in the English Revolution*, London 1970.

Mullett, M. A., *Radical Religious Movements in Early Modern Europe*, London 1980; (ed.) *Early Lancaster Friends*, University of Lancaster 1978.

Nickalls, J. L. (ed.), *The Journal of George Fox*, London Religious Society of Friends 1975.

Nuttall, G., *James Nayler: A Fresh Approach*, *Journal of the Friends Historical Society*, Supplement Series 26, 1954; 'The Last of James Nayler, Robert Rich and "The Church of the First Born"', *Friends Quarterly* 60 (1985) 527-534; *The Holy Spirit in Puritan Faith and Experience*, Oxford 1946; *Studies in Christian Enthusiasm Illustrated from Early Quakerism*, Pendle Hill Publications, Pennsylvania 1948.

Penney, Norman (ed.), *The First Publishers of Truth*, *Journal of the Friends Historical Society* Supplement Series, 1-5, 1907; (ed.) *The Household Account Book of Sarah Fell*, Cambridge 1920.

Powell, C. L., *English Domestic Relations 1487-1653*, New York 1917.

Punshon, John, *Portrait in Grey: a Short History of the Quakers*, London Quaker Home Service 1984.

Reay, B., *The Quakers and the English Revolution*, London 1985; 'Popular Hostility Towards Quakers in Mid Seventeenth Century England', *Social History* 5 (1980), 387-407; 'The Authorities and Early Restoration Quakers', *Journal of Ecclesiastical History* 34 (1983), 69-84; 'Quaker Opposition to Tithes 1652-1660', *Past and Present* 86 (1980), 98-120; 'The Social Origins of Early Quakerism', *Journal of Interdisciplinary History* 11 (1980), 55-72.

Reay, B. and McGregor, J. F., *Radical Religion in the English Revolution*, Oxford 1984.

160

Rogers, K., *The Troublesome Helpmate: a History of Misogyny in Literature*, Seattle 1966.

Ross, Isabel, *Margaret Fell, Mother of Quakerism*, London 1949, 2nd edn. York 1984.

Ruether, R. R., 'Prophets and Humanists: Types of Religious Feminism in Stuart England', *Journal of Religion* 70 (1990), 1-18.

Scheffler, J., 'Prison Writings of Early Quaker Women', *Quaker History* 73 (1984), 25-37.

Shepherd, S., *Amazons and Warrior Women*, Brighton 1981; *The Womens Sharp Revenge*, London 1985.

Smith, H. E. and Cardinale, S. (eds.), *Women and the Literature of the Seventeenth Century: an Annotated Bibliography Based on Wing's Short-Title Catalogue*, New York and London 1990.

Smith, H. L., *Reason's Disciples: Seventeenth Century English Feminists*, Chicago and London 1982.

Smith, Joseph, *Bibliotheca Antiquakeriana*, New York 1968.

Smith, N., *Perfection Proclaimed · Language and Literature in English Radical Religion 1640-1660*, Oxford 1989.

Smith, Roberta, *Female 'Intransigence' in the early Quaker movement from the 1650s to about 1700, with particular reference to the North West of England*, unpublished dissertation as partial requirement for M A. degree, University of Lancaster 1990.

Speizman, M. D. and Kronick, J. C., 'A Seventeenth Century Quaker Women's Declaration', *Signs. Journal of Women in Culture and Society* 1 (1975), 231-245.

Stone, L., *The Family, Sex and Marriage in England 1500-1800*, London 1977

Stroud, J., *The History of Quaker Education in England 1677-1903*, unpublished MA degree thesis, University of Leeds 1944.

Thomas, Keith, *Religion and the Decline of Magic*, London 1973; 'Women and the Civil War Sects', *Past and Present* 13 (1958), 42-62 and in T. Aston (ed.) *Crisis in Europe 1560-1660*, London 1966.

Trevett, C., 'The Women Around James Nayler, Quaker: A Matter of Emphasis', *Religion* 20 (1990), 249-273.

Tual, Jacques, 'Sexual Equality and Conjugal Harmony: The Way to Celestial Bliss. A View of Early Quaker Matrimony', *Journal of the Friends Historical Society* 55 (1988), 161-174.

Underdown, D., *Revel, Riot and Rebellion: Popular Politics and Culture in England 1603-1660*, Oxford 1985; 'The Taming of the Scold: The Enforcement of Patriarchal Authority in Early Modern England' in A. Fletcher, J. Stevenson (eds.), *Order and Disorder in Early Modern England*, Cambridge 1984, chp. 4.

Underwood, T. L., 'Early Quaker Eschatology' in P. Toon (ed.), *Puritans, the Millenium and the Future of Israel: Puritan Eschatology 1600-1660*, London 1970, 91-103.

Vann, R. T., *The Social Development of English Quakerism 1655-1755*, Cambridge Mass. 1969.

Watts, M. R., *The Dissenters from the Reformation to the French Revolution*, Oxford 1978.

Wilcox, C. M., *The Theology of the Early Friends and its Implications for the Ministry of Women in Seventeenth Century English Quakerism*, unpublished PhD Dissertation, King's College London, 1991.

Williams, E. M., 'Women Preachers in the Civil War Sects', *Journal of Modern History* 1 (1929), 561-569.

Index

The following index covers personal names and subjects. Persons who were Quakers of the seventeenth to nineteenth centuries (but not present-day writers who happen to be Friends) are listed with a following Q.

162

Grigge, William, 141
Grindletonians, 2, 17
Groves, Mary Q, 63
Grubb, L., 136
Gubar, S., 135

HALHEAD, Miles Q, 66, 68
Halkett, Lady Anne, 8
Hambly, Loveday Q, 62, 71
Hambrick-Stowe, C. E., 136
Hamilton, A., 132-3, 148
Hamilton, R., 151
Harris, Elizabeth Q, 19, 24, 39, 65, 142
Harwood, John Q, 36, 39
Haslam, Elizabeth Q, 112
Hawkins, Jane, 6
Hayes, Alice Q, 53, 66-9, 146
Hebden, Roger Q, 25
Henderson, K., 141
Henton, J. W., van, 133
Herbert, George, 144
Heresy, 1-3, 15, 47, 54
Herrup, C. B., 134
Higgins, P., 134
Hill, Christopher, 13, 37, 132-3, 136-8, 140-1, 155
Hit-Him-Home, Joan, 7
Hobby, Elaine, 135-6, 146
Holme(s), Elizabeth (see Leavens), 24
Holme(s), Thomas Q, 98-9, 144
Holmes, Jane Q, 16, 19, 25-8, 139
Homan, W. J., 155
Hookes, Ellis Q, 68, 103
Hooton, Elizabeth Q, 16-22, 26, 40, 52, 65, 102
Hooton, Oliver Q, 16, 61, 139, 145
Hopkins, Matthew, 1
Horle, C. W., 137, 145, 151
Houlbrooke, R. A., 144, 147
Howgill, Abigail Q, 95-6, 128
Howgill, Francis Q, 30, 32-4, 95-6, 128, 140
Howgill, Mary Q, 142
Hubbard, D. G. B., 124, 156-7
Hubberthorne, Richard Q, 33-4, 59, 145, 149
Huber, E. C., ix, 134, 138

Hull, S. W., 136
Hunt, W., 132
Hurcombe, Linda, vii
Hurwick, J. J., 145
Hutchinson, Anne, 138
Hutchinson, Lucy, 8

IMPRISONMENT, 2, 17-21, 23, 26, 43, 58, 61-2, 65, 94-6, 100-106, 113, 124, 138, 150, 153-4
Independents, 20, 45
Inman, The widow Q, 69
Inner Light, The, 15, 17, 30, 50, 53, 136
Inquisition, The, 1, 61, 65
Insanity (see madness)
Ireland, 32, 40, 64, 104-5, 125, 138-40
Irwin, J. L., 134, 136, 143, 148
Isichei, E., 147, 150

JACKSON, Barbara Lupton Q, 105, 154
Jackson, Catherine Q, 94, 152
Jackson, Henry Q, 94, 152
Jamaica, 22
James II, 77, 92
James, Martha Q, 107
James, M., 133
James, William Q, 145
Jenkins, James Q, 154
Jews, 52
Joceline, Elizabeth, 6
Joel, 15, 47-8
Jones, J. G., xi
Jones, Marcia Bell, bibliography
Jones, R., 153
Jones, Rice Q, 140
Jones, Tabitha Q, 107
Jonson, Ben, 144
Judy (Crouch) Q, 32, 38, 40, 142

KABER-RIGG Plot, 107, 154
Kaplan, L., 134
Katz, D. S., 144
Keith, George Q, 118, 124
Kellett, Priest, 137
Kenney, K. S., 148
Kent, Frances Q, 60
Ker, Margrett Q, 124-5

166

171

SI SONENT TUBÆ PARATUS